Country Doctor

D1132459

Country Doctor

A MEMOIR

Bess Dlin

CAITLIN PRESS INC
PRINCE GEORGE, B.C.

Caitlin Press Inc.
Box 2387
Station B
Prince George, BC   V2N 2S6

All photos supplied from the authors personal collection.
Cover design by Warren Clark
Typeset by Warren Clark
Edited by Betty Keller and Candice Dyck

Printed in Canada

Canadian cataloguing in publication data

Dlin, Ben, 1924-
    Country doctor, a memoir

    ISBN 0-920576-85-0 (pbk.)

    1. Dlin, Ben, 1924- 2. Physicians—Alberta, Northern—Biography,
3. Alberta, Northern—Biography, I. Title.
R464.D54A3 2000   610.92   C00-910962-5

Caitlin Press acknowledges the support of the Canada Council for the Arts for our publishing program. Similarly we acknowledge the support of the Arts Council of British Columbia.

AUTHOR'S NOTE

WHEN I DECIDED THAT IT WAS TIME TO WRITE A STORY FOR my grandchildren about my medical memoirs it never dawned on me that this would be something that would be published. Memories poured forth, and I wrote with a sense of urgency, after all I was 74 years old and time was running out. My wife, Lorna, read my rough material and encouraged me to continue while my brother, Norman, focused on correcting my many spelling errors.

Friends that I trusted, interested in what I was doing, read parts of the early material offering unsolicited comments and suggestions. All of them urged me to continue and suggested that it would be an interesting book. Those from Philadelphia included Harold Bershady, Janice Booker, and Stephani Levin as well as my Canadian friends in Pender Harbour, Victoria Campbell and Edith Iglauer Daley. Martin Nicholes rescued me by patiently showing me how to format the material on the computer.

Howard White, a friend and publisher of Harbour Publishing, heard that I was working on a book. He called and offered to read and critique it. He then suggested that it was good and that it needed the help of an editor. That is how I came to work with Betty Keller who lives and works about a fourty minute drive from my British Columbia home.

After we met and agreed to work together, I suggested that I was now 75 and that I wanted to get this done before I die. The lions share of the work was completed in the summer of 1999. She worked very hard at sorting through the jumble of disconnected memories and had it sorted out and smoothed over without changing my style or my message. She just made it all clear. Betty reminded me of Mrs. Francis, my 5th grade teacher, in bringing out the best in me.

I am indebted to you all and forever grateful because now my grandchildren will be able to read my story of what it took to become a doctor and what doctoring is all about.

PREFACE

GENERAL PRACTITIONERS, FAMILY DOCTORS, COUNTRY doctors—call them what you will—are the doctors who work on the front lines of medicine. They are the ones to whom most people turn to for care, guidance and treatment, or for referral to a specialist.

Before WW II, the great bulk of practicing physicians worked in general practice. Most worked alone, turning to a nearby doctor to cover for them during vacations or periods of illness. They loved what they did and enjoyed their independence, but were generally poor business people who tended to end their careers not much wealthier than when they began. Traditionally, these doctors looked after entire families for as long as they remained in active practice. They knew more about the health, personalities, and social and economic vicissitudes of their patients than any other person.

In the past five decades medicine has experienced many changes. The most dramatic changes have been the rapid advances made in all branches of medicine. More advances have happened in the last five decades than have occurred in the entire five thousand year history of medicine. This increase has happened so rapidly and in so much abundance, that it is virtually impossible for a single physician to keep up with all of it.

At the same time as this growth in knowledge happened, a slower change was going on within the medical community: young doctors were being lured toward specialized areas of medicine. As general practitioners, they were being squeezed to the margins of the profession by having limitations placed on what they were allowed to do in city hospitals. The general practitioners' value to the profession was not recognized by faculties of medicine, where they were not even included on the teaching staff. Instead, their training was left in the hands of the specialists. This situation was not rectified until general practitioners organized to form the specialty of Family Practice. The universities then wisely encouraged and supported this change, belatedly realizing the vital role such doctors play in the practice of medicine. However, by this time specialists had come to dominate medicine, and today, finding a good family doctor is becoming a critical problem in this era of government and insurance managed medicine.

My story is about the "real" doctors of medicine, who do not get written up in newspapers or scientific journals like those in specialties or those doing exotic medical research. It is the true story of my time spent with such a doctor, Frank Coppock. Frank was born in 1896 and after completing his internship, started to practice medicine in 1926 in rural Saskatchewan, later moving in 1938 to the small town of Eckville, Alberta. This is a glimpse into the life of this seasoned country practitioner, as well as a study of the making of the novice doctor who went to work for him. I soon learned what it was like to take on the twenty-four-hour-a-day job that this remarkable man had been doing for more than thirty years before I met him. I also discovered what it was like to step into his shoes when he was away, with 10,000 patients scattered over a huge rural territory. I discovered that doctors like Frank Coppock are called upon to do things that I never even dreamed of when I was a medical student or even when I was an intern. I learned that I had to be prepared to do anything, anytime and anyplace without regard for the hour, the inconvenience, the exhaustion or the absence of assistance.

This book is also about my childhood dream of becoming a doctor and what it took to overcome obstacles in my path. Like me, most of my classmates in medical school wanted to enter general practice, but in the end, most of us left to specialize. In my story, I try to explain why this happened to me and how I made the decision to get more training. Frank Coppock knew that I would not be returning to general practice, and I'm sure he understood why. We are therefore two symbols: Frank, the country doctor who stayed, and Ben, the country doctor who left.

I believed then, and still believe now, that every student of medicine should spend time in rural practice; it is the place to discover what you are made of. But more importantly it is the best place to learn the profession, working with a seasoned doctor who will teach the apprentice all that he has gained from his years of solo practice. Within the novice, it creates a lifelong humanistic approach to medicine that remains no matter what specialty is pursued. The baton is thus passed on and on to future generations of healers.

I KNEW BY THE AGE OF NINE THAT I WANTED TO BE A DOCTOR. That doesn't mean I didn't consider other occupations. I also recall wanting to wear a uniform and sing with the Salvation Army, to be a cowboy, a boxer and a farmer. But all these and other possibilities were short-lived, and eventually became interests or hobbies in the form of music, sports and gardening. I was a wild, unruly child, yet experiences and other influences forged my resolve to lead the life of a doctor.

If people who knew me as a child in the 1920s, growing up in the Alberta farm community of Bruderheim, were asked, "What was Bennie like as a kid?" they would say that he was a little devil, a trouble maker, a rebel, a terrible student, and certainly the last person to become a doctor. I was a child full of mischief; filled with curiosity and a desire for adventure and freedom. I plucked the feathers off a live chicken because I felt it would suffer from the heat of the day. When my brother Howard complained of being cold, I helped him into the oven of our large kitchen stove. He went willingly but when mother saw what I had done I got a spanking, even though my intentions were good! I was wildly inaccurate with my slingshot and recall twice smashing the plate glass window of the butcher shop.

I liked starting fires and nearly succeeded in burning down Fogelson's wooden store by lighting a fire in their woodpile. I was a forever taking the farmers' horse-drawn wagons for joy rides because I loved to control the big horses. I climbed onto box cars, turned the big wheel on top to release the brake and went for joy rides as they rolled down the gentle slope leading from the station. I recall Mr. Sherman, the station agent, running after the runaway car to stop it. He would give me hell and send me home, but that didn't stop me. For a little extra excitement, I'd climb the fence of the pig farm at the end of the block, jump on a pig's back and go for a quick ride.

I gave no thought to the spanking I would receive for each naughty action, nor did I seem concerned about the problems I was causing others. I rebelled against the discipline imposed on me by my mother. If I swore, she would wash my tongue with soap, but it happened so often that I actually developed a taste for carbolic soap. If she was really frustrated with Howard or myself, she would tie both of us to a large tree in our back yard. I could untie the knots and escape; poor Howard couldn't.

Dad spanked me often by swatting me on the rear end, but his spankings were more symbolic than painful. He never raged at me or lost control. Sometimes he would suddenly take off his belt and shake it at me as if to say, "You're going to get a good whipping if you don't behave!" But he never did hit me with it. Usually what happened was that his pants would slip down and he would hold onto them while everyone around would start to laugh. Good thing dad had a great sense of humor.

I once stole ten dollars from his pants pocket and spent it all on penny candy in Mr. Loomer's store, then shared my loot with all the kids in town. Dad found out and I got a real spanking this time; he would not tolerate stealing. I felt terrible. Next morning I saw a lot of loose change sitting on top of our bureau. I picked it up and brought in to dad who then thanked me and reminded me once again that stealing was a very bad thing to do. That is one lesson that I have never forgotten

One day I was so naughty that some of the village elders locked me up in the small "jail;" a one-room shack usually reserved for drunks to sleep it off. I do not recall the sequence of events that brought this on, but I do know that it was the station agent, Fred Sherman, the butcher, my dad and some others who collectively decided to lock me up. I remember looking out a small glassless window and talking to visitors; mostly my playmates and curious kids from school. Once in a while dad or some other adult would peek in and not say a word. I guess I was being shunned, but at the time I felt more like a celebrity than a naughty boy.

When I was about four years old, my elder sister Sarah and her friend Joe Loomer took me to see the remains of the first schoolhouse in

Bruderheim that had just burned down. Only a big hole in the ground remained, cluttered with black smoldering embers of charred wood. I recall thinking that I didn't do it and that it must have been some other kids playing with matches.

A brand new, four-roomed school soon covered the spot. A simple wooden building, it was called "Walker School." I never did learn who Walker was. Our gleaming white school stood out, easily seen from all directions as it sat alone, surrounded by fields of grass and scrub trees. Sarah took me for my first day at school, registering me with a brand new name.

I had been given the Hebrew name of Dad's father, Baruch Mordechai, which when Anglicized, can be Barney, Bernard, Ben and even Baruch. My mother intended me to be registered for a birth certificate as Barney Martin, but it happened that on the event of my birth Dad was a little tipsy so he registered my name as Benjamin Maurice. Mother was not aware of what he had done and continued to call me Barney.

Sarah, however, being sensitive to the fact that the most popular names for horses were Rose and Barney, which just happened to be mother's and my names, took it upon herself to register me at school as Benjamin, which was soon shortened to Ben. As a result, I went through my life being called Ben by my siblings and friends while Mother and her friends called me Barney. While this was a little confusing, the real complications to my life came in later years. When I was to travel to United States, I found that my birth certificate did not line up with my understanding of who I was. It said I was Benjamin Maurice but all my documents and certificates said I was Barney Martin. So at that point I changed my name legally to what my mother had intended.

At the Walker School there were three classes to each room and a busy teacher trying to work at all levels to keep us occupied. For me the only exciting object was a big clock that hung in front of the teachers' office. It had my dad's name painted in gold on it because he had donated it to the school. He was a member of the school board.

There were two outhouses in the back of the school: one two-seater for the girls and another for the boys. Each was equipped with one large hole for the big kids and one small hole for the little kids. We boys also had a crude trough that was used for pissing. No way would the school authorities take the chance of leaving boys to pee into the holes. Even so, the seats were perpetually wet in the summer or covered with frozen piss in the winter. To use the outhouse, you had to raise a hand and signal the teacher with one finger or two, so the teacher would know what we needed to do. Lord knows why the teacher had to know this; certainly not to report toilet habits to our folks.

I spent a lot of time gazing out the windows, running to the toilet and staring at Miss White. She seemed so beautiful and kind. I guess she was in her mid-twenties, even though she seemed old to me. I can't recall her becoming impatient or angry as she shifted her focus from the first graders to the other grades sitting just one row from each other, nor do I remember learning anything from her.

For us, school meant memorizing letters and numbers and practicing script with old fashioned, wooden-handled pens. At one end of the pen was a metal nib, which in turn was dipped into ink that was stored in an inkwell at the top right hand corner of each desk. Although it had a lid to prevent spilling, somehow my hands and clothes were always covered with ink. It seemed impossible for me to get the right amount of ink onto the nib. It just dripped off and smeared over my papers, clothes and fingers. No wonder I never learned to write or spell well; I was just too busy handling the messy ink.

Miss White used two forms of punishment when she needed to discipline the children. The first was to order us to sit on our hands and the second was to stand us in the coat closet at the back of the room. When I was given the coat closet treatment, I'd stay for a few moments, then just walk outside. I wanted desperately to explore the world around me and understand everything that I observed. Everything that held my interest required investigation and exploration. The list was long; it included the fields, marshes, woods, and all the birds and animals that lived and thrived in these places. Most of the time I was alone as I explored the grain elevators, trains and train tracks, the cheese factory, blacksmith shop, pool hall, beer parlor, farms, animal pens and chicken coops. The creamery man showed me that milk could make cheese by a process of separation, agitation and fermentation. Farmers taught me about the cycle of life; about birth and death and the necessity for reproduction in the kingdoms of birds, animals and plants.

When I roamed the countryside, I foraged for wild gooseberries, chokecherries, and blueberries in patches that I knew well. Wheat kernels made good "chewing gum," and everyone's garden had plenty of fresh peas, carrots, potatoes and radishes. If I was thirsty, there was always a well or pump that produced clean, ice cold water. I could get milk by squeezing a cow's teat and squirting the warm liquid into my mouth. Chicken coops always had a few recently laid eggs that I would guzzle by poking holes at either end and sucking out their contents.

This natural world held far more allure for me than what I was exposed to in school, and as a result, I don't recall much of what happened there. I did not recognize that my boredom was due to the lack of any challenge or excitement from the teacher. One year just blended into the other. I have a memory of Joe and Bill Lutsky sitting near me in first grade. They stick in my mind because they were recently arrived immigrants and had such peculiar dress and speech. I just remember being in the classroom for grades one to three, then one September moving into the next room with the bigger kids who were in grades four to six. I recall little else, except feeling bored.

Understandably, my folks only hoped that I'd somehow manage to finish school and with a little luck stay out of jail. Certainly they never said, "Ben, you should be a doctor!" Yet I'm convinced that the influence of my parents was the most potent of all the factors that contributed to my determination to become a physician.

My dad, William or Bill Dlin, was warm, loving and generous— almost to a fault. He was a handsome man, short and powerfully built. His ruddy complexion made his blue eyes stand out. My mother always neatly trimmed his mustache after she gave him his morning shave. He would sit on a straight-backed chair set in the middle of the kitchen. Mother would soften his tough beard with a hot steaming towel, then proceed to lather his face with his favorite shaving brush and with bold strokes, shave off his whiskers. She rarely nicked his skin. Dad luxuriated in this indulgence by mother.

Dad was born in 1889 and grew up in the Ukraine, in the hamlet of Yerki, a farm community situated about 200 miles west of Kiev. From his description, I think that Yerki had a population of no more than 50 people. Although most of them were Greek Orthodox, dad's family were orthodox Jews. Everyone in the village was poor and struggled to put food on the table. Dad had no schooling except for a few individual lessons in Ukrainian and Hebrew, so as a boy he could barely read and could not write at all.

Being Jewish put the family in constant danger of violent anti-Semitism. My dad explained that when there were uprisings, "My father and we four boys would gather at our family's tanning factory and fight off the peasants by swinging fresh hides as weapons, as well as using them for protecting ourselves. When I was a teenager [probably between 16 and 19] a few of my braver young friends and I would go out at night and attack Cossacks. I would grab a man and pull him off his horse and beat him to a pulp. Sometimes I even pulled the horse down with the rider. Afterwards we would run and hide."

Dad's physical strength came from his work at Yerki's lone grain elevator. His job was to weigh in the farmer's wagons filled with grain. This was done on an old-fashioned balance scale, which meant that he was lifting weights all day long. His good friend Chaim was a blacksmith and so must have been powerful as well. Dad never told me that Chaim was one of his group of vigilantes, but he did say that "when the violence grew to the point where Jews were being killed and my life was in danger, Chaim and I fled." They left their homes in 1909, traveling by foot, horse, train and ship. Eventually they found their way to the English Channel and were smuggled into England where they boarded another ship and travelled steerage class to Montreal. "Other Jews from our village had settled in Edmonton, Alberta, a few years earlier," he told me, "so that's where we went, too. When I left home, I said good-bye to mother and father and my sister and three brothers. I never knew if I would see any of them again." But after a while he was able to bring over his younger brother and sister and later an older brother and his wife and their seven children. His widowed mother and one older brother refused to emigrate. He never did see them again.

He arrived in Alberta in early 1910, just five years after Alberta separated from the Northwest Territories. A 19-year-old illiterate who could speak only Yiddish and Ukrainian, he worked as a labourer on the railroad. But he was not content with being a mere labourer. He bought raw cowhides and wild animal skins, salted them and shipped them to wholesalers. He staked a 160-acre homestead in the bush just four miles northeast of Bruderheim, which is about thirty-five miles northeast of Edmonton on the 53 parallel of latitude. It was his land, provided he cleared it of bush. I recall horses still pulling out tree stumps from the remaining uncleared acres when I was a kid.

The topsoil was wonderfully rich in nutrients, coal black and very deep; it produced bountiful crops of wheat, oats and barley. Even after he opened a general store in Bruderheim, he continued to farm the land by contracting the work out to neighbours. Times were good, and he worked hard and prospered. By the time the great depression hit in 1930, he owned his farm, the Bruderheim store and two other stores; one in Lamont, the other in Mundare.

During those early years in Canada, he learned to speak Russian, German and English, and he taught himself to read and write in both English and Yiddish. [Before he died he was studying French.] Eventually he spoke English without a European accent and could pass for a native Canadian. At home mother and dad conversed mostly in Yiddish, but they also spoke in Russian, Ukrainian, and German if they didn't want us to understand what they were saying. We children communicated with them in English.

Dad was a generous man. He believed that charity was both a virtue and an obligation. He told me over and over again that all a man had was his word, and that this and charity were the true measure of a man's character. He was always quietly helping others. Fellow Jews who traveled by horse and buggy through our town on cold winter nights were welcomed to lodge in our spare room until it was safe to travel further.

He had great respect for men of learning. Though he had little education himself, he served on our village school board. He brought two young lawyers—Abe Miller and Leo Pekarsky—to our village and gave them a place to see clients. He always had room in our house for travelling religious Jews who needed a kosher home in which to rest and eat. But above all others, he admired doctors for their ability to heal, and he was always transporting sick country folk to his Edmonton doctors. When he found a doctor he liked, he brought him gifts of turkeys and farm produce throughout his entire life. I recall two of them: Dr. Morris Weinlos and Dr. Walter McKenzie, both good surgeons. Dr. McKenzie went on to be chief of surgery and later Dean of Medicine at the University of Alberta.

My mother, Rose, was also born in 1889, the same year as Dad, but was raised in the cosmopolitan city of Odessa in the Ukraine. She was the third in a family of six children, the one referred to as the "sensible" and "bright" one by her siblings and their spouses. She graduated from a *gymnasia*, the equivalent of a college education in Canada, and became a socialist with a strong identification with the working class. Being a feminist as well, she believed in equal rights between men and women. She was also an agnostic. She loved music and theatre, and treasured an old poster from Odessa in which she was billed as the lead in a semi-professional play. A handsome woman, she had coal black hair that hung down to her waist when it was combed out, dark eyes and strong facial features. Her frame was big-boned and she stood as tall as Dad did.

Mother told us stories of her time in Odessa. It sounded like she had a great social life with many friends, some of whom also immigrated to North America and with whom she continued to be close all her life. As a teenager and young woman, there had been much fun in her life with music, theatre, dancing, boating and partying. She told me that she was in love with one young man but was separated from him when they immigrated to different parts of the world.

Then there were the bad times; the pogroms. "When conditions were very bad and the danger of death very real, my mother gave me to Russian farmer friends. I was a little past two years of age. The Russian family took care of me for two years. I only remember that the house had one room and a dirt floor and that the people who took me in treated me as if I was their own child. Then my mother came and took me home. I remember how we would hide in the dirt basement of our apartment building when hoodlums searched the area to find and kill Jews. It was small and cramped with a wooden trap door that was pulled shut, leaving us in complete darkness. I was only a little child, but I remember my mother having me hold my newborn baby brother. My job was to cover his mouth if he cried. We could not allow any noise for fear of being discovered. I remember how terrible I felt when the baby died a few months afterwards."

Like my dad, she fled to Canada around 1912 when Jews were being killed indiscriminately by roving gangs of hoodlums that had the blessing of the Czarist government. Mother's aunt, a nurse and midwife in Toronto, sent for mother, her two oldest sisters and their brother and his family. They came by ship, travelling steerage, packed in the lower decks with little to eat and in overcrowded quarters. Mother made friends with the crew and was able to get fresh fruit and vegetables to share with her family. Shortly after World War I, she was instrumental in getting her youngest sister out of the Ukraine and safely into Canada. She did this by working as a seamstress in a dress factory, a trade she learned in Canada; it was a far cry from the cultural and academic life of her youth. Around 1930 she brought out her youngest brother and his family.

She met my dad in 1919 while he was on a business trip to Toronto. "I met her at a party and fell in love with her instantly, especially because of her singing voice and her long hair." Apparently mother was singing songs in Russian and Yiddish and had her unbraided hair combed out so that it hung below her waist. He proposed marriage within a few days. I don't think mother felt the same as dad, but she was a very practical person and she saw that he was a "good man" and so accepted his proposal. He told her all about the beauty and wonders of life in Alberta, although he failed to describe the primitive living conditions and the wilder-

Rose and Bill Dlin, 1920, in Bruderheim, Alberta

ness of the north country. Shortly after mother came to Edmonton, they were married at the home of dad's good friend Chaim, the blacksmith, and his wife, Shaindel.

As practical and courageous as Mother was, however, she was not prepared for Bruderheim. As she stepped off the train, it must have looked much like the frontier towns depicted in old Western movies. This, however, was no Hollywood set. What she saw was a primitive prairie village of less than fifty people. A few clapboard, false-fronted buildings lined the dirt streets. The wooden sidewalks were elevated about a foot higher than the road to be above the mud in summer and the snow in winter. Few families had a motor car or truck. Instead, they drove horse-drawn buggies and wagons, though some people rode to town on horseback—generally bareback. As a result, there were hitching rails fronting the few buildings. Said Mother, "My first impulse was to get right back on the train and return to Edmonton."

Although dad continued to farm his homestead, my parents settled into a tiny house in the town. Some local women welcomed mother and became lifelong friends of hers, making her adjustment easier. They had all been forced to adjust to this life. It was especially demanding on the women who had to pump water and carry bucket after bucket into the house, stoke up the stove, cook, clean and wash everything by hand. Every house had a garden, a well, an outhouse, a root cellar, and often a cow and a chicken coop. We also had an icehouse and our woodpile was often bigger than our house.

My own memories of Bruderheim begin in 1928 when I was a little less than four years old and the place had reached its zenith with a population of a hundred and fifty. Since my mother's arrival, the town had acquired a cheese factory and a lumberyard, and many of the older farmers of the district had settled for the easier life in the town, leaving their farms to the younger generation.

The approach to our little village was down a two-mile stretch of dirt road from the main gravel highway. We called that spot the "two mile corner." It was where the bus stopped and left off parcels, papers and passengers. Just seeing that bus was like having a link to the outside world. It was a big adventure for my brother Howard and I to go with Earl Sherman to meet the bus and pick up the Edmonton newspapers. It was Earl's job to

Bruderheim, Alberta in the 1930's when the motor car finally replaced the horse and buggy

deliver them to his few customers, but he magnanimously allowed Howard and me that "privilege."

I knew everyone who lived in the homes and farms that we passed as we walked back to the village. No one carried weapons and we never locked our homes; everyone lived on the honor system. When it came to outsiders, we felt safe with those we knew, like when Mr. Newhouse, a wholesale grocer, came to town to sell his merchandise, and we flocked around him because he always had Russian bon-bons in his right hand jacket pocket for each of us.

Whenever a troop from the familiar Salvation Army came to preach and sing, we kids tried to join in as best we could. I loved singing with them because in my entire life they were the only people who never complained about my inability to carry a tune. But when a perfect stranger came to town, the kids would follow him everywhere, staying out of sight in the bushes and behind fences and buildings. I think it was a combination of curiosity and a little fear mixed with distrust until we could be sure that it was safe to reveal ourselves. We had to be satisfied that the stranger would bring us no harm.

The most striking sight as we came into town were the five majestic grain elevators that filled the skyline on the right side of the road, each elevator sitting next to a railroad siding so that the grain could be loaded into boxcars. We turned left after crossing the railroad tracks, passing a few homes, a lumberyard, a machine shop, and a small shack that served as the fire hall and housed a big container of water suspended between two large, wood-spoked wheels. It took only one man to pull this water barrel to a fire and two men to pump the water that squirted through a short fire hose, but having the town's men stand and piss on the fire would have been just as effective.

Fires were frequent because our wooden homes were heated with old-fashioned wood-and-coal burning stoves, stoked high to shut out the freezing winter cold and set just too close to the wooden walls. Every fire I saw resulted in a lot of heroic effort on the part of the neighbors, but each and every building, including my father's store in 1929, inevitably burned to the ground. I remember being carried from our home by Mr. Gillespie and watching the flames leaping toward our house, although fortunately it didn't catch fire.

Further along this road was the railroad station; the station agent, Fred Sherman, his wife, Maude, and their children were our family's best friends. After that, came two more grain elevators, Strong's lumberyard and the cheese factory that was tops in the province for its cheddar. It was a favorite place to play and eat all the cheese we wanted. The manager never seemed to mind us hanging around. My friend Ashley Strong and his kid sister Velma—my first girlfriend—lived between the lumberyard and the cheese factory. My most vivid memory of Mrs. Strong was that she could grab hold of a screeching chicken and chop off its head. We would all watch as the chicken ran around the yard headless and spurting blood.

Looking down the cross street that held the commercial center of the town was like viewing a scene from the old west, with its hitching rails and false-fronted buildings. One of them was a two-story hotel with a beer parlor and next to it, a tiny two-room bank. Donnie Dunlop, who was the son of the bank manager and lived above the bank, Ashley Strong and I would have our ritual pissing contests onto the back wall of the bank. Dad's general store was next to the bank with a yard separating it from our house.

Across the street was a tiny one-room post office, Stewart's apothecary, and Loomer's confectionery. Further down the road was Sam Fogelson's general store and Palutzki's butcher shop. (It was his plate glass window that I smashed with my slingshot.) A two-story building housed a barbershop with a pool hall in back on the ground floor, and the town hall on the second floor; this was also where we went to watch silent movies. Kroenig's farm equipment shop was at the corner, surrounded by wonderful tractors, plows, binders, harrows and discs, all the toys a kid could ever dream of having and all of them unbreakable. We were very friendly with the Kroenig kids.

My very favorite place of all was Shultz's blacksmith shop. He could do magic things with metal when it was heated red-hot in his charcoal-filled hand-driven forge. He always had a piece of iron heating up in the forge, preparing it for shaping and molding, and he would grasp that red hot metal with a large set of tongs, take it to a huge anvil and then pound it into shape with one of his metal sledge hammers. The showers of sparks and the ringing of metal against metal made just the best show on earth. He could fix anything that was broken or in need of a part, and when he made horseshoes, which he nailed onto the hooves of the huge Clydesdale workhorses, I got to crank the handle that worked the bellows fanning the coals in the forge. Sometimes, Mr. Shultz would give me an old horseshoe nail that I would force through a cork and then use as a dart. There wasn't a board fence or building in town that I didn't leave my mark on.

There was no electricity in Bruderheim, so kerosene lanterns provided light. Most homes had root cellars to keep food from freezing in the winter and icehouses to keep it cool in the summer. There was also no running water, so everyone had a well. Lucky people had hand pumps to draw their water but the rest of us used buckets attached to windlasses. I recall the excitement in our house when we got a pump. It made collecting water so much easier, but of more importance to me, it meant that we could make our own little patch of ice in the back yard to skate on in the winter and even play hockey.

Cold winds arrived by the end of October each year, accompanied by a rapid drop in temperature. It stayed below freezing for the duration of the winter, often going as low as 50 and 60 degrees below zero centigrade. Once the snow arrived, it did not leave until the thaws of late March or early April. Since none of our homes had insulation, the cold air seeped in through the walls and over sills. In our house, snow would blow in under the doors, so Mother would seal them with old rugs or thick cloth rags. Our basement was a dirt hole that had a coal-burning furnace with one galvanized pipe leading to a grated vent in the middle of the living room floor. The only way one could stay warm in the front room was to stand directly over the open grate. The upstairs was always cold because the heat had to travel up through the floors or up the narrow stairwell.

As it would be dark by 4pm in winter, we children were ready for bed shortly after having our evening meal. We would rush to the cold upstairs, leap into our cold beds and quickly snuggle under thick, homemade down quilts that would keep us warm no matter what the temperature dropped to. Howard, Norman and I slept in a room that was just big enough for a small bureau and two cribs, later replaced by two single beds, one of which Norman and I shared. We had to go through our parents' bedroom to get to our room. They had a double bed and a bureau and a tiny clothes closet. Rita slept in a crib in the corner, but Sarah had a room all to herself. In the morning when we rose, the urine in the chamber pots beneath our beds was always frozen. When conditions got too cold, or if there was a blizzard, instead of heading for the outdoor privy, we would use a large bucket fitted with a wooden seat.

The business and social center of our house was the kitchen, where mom cooked, washed, sewed, darned, and ironed, and where we ate all our meals, played games, read and did our homework. It was also the room for washing and bathing. We children bathed in a small metal tub and I suspect it was where our parents took sponge baths. You would think that the kitchen, the hub of our home, would be large but it was not. It was furnished with a wooden kitchen table, a bench, a few wooden chairs, a large stove, a washing basin, and a small cupboard for the kitchen dishes and utensils. The floor was wooden and covered with linoleum. There were two windows, never opened, and a door that led to the back yard. Our prime source of light was from a coal oil (kerosene) lamp that hung over the kitchen table. We carried candle lanterns that provided light when we went from there to one of the dark places in the rest of the house.

Our big cast iron stove with its warming oven on top and water tanks on the side was a work of art, coal black with strips of silver metal to give it a touch of class. In winter we usually had the oven door open for maximum heat, but the house never seemed to get dry because there was always steam rising from the copper boiler filled with laundry, from kettles, basins, and pots filled with soup. As a result, the windows were often an inch thick with ice on the inside, but I loved inspecting the lacy patterns it formed.

Our tiny living room had only room for a sofa and an old-fashioned Victrola on which we played classical music. Mostly I remember Caruso's voice filling the house. We children would fight to see who got to crank the record player. A wonderful rocking chair was Mother's favorite piece of furniture. It was here that she nursed us all, held us on her lap and sang songs in Yiddish and Russian and told us stories. Howard and I loved standing on the rockers on either side of the chair as she rocked and sang to Norman and Rita. I remember when Ma was nursing Rita, my brother Howard and I would lie on the floor and drink milk, each from his own beer bottle with a nipple attached, the openings greatly enlarged so that our regressive needs would be quickly satisfied.

Sarah was too grown up for all that. Though she was only four years my senior, from my earliest memories she always seemed much older and wiser. One of my earliest memories is of Sarah and her girlfriends playing house and dressing me up in girl's clothes. I didn't mind because I sort of liked the attention. But I always envied her because she was the pet of both parents, the one who had her own bedroom in Bruderheim and the one our folks would take with them on vacations. It was easy to understand why they would indulge her. She was very pretty, had lots of girlfriends and was well liked. She was also tops in her class and a model student. I did not like it when teachers would say, "So you are Sarah's brother. We hope you will be as good a student as she was." They were, of course, in for a disappointment. Nor did I like it when she got to travel with our parents. I still recall how jealous I felt when they took her to Banff.

My brother Howard was born on Nov. 12, 1922. Much to Mother's dismay she became pregnant with me while she was still nursing my brother, and I was born just sixteen months later on March 13, 1924.

Howard was sick a lot as a child, forever getting colds and always going round with a runny nose. His shirttails hung out and he was constantly hitching up his pants. He was bashful and timid, but good-natured and very kind, and from his earliest childhood, a tireless worker. Even as a little boy he would bring wood and water into the house without having to be asked.

It is strange that I have almost no memories of him in school, though I know that we were in the same room in the Walker School in Bruderheim, and it's possible we were even in the same grade. In those days I had no idea that he was struggling with learning and that he had serious difficulties with reading. But who was I to be a judge when I was such a bad student myself?

For a time he did play some sports such as tag and hockey but soon gave them up. He did, however, enjoy walking. If he got into any trouble, it was almost always because I instigated it. He just went along with me trustingly, with no thought about what I was getting him into. When mother tied us both to a tree after we'd been misbehaving, he stayed right there until she released him. If teased or picked on, he did not defend himself, so from an early age I acted as his protector. Though younger, I was bigger and much stronger than he was so I fought his battles for him.

Occasionally I also fought battles for my younger brother Norman, but for the most part he was able to take care of himself. Norman did not finish high school, although years later he decided to pursue an education, eventually surprising everyone, including himself, when he got his Ph.D. in geography and went on to become a college professor. From the time he was a toddler, he tagged along with me, doing anything that I asked him to do. He seemed to be fearless. I could put him inside a tire and roll him around the streets and even down some hills. He climbed trees and wandered among animals in the same manner as a barnyard dog. At the same time he was meticulous about his appearance.

Our baby sister Rita was a lovely baby and everyone's pet, especially Dad's. She had a great sense of humor, cried easily and was quick to make life long friends. Even though she was not a good student, she did go on to

Dad, (left to right) Howard, Rita, Ben, and Norman (bottom) 1929

become a registered nurse.

As my dad was a practicing Jew, we followed some of the rules and rituals associated with food, and mother, though an agnostic, fully shared his wish to have a kosher home. Because it was against Jewish dietary laws to mix meat and milk, we had two sets of dishes, one for meat, the other for milk. And since it is forbidden for orthodox Jews to eat blood, the symbol of life which only God can give, all our meat had to be killed by a shochet, a religious man who traveled to the small towns of the province to kill animals required for food. The shochet's basic technique is to sever the carotid artery so that the animal rapidly bleeds out; this not only satisfied our religious requirements but also reduced the chances for bacterial growth in the tissues. The shochet is also responsible for accepting or rejecting the bird or animal for food depending on the absence or presence of disease. To give us additional variety, two or three times a year dad would also order a box filled with wieners, salamis, and corned beef from Winnipeg. We didn't mind the inconvenience of this system; it just seemed normal.

For the high holidays of Rosh Hashanah (our New Year) and Yom Kippur (the Day of Atonement), dad would stop all work and take us to Edmonton. There we stayed in one room at the Royal George Hotel on 101 Street and walked to attend services at our synagogue on 95th Street. Dad was one of the founders of the synagogue and so was honored by having a place in the very front row.

Passover was celebrated at the home of dad's older brother, Beryl, who lived in Chipman, about 25 miles east of Bruderheim. We looked forward to being with dad's extended family and sharing in all the festivities. Much of the excitement for us was driving in dad's old Dodge over frozen snow-covered roads while we all snuggled under blankets and hides to keep warm. When we got to Chipman, the first thing we did was run into my uncle's general store, where after greeting us, he would give each of us boys a nice red handkerchief. Then we would run up the outside staircase to enter the home and meet all the other Dlins. The place would be humming with activity, lively chatter and the smell of wonderful pastries, although for me the best part of the excitement was wrestling with my older cousin Mickey. The big item of the occasion was the Seder and the retelling of the story of our exodus from slavery in Egypt. My Uncle Beryl, who presided over the ritual feast, conducted everything in Hebrew and Yiddish and was so very serious that he wrecked that portion of evening for the children. At the end of the day we were happy to get under the car's warm robes again and fall into a sound sleep. It would be late at night by the time we arrived home.

Minor holidays were celebrated at home. On Chanukah we would light the candles each evening, enjoy the songs and make wagers on which candle would be the last to burn out. Our traditional gift was a 25-cent coin. We didn't celebrate Christmas with its tree and lights, but we attended the local celebrations in our town hall, where dad or Mr. Kennedy from the grain elevator played Santa, distributing gifts to all the children. And my brothers and sisters and I did hang up stockings just in case Santa might even make a visit to an orthodox Jewish home. One year to make sure he left plenty for me, I asked Mrs. Fogelson for one of her stockings because she was the fattest lady around. She hollered and chased me away.

The only bad things about those early years were my first encounters with anti-Semitism. I was not yet in grade one when some boys called me "a dirty Jew" and accused me of killing Jesus Christ. Our being Jewish had never been hidden nor was it imposed upon others, so I thought people were intrinsically respectful of others just as my parents taught us to be. I returned home quite upset because of these accusations and told my mother, "I didn't kill anyone! I never even knew Jesus Christ."

This racial hatred never came from the people in town, but instead came from the farm boys whose parents had emigrated from central Europe. They must have learned this stuff at home or even in their churches where it was preached that the Jews killed Christ. I do know that there was strong support for Adolf Hitler from many of the German people in the Bruderheim area.

All this had to be upsetting to my parents because of the virulent anti-Semitism that they had faced in their youth, but they explained calmly that this behavior was not nice and told me to avoid these boys. That, however, did not work. The taunting became threatening to me and to my two brothers. Though scared and bewildered at first, I finally became furious and vowed that I would not run from them. When it got to the point where their threats became physical, I responded by fighting to protect myself and my brothers and proceeded to have so many fist-fights that it became almost routine. The only advice my dad ever gave me was "If you are attacked, protect yourself!"

I got to be a good fighter. I fought with a terrible rage with only one thing in mind and that was to beat my opponents. Even though I suffered cuts, bruises, and a broken bone, I never lost a fight. By the time I was 8 or 9 years old, dad was calling me Little Jack Dempsy. I knew that he took great pride in my being able to stand up to my tormentors just as he had while in the Ukraine.

There were two churches in town, one Lutheran and the other Moravian, and every Sunday most of the people of Bruderheim would attend one or the other. I loved to sit outside the Lutheran church with the farmers who pitched horseshoes, whittled away at wood and just talked while their womenfolk attended service. They spoke about women, sports local gossip, and sometimes told dirty jokes, but mostly talked farming. "So what did you feed that sick cow of yours?" Or "How much grain did you haul this week?" Or "Looks like we should get a good crop this year provided it don't hail. I sure hope this warm weather stays around for just a few more weeks." The quiet tone of the conversation conveyed a sense of serenity. It all seemed so simple and so intimate.

At the Moravian Church, I hid in the adjoining cemetery and watched their burial ceremony. I never actually saw the dead person, although I knew that someone had died because men and women dressed in dark clothing stood quietly next to a freshly dug grave, crying softly and praying as the coffin was lowered into the ground. Then I watched as some of the men stayed behind when the service was over and shoveled dirt back into the deep hole. I can still hear the sound of the first shovelfull hitting the wooden coffin.

That burial started a whole chain of thoughts and feelings for me that was somehow tied in with the animals and birds that were killed for food and the lives and deaths of pets. No one said prayers or cried when the head of a chicken was cut off or when a steer was butchered, yet when our dogs or cats died or were killed in accidents, intense grieving followed. I had already suffered the loss of my dogs Prince and Queeny. Both had been car-chasers and had their necks broken as they locked their teeth onto the wheel spokes. Now they were no longer around to hug and to play with.

I had more difficulty understanding about people who died. I knew some children who became ill, died and were buried so I understood that sickness and deformity could lead to death. I recall a pale-skinned, hunch-backed boy, a few years older than I, who couldn't play sports, and who one day just died. It was years later before I understood that he had suffered from tuberculosis of the spine. But as neither he nor any of the others who died had been my playmates, I couldn't understand the emotion and the significance of the loss. Therefore, I did not feel sadness for the dead person, only curiosity about those who grieved.

No one in our community had any formal medical training. We did not have a doctor, nurse, vet or dentist, and it was rare for a doctor to make a house call from Lamont, although it was only about 10 miles away. In fact, I have no memory of seeing a doctor visit our town, and though the people of Bruderheim were a relatively few miles from medical help, the weather could keep us isolated from that help for days or weeks at a time. Drifting snow often covered the roads, and when it rained, the local clay turned into a sticky gooey mess—gumbo—which would bog down all forms of motor transportation. In any case, a horse-drawn buggy or sled was generally the only form of transportation available, though not exactly the best choice for a very sick or badly injured person. By the time we traveled to the doctor, either it was too late and nothing more could be done or the crisis was passed and treatment was directed to healing complications.

As a result, those who lived in the community provided primary medical care. If they needed a vet, folks relied on a resourceful local farmer who was skilled and self-educated in the care of large animals. The same principle applied to human illness; sick people called on the neighbor with the most skill and practical knowledge. In our small community, people turned to my mother, the designated village nurse.

Medicine in the 1920s was still very primitive and really not far advanced from what had existed in the Middle Ages. Other than steam, cough medicine, aspirin, chicken soup, herbs, molasses and bed rest there was little to combat illness and disease. Mother did, however, understand that germs invisible to the naked eye caused illness and she was adamant in adhering to the principles of isolation and sterilization.

She was very good at diagnosing and treating sickness during the very early stages of development. Whenever one of her own family was ill, she attended to our needs around the clock. She would sponge our burning bodies to keep fever in check, encouraging us to drink quantities of water and chicken soup for the fluid and nourishment. She would feed us a "gogle-mogle"—a home mixed drink of hot milk, honey, butter and a little scotch or rum to ease a cough or sore throat. When one or more of us were ill from anything that seemed contagious—flu, measles, chicken pox—Mother had us stay in the "sick room," the tiny cubicle just off the kitchen where our indoor winter toilet was kept. It was just big enough to house a tiny metal-framed bed, a small table and one chair. There we were isolated from everyone except mother. The shade on the lone window would be drawn to cut down on the light if we had any photosensitivity or just needed to sleep without interruption. She would keep us clean and change the bedding frequently. Her great nursing skills kept us from succumbing to the ever-present potential for serious complications.

She used steam with aromatics added to it to counteract the dry atmosphere and ease breathing. Her mustard plasters were made with a hot mustard paste laid within a fold of linen and applied to the chest to draw out whatever was causing pulmonary congestion. It felt good as the burning on the surface took our minds off the coughing and pain, but it left the area with a red burn that stayed for days. Rashes caused by measles, chicken pox and other skin ailments were soothed by tea or starch solutions. Raw grated potato poultices did wonders for burns. She

21

had a variety of awful tasting expectorants for coughs that must have had a positive placebo effect.

My mother believed in prevention. Whenever we had a cut or scrape, she would wash the area with soap and hot water and then paint it with iodine that hurt like hell. She was forever warning us about the dangers of infection. "I don't want you to get blood poisoning!" she would say. This was something that we all listened to. I for one did not want to get a "sore ear" or a raging fever. I knew that lots of kids and grown-ups died from blood poisoning and that frightened me; I did not want to be buried in the ground.

Once my little brother Norman and I were playing on our homemade raft that we floated on the slough near the grain elevators. We were both barefoot and Norman stepped on a protruding rusty nail. I helped him back home and watched as mother cleansed the wound. She probed to remove dirt and rust, then flushed it out with water from the kettle to which she added a liberal supply of salt. When she was satisfied that it was clean she added some iodine and covered it with a sterile bandage. She was not taking any chances of having Norman get blood poisoning. When she treated any of us, we listened and cooperated. I was totally accepting of her care and never recall any sort of misbehavior. Now I marvel at her devotion and I see that I wanted to be like her when I grew up.

When the locals got scarlet fever, whooping cough or diphtheria, mother would cook for the family and advise them on the techniques of nursing care. It took great courage for her to enter the house of a diphtheria victim when she knew that it could cause death to her and hers. As I look back on what she did, I am amazed that she did not bring any illness home to us. I attribute that to the attention she gave to isolation and quarantine and to being scrupulous about cleanliness and sterilization techniques.

When my mother chatted with other women, they talked about recipes, canning and sewing, but my ears always perked up when the conversation turned to health or illness. In later years she told me that they would discuss the handling of such personal matters as child rearing, marriage, and birth control and said that she was openly opposed to reliance on the local abortionist. Although she didn't go into the specifics with me, she told me that she tried to educate the women on the methods of contraception available then. I believe these included crude diaphragms, cervical caps, condoms, douching and withdrawal. I think that her advice would still be totally appropriate today.

My dad's approach to medical care had more to do with magic than medicine. Our home had all sorts of his "secret" liniments for whatever ailed one. His favorite was a product created by John Schneider, a local farmer who in Russia had been a "feltsher," a lay person trained to do simple medicine like setting broken bones and relieving pain for those who could not get to a physician. "John's Liniment" was a creamy thick liquid that could blow the top of your head off with its powerful aroma of ammonia. If that weren't enough, it could also make your skin burn for hours after being applied. Dad would administer this concoction with great care and belief in its magical powers. When I visited John, I saw him use the same stuff on his horses.

Dad also insisted on having mother administer "cupping" to heal his illnesses. She would heat the inside of these specially designed glass beakers by holding the open end over the flame of a candle. She then placed each heated beaker on the area to be treated, sometimes six or more of them being applied to his back. After a while the cooled beakers would be removed, leaving bright red, round areas on his back. After this procedure was repeated a few times, dad would pronounce himself better. I was really impressed by this treatment and at the time believed that it did cure him of his sickness. I could relate it to sucking the skin on my arm to ease the itching of mosquito bites or the redness caused by bloodsuckers when I went swimming in the lake at Elk Island Park. Of course, the redness was actually caused by bleeding!

In our community, chronic conditions affecting the heart, rheumatic fever, kidney diseases and infected bones were commonplace. Many people just died after brief or prolonged periods of debilitation. I remember some of my friends being laid up in bed for months with rheumatic fever. They seemed so weak and pale when I visited them. Some of them died. I also recall people with broken limbs covered with a putrid smell of green and yellow pus. Epidemic diseases of measles, mumps, chickenpox, scarlet fever, whooping cough, diphtheria, and poliomyelitis constantly plagued the community, leaving a swath of fear, death and deformity behind.

In our family we all heeded mother's warning to stay away from these sick people and, of course, avoid going to school when there was an outbreak. The return to health was always greeted by a great sense of relief by everyone in the community.

Tuberculosis with all of its complications was endemic. There was always someone with a cough and bleeding from the lungs that resulted in their being sent off to some distant place for a cure. Mother was always attentive to our complaints of a tummy ache in case it was appendicitis; if the appendix ruptured, it was likely to result in death. Tonsils were routinely removed. We were told that this was done to prevent further infection of the tonsils and recurring sore throats. Ear infections and mastoiditis were extremely common; Dad had a depressed area behind his left ear from an operation for a mastoid infection. He satisfied my curiosity by letting me poke my finger into the hole.

Pneumonia was routinely associated with death especially if the victim was very young or very old; when I was told of someone having pneumonia, I just figured that they were going to die. People with arthritis ended up crippled and disfigured and often relegated to crutches or to limited activities around the house. Metabolic disease was evidenced by those who went around with large goiters from lack of iodine or with loss of limbs due to poorly managed diabetes.

As a kid I was intrigued by rotten and absent teeth. Most adults I knew had spaces in their mouths where teeth used to be. If there were too many spaces then the person had the remaining teeth extracted. Some were fitted with false teeth and some simply managed without teeth at all. When they closed their mouths their lower jaws almost touched their noses, and when they tried to chew food it seemed almost comical. I know that both dad and mom had partial dentures that they would take out at night and leave in a cup of salt water at their bedside. Mother urged us to brush our teeth each morning with a mixture of salt and baking soda, insisting that if we brushed each day we would save our teeth from falling out. This was one piece of advice I listened to.

Family, learning and sexual problems and cases of abuse were ignored or not even recognized because there was little understanding that early life experiences had an effect on later emotional and social development. People with mental illness ended up in insane asylums, killed themselves or simply wandered around in their communities where they were known as the local "crazies." There were a few of these people in Bruderheim, and I marvel now at the way the community extended itself to help these neighbors in distress, though every once in a while that help would not reach someone in time.

I recall two suicides. One was the first Mrs. Strong who jumped to her death in a grain elevator; the other was a farmer who laid on the railroad track to be run over by the train. I was about six when I heard about the farmer's suicide, but although people talked about the horrors of the event, they never spoke about why he did it. It was as if tragic things just happened.

Throughout my childhood I was conscious of the concern, fear and superstition that was attached to illness, and the frantic methods to which people resorted to protect themselves. They did everything that was done in the Middle Ages short of burning peoples' homes and throwing them into the inferno. Even mother would hang some camphor or garlic on a string around our necks to ward off evil vapors. Other people ate garlic, swallowed tonics and purged themselves with laxatives and enemas to cleanse their insides. They prayed for protection and shunned the ill as if they had leprosy or the bubonic plague. When I look back on those times, I wonder why more people did not die of infections and communicable diseases.

Periodically, our family took a trip to Edmonton to see Doctor Boulanger, our family doctor. His office building, right next door to the old YMCA, though very small by today's standards, really impressed me because it was made of brick. It had a small waiting room, which led into the doctor's consulting room; off to one side was the examining room.

We children always had brief examinations—a quick throat check or an examination of a sore ear—while he always spent more time with mother. It did not occur to me then that a mother of five might have more than an ear or throat examination. I used this extra time to wander around his consulting room "museum" that so intrigued me by its wonderful odor of medicines and disinfectant. I wondered about the strange set of tools he kept there, weird-looking saws, knives, forceps and retractors. They were like no other tools I'd ever seen, and it was some years before I realized this was his collection of medical antiques.

The shelves lining one wall in his waiting room were filled with bottles containing surgical specimens. The bottles, although well sealed, still gave off on unforgettable whiff of formaldehyde. I recognized fetuses at varying stages of development. Brains and such things as fingers and toes proved no mystery, but there were also appendices, gall stones, internal organs, growths, all devoid of color and lacking any resemblance to the bloody tissue I saw whenever animals were butchered. I wondered where they came from. Did the good doctor take the parts from the dead as farmers did when they butchered an animal?

Dr. Boulanger with his scientific knowledge and power was my first model of a physician. The perfect picture of the old-fashioned doctor, he had white hair and a neatly trimmed mustache, and he wore a wing-collared shirt and a dark suit. Although he was slight of build and much smaller than most of the farmers I knew, he oozed dignity and yet was warm and gentle and spoke in a soft voice. I knew he must be good if my mother went to see him for consultation, and by the time I was six, the idea of being like such a man and becoming a doctor began to dawn on me, though I must admit that at that time it was no more powerful an urge than my wanting to be a farmer or a singer in the Salvation Army.

It was around this time that Dr. Boulanger said I should have my tonsils taken out. This was usually done around that age as a means of preventing throat infections, but it was my very first experience with being admitted to a big city hospital. I had no idea what was going to happen, but I had no fear because I was with my parents and would be treated by my hero doctor. When I got to the operating room, my kindly old doctor was all decked out in a white gown, mask and cap. The anesthetist, whom I had never seen before, asked me to count out loud as long as I could. I think I got to 10 when the swirling began in my brain. I was being drawn into a vortex as the ether dripped onto the mask covering my nose and mouth.

I had a sore throat when I woke but my mother was at my bedside. My Uncle Jack, dad's younger brother, was there to give me a package of dried figs which I kept under my pillow and ate an hour or so later with some nice cold milk. I think that my kid sister Rita was also in the hospital that same day. Dad would be with her because she definitely had become his favorite child. All things considered, it was an interesting experience.

There was no residue of anxiety or concern, even though the swirling vortex induced by the ether would visit me in the form of dreams from time to time.

Before I was nine I had soaked up a tremendous amount from my parents about the broad approach to health and sickness, emotional as well as physical. I incorporated my dad's awe, respect and reverence for doctors and my mother's practical, straightforward approach to all things that confronted her. Even if there were no answers, she never gave up. She always strove to learn as much as she could. She was especially good at being objective and combined an unusual intuitive skill with being a good observer.

I am convinced that the seeds of my choice to enter the field of medicine were germinating and fermenting within the deeper recesses of my mind before I was nine. By the time I was in high school they had become a conscious part of my private thoughts. I am equally convinced that my parents had not the slightest idea that they had any special effect on my career selection. They just saw me at that time as a wild, unruly child.

BY THE SUMMER OF 1933 MY SISTER SARAH WAS READY TO enter the ninth grade, and our folks felt that all of us, especially Sarah, needed to have better schooling than what was available in Bruderheim's four-room schoolhouse. They also wanted us to have stronger ties with the Jewish community to help ensure the continuity of our Jewish identity and to promote marriage within our faith. Therefore, a few months after I turned nine, dad packed up the family and moved us to Edmonton.

After the move, dad spent his weekdays operating his general store in Bruderheim, commuting to Edmonton on Saturday nights for Sunday with the family. Our new home in the city's east end was huge in contrast to our country house, and it seemed so luxurious to have running water, electricity and gas. But most of all, I loved not having to run to an outdoor privy. I'll bet I flushed that toilet a dozen times for every bowel movement just to watch the water gush out of the tank and then load up again.

Much of my unruly behavior changed after leaving Bruderheim. I think it was because more structure was introduced into all aspects of my life—school, recreation and community. My school and street fighting slowed down dramatically. Although I had two great fights that first year in the city, both of them were precipitated by bullies who attacked me simply because I was a new boy at the school, not because I was a Jew. I found it rather novel to be surrounded by a huge crowd of kids in the schoolyard during those fights, but after both bullies were whipped, all my fighting stopped. I found new interests.

Our new house was across the street from a huge field in which there was an old-fashioned open-air skating rink. It was there I met Charley, the manager, who let me run the hand-pushed ice scraper and pull the barrel that sprinkled water over the ice surface.

I was enrolled in McCauly School, a red brick structure that was huge in comparison to Walker School. It seemed really novel to have an entire room just for a single grade. On the first day, the principal of the school, Mr. Humphries, had all the children line up in the main corridor and sing the Canadian national anthem and then put us through some drills in which we would chant things like "Look both ways before crossing the street." That all seemed like fun. Then I found out, without any warning, that I had to repeat the fourth grade. I guess the authorities figured correctly that my schooling had been inadequate to that point. My ignorance was graphically reflected in my first IQ test. I scored a 90, a low that became part of my school record for the next eight years.

My new teacher was Miss Hood, a woman who always seemed to be bitter or angry about something. I remember that one day she wanted the class to spell the word "curb." I raised my hand to ask, "Miss Hood, what is a curb?" Suddenly, as if she were propelled by a rocket up her ass, she ran down the aisle toward me, pulled my hair, hit me with a ruler and yanked all the books and papers from my desk. She screamed, "You're just a smart alec!" In reality, I was merely ignorant; there were no curbs in Bruderheim. I learned an important lesson from that experience with Miss Hood: "Don't ever ask an ignorant, mean-spirited teacher anything." Fortunately, she was the first and last of my evil teachers.

I started Hebrew school when I was ten and continued for the next eight years. The school was called Talmud Torah, which means "student of the Torah." Dad was one of the founders of the school, located on 103 Street just off Jasper Avenue, less than two miles from where we lived. We would walk there three times during the week and again on Sunday mornings.

At this time, although barely able to read English, I was confronted with the totally strange and ancient language that I would need in order to read and understand the Old Testament and be prepared for confirmation or Bar Mitzvah. Hebrew writing is entirely different from English even though the alphabet is similar to, but preceeded, both the Greek and Latin alphabets. For example, the vowels are symbols placed below the letters, and one reads from right to left, which just seemed backwards to me as a child.

After being enrolled in Hebrew school, we became active in the synagogue and joined Jewish clubs; for the first time in my life I met groups of kids who were Jewish. We began to develop a group of boy and girl friends that became the nucleus of our social group well into our adult lives. In the first club I belonged to, the Young Judeans, our activities centered on raising money for charity and having fun in the form of dances, picnics and parties, but we also elected officers, had executive meetings and a club newspaper. My sister Sarah acted as advisor to our young club and was the one we turned to for help with our little newsletter.

I was elected to be our representative on the executive committee of the Jewish Council which had just been formed and therefore became one of its charter members. This council's function was to coordinate all Jewish charities much as the United Way operates. I remember sitting in with the adults who were responsible for all local Jewish community activities as well as issues dealing with world Jewry. This was especially important because of the growing threat of Hitler's Nazi party in Europe.

However, none of this changed our family's participation in the non-Jewish community, so we had the best of both worlds, and I found this arrangement very satisfying. Soon after we were settled into our city life, dad enrolled Howard and I in the YMCA. On the way there he told us that when he first came to Edmonton, he had competed in wrestling at the Y and enjoyed having a good steam bath there. Although my brother Howard dropped out after the first year, I made great use of the facility. It was there that I learned to swim, play basketball and volleyball, and enjoyed friendly competition with a bunch of nice guys. After the first year I managed to earn a life membership at the YMCA by points gained through bringing in new members.

Dad also encouraged us to become involved with scouting. I well recall the thrill of joining Cubs and working to earn merit badges. We would meet weekly in the basement of our synagogue and later at the McDougal Presbyterian Church on 105 Street. A major event that still stays in my mind, happened on April 26,1935. It was the day 2500 cubs, brownies, guides and scouts gathered to meet Lord Baden-Powell, founder of the world scouting movement at the Edmonton Arena. We paraded around the center of the Arena while 3500 adults sat in the stands to watch the events.

Both my parents also joined new activities when we moved to the city. Dad was elected to the board of the Hebrew School. I felt very proud of him, especially since he never went to school himself. That same year mother became active in the Jewish theatre and in an organization called Pioneer Women, which raised money to aid women's labour groups in Israel. Around 1937 she became president, and I recall her having a group of her women friends to our house to meet with Golda Meir, then national president of the Pioneer Women's organization. Mrs. Meir looked and acted like a typical middle-aged Jewish mother, and when they all sat around the dining room table, she said to my mother, "Rose, why are the children sitting in the kitchen? Have them join us!" We were delighted because it meant more pastries for us. It wasn't too many years later that Mrs. Meir became prime minister of the State of Israel.

One year after coming to Edmonton, we moved to the west end of the city, remaining in that house until Dad purchased a permanent home for us on the same street. It was a great location. We were on the corner of 113 Street and 103 Avenue, just four blocks from Oliver school and the Westend pool and skating rink and one block from Gyro Park.

At the new school, Dr. Willis, the school psychologist, tested my brother Howard and decided that he was retarded. Without any consultation with my parents, the school authorities put him into the slow learner's class, a room that all the kids knew was for the "dumb" ones. Howard's demeanor changed overnight. He became even more bashful, resisted socializing and lost all interest in school. His activities became almost entirely related to work. With me as his helper, he got jobs shoveling sidewalks and emptying ashes from people's furnaces, collecting anywhere from 10 to 25 cents for the jobs, depending on how much was involved. His main joy, however, was in helping our milkman, Art Paquin, by driving the horse along Art's route and in helping deliver the milk. Art was a good man who genuinely liked Howard. As time went on gave him more and more responsibilities, finally introducing Howard to the management at Woodland Dairy as a prospective employee.

My mother, however, was not about to accept Dr. Willis's decision without a fight, and I recall her taking Howard to one doctor after another and finally to Dr. Levy, the chief of ENT at the University Hospital. After repeated visits, the doctor announced that Howard's problem was that he was hard of hearing but that nothing could be done about it. Mother was still not satisfied, but it would take money to get more medical help for Howard, and by this time dad had lost the store in Bruderheim.

When the Depression hit, the same farmers whose kids had taunted me in school had needed credit to survive. My dad had given it willingly, saying simply, "pay when things get better". Only about five percent of those farmers honored their debts. The rest took delight in not paying their bills to the "Jew."

In the end, dad had been forced to shut down his store, losing everything. But in spite of the difficult times, mother found the money to take Howard to the Mayo Clinic in Rochester Minnesota, the Mecca of Medicine at that time. She had been to the clinic herself on an earlier occasion for a checkup when she was visiting relatives in Minnesota.

After a few weeks mother and Howard returned home, having arranged that he would return for treatments to remove polyps that filled both middle ears. These growths had caused him to become progressively deaf, giving the impression that he was retarded. I don't know how mother scraped together the money for Howard's treatment or even how much the clinic charged, although I do know that they used a sliding scale in those days.

On his second visit to the Mayo Clinic, Howard remained in the hospital there for months. I recall how different he seemed when I met him at the CPR station on his return. He had grown taller and his voice was changing, but although his hearing was cured, the emotional damage he had suffered remained. He did gradually begin to read on his own and became a voracious reader, but he had lost all interest in school and now spent most of his time with our milkman. I recall feeling furious and disgusted with both Dr. Levy and Dr. Willis for the casual and incompetent way in which they had dealt with my brother.

It was not long after the recovery of Howard's hearing, when I walked into our house to find mother crying. I was alarmed because I'd never seen her cry before. "Mom, why are you crying?" I asked. She then told me that she had recieved news from Odessa that her parents had died. I

Howard and Ben Dlin, 1927, ages 5 and 3.

was a young teenager then. It one one of the few times that I ever saw her cry. I often felt that she had to be very strong in order to cope with all that she faced in life. Dad had an easier time letting his feelings out. He was more sentimental, and would cry from both sadness and joy.

We children knew no grandparents. Dad's parents had died before I was born, and mother's parents never immigrated here. All of our relatives in Canada were alive and well, so I did not experience what it was like to lose a close member of the family. However, I was able to feel concern and compassion for the suffering of others. This included family, friends, and even people I did not know.

As a young adolescent, I recall tending to mother when she was bedridden with the flu. She was having a severe bout of vomiting and diarrhea. I sat by her bedside all night, helping her to the bathroom, supporting her as she vomited into a basin, giving her sips of ice water, and applying a cool compress to her fevered brow. And yet, as weak as she was, she said, "Barney, why don't you get some sleep? You have school tomorrow." My answer was, "Mom, how many nights did you sit up with us kids when we were sick? So let me do the same for you." After that, she accepted my help.

One night I made Howard a mixture of hot milk, whiskey, and sugar for a severe bout of coughing and a sore throat. I know that is what mother would've given him, but he took one sip of the mixture, gagged, and refused my further help. I couldn't throw out the mixture, so I drank it myself.

After dad lost the store in Bruderheim in 1934, we had very little to live on. Food was limited to the cheapest items that would provide some nourishment, and dad would buy caselots of canned stuff, which we stored in our basement preserves room. On one occasion when he got a good buy on dried lima beans, they served as a staple for years. I've not eaten lima beans in the fifty years that have passed since then.

If we had meat, it was generally beef bones with some attached meat that mother used for soup stock. The Sunday "roast" was often lung and occasionally brisket. And I remember going to the Four-X Bakery a few blocks away at five in the morning to buy a full carton of day-old bread for 25 cents. We kept the bread in the snow during winter because that was our freezer. For my first two years of high school my lunch consisted of bread and butter sandwiches. We ate better during the summer because our garden gave us plenty of good vegetables, and when Howard worked for the dairy, he brought home milk and cottage cheese.

I think we hit our lowest spot the day that mother served us a tasteless soup made of dough dumplings floating in water. Having never seen anything like it before, we asked what it was. Without a moment's hesitation, Mother responded, "Why, it's Prince of Wales Soup! It's one of his favourite dishes!" Since we all admired the dashing prince and had his photo hanging just left of the front door, we all ate the soup without further complaint. It did fill our bellies and staved off hunger.

Mother made all the girls' dresses, and was constantly altering and repairing hand-me-downs. She patched our clothes and darned our socks so that nothing was wasted. Once in a while dad would take us to the G.W.G. manufacturing plant and buy us blue jeans at wholesale prices.

Everyone pitched in to help at home. Doing chores had always been a natural part of our daily routine. From the time that we were little, our folks had encouraged and expected us to contribute. I remember both Howard and I carrying firewood into the house in Bruderheim and bringing water from our pump. But after dad lost the store, my tasks in our Edmonton home increased to include digging and weeding the garden, washing and waxing floors, hanging out the wash and bringing it in to be ironed. I also ironed shirts and dresses, washed windows, helped with canning and whatever else needed doing. Mother's arrangement for dealing with the dishes was to have us draw straws. Each different length was designated for clearing, washing or putting away the dishes.

Any money that came into the house was put into a gravy dish in the kitchen cupboard, and was used to pay the mortgage, taxes and utilities first; anything left over went for food and clothing. Dad got a job managing produce warehouses where he graded potatoes, eggs and turkeys. Howard became good at lining up customers who needed ashes removed from furnaces or sidewalks shoveled. I made money doing stage makeup. My teacher was Harvey Kagna, a family friend who was an executive with the Edmonton City Bakery by day and a make-up artist in his spare time. He had trained with the famous Hollywood makeup expert Perc Westmore, and whenever us kids put on plays for Jewish holidays he put makeup on us. Since we were protraying characters from the Old Testament, we had to be made up to look like King David and Moses and the pharoahs of Egypt.

I was fascinated by the way Harvey could take a ten or twelve-year-old child and completely transform their features. Seeing my interest, he asked if I would like to be one of his assistants, and I was given the honour of applying the cold cream to the kids' faces. When I mastered this, I was allowed to apply the makeup base, then the shadows and lines, then nose putty and false hair. After a while I became part of his crew whenever operas and carnivals were performed in Edmonton, and by the time I was in high school, Miss Eva Howard, our drama teacher, placed me in charge of makeup for all our school productions.

In high school I also worked every Saturday selling shoes at the Army and Navy Department Store. Then one day I was called into the office of Harry Cohen, the owner, for a little chat. A big man with a deep horsey voice, he was always puffing on a big fat Cuban cigar. "You're a good hard worker," he told me. "How would you like the job of delivering the company's cash to the bank?" After that, each Saturday I would carry two big canvas bags loaded with thousands of dollars to the bank. My pay was four dollars and some change. I put the bulk of the money I earned into the family gravyboat, keeping only enough for spending money.

In spite of the family's economic setback, our morale was good. We could still enjoy listening to good music, playing cards and having a cup of tea together. We took pride in being able to manage without having to ask for assistance. I never saw or heard any evidence of complaint on the part of my parents; they had both seen far worse times.

It was when my friends and I were somewhere between ages eleven and twelve that we started having parties and dances. It was awkward but fun. In the beginning the boys and girls stayed to themselves except for a few brave kids who would ask each other to dance, but it wasn't too long before we had boy/girl parties at each other's homes. I remember getting aroused by holding a girl in my arms, especially when they had breast development. We boys would talk about what they felt like and how exciting it was as if it was the first time we ever saw or felt a set of mammary glands. I never recall getting so excited about my older sister Sarah or my Mother's breasts. During these parties, one or both parents would sit in the kitchen, preparing snacks and some non-alcoholic drinks. They knew quite well what was going on.

Of course, being around animals when we lived in Bruderheim, I wasn't entirely ignorant about sex. I remember one incident when I was no more than three or four—I stood about a head taller than my dog Prince so I know that I was very young—that I came upon Prince vigorously humping another dog. I knew what he was doing because all the farm animals and chickens were constantly humping each other. What bothered me on this occasion was that I couldn't separate Prince from his girlfriend no matter how much I beat him with a stick. In disgust, I left them and was sauntering down the road when I saw an adult couple walking, talking, holding hands and gazing at each other with strange intensity. I came to a shocking realization. *They do it too!* I thought. *Humans hump each other!*

It wasn't long after this realization that I felt sexual passion for the first time. I kissed blue-eyed, blonde-haired Velma Strong, my only female playmate. I was no older than five at this time because I know we were not yet in first grade. She became my first real girlfriend.

Around that time, I have this memory of my sister Sarah lying in bed with a hot water bottle on her tummy and crying while she read *Gone with the Wind.* I knew something was wrong because she was not going to school. I asked mother and she said something like, "Sarah is not feeling well. She is having female problems that she will have once a month." I was satisfied with the explanation and understood that Sarah was menstruating. She had just turned eleven.

I was about twelve, just a few months short of puberty, when my friends and I started to become more sexually active at our parties. This took the form of playing kissing games such as spin the bottle and postman's knock. We then advanced to turning off the lights, pairing off, and doing some kissing and hugging. If we were lucky we got to feel a girl's breast. Wow! What's interesting is that when these kids grew up, a good percentage of them married each other.

The major event in my life at age thirteen was being called up to the Torah to chant the portion of the week, as Jews have done for thousands of years. By then I had spent four years preparing to stand up there in front of the congregation to perform this task with everyone checking to make sure I did not make a single mistake. This was my official introduction into manhood, but I think it would have been easier to take a spear and go out and survive a week in the wilderness as was the custom in some societies.

As soon as I finished, women sitting in the balcony threw down paper wrapped candy at the boy-turned-man. Kids scrambled to pick up the goodies and then the celebration began. In those days that meant the grownups in the congregation gathered in the basement of the old synagogue to share in a drink of whiskey and eat herring and simple pastries. A party for my boy friends followed with a movie, more food and a baseball game. In the evening, friends and relatives came to our home to bring gifts and congratulations and to have more to eat and drink.

I recall the gifts of money totalling the huge sum of $14, enough to buy a brand new, sturdy, blue CCM bicycle, a major luxury for a kid like me. Norman was as delighted as I was for he soon learned to ride it even though he could not yet reach the pedals from the seat.

From the time I enrolled in Oliver school, I really liked my teachers. A few were outstanding and had a great influence on my life. The first and the best of all was Mrs. Francis, my sixth grade teacher. She was a loving person who recognized something in me that led her to assign me a major classroom project that took months of my time. For my workplace she set up a 4x8 foot piece of plywood on a couple of sawhorses at the back of the room.

My assignment was to make a giant relief map of India, which was to include all geographical landmarks, natural resources, cultures, religions, industries, and agriculture. I remember using large amounts of flour and water to make mountains and painting the rivers blue. I did not know why Mrs. Francis picked me out, but I was the only student in class assigned an independent project.

While she taught the other students, I had the freedom to spend all the time I needed on my assignment in the back of the room, although she did expect me to keep up with my regular class work. I worked at my own pace, adding information as I researched it. When the year was over Mrs. Francis gave me 110% for my project, the highest mark I ever got in school. But what was more important was the feeling of excitement and enthusiasm in working with a teacher who inspired me in some mysterious way to do the best I could for her and for myself. It was easy.

Mrs. Francis seemed quite old to me, yet she was only in her mid-forties then, a widow without children. I would describe her as thoughtful, sincere and dedicated to the task of teaching. Every once in a while she'd bring us a batch of cookies or some homemade caramel candy, and she always had an interesting book to read aloud to the class. We would listen with total attention and even rapture. She commanded respect without seeming to make any special effort to get it.

As the years went by, we wrote to each other on a regular basis. Her last letter was from an old folks' home in Edmonton. She wrote, "I was sitting in my wheel chair delighting in watching sparrows flying freely about as big fluffy flakes of snow dropped from the skies, when suddenly this lovely tranquil scene was interrupted by this old geezer who came over and made a pass at me. I told him to get lost!" Mrs. Francis died a few weeks after she wrote that letter. In her will she listed the names of her special students, requesting that they be notified of her death. I never did discover what led her to assign me the India project.

In 1938, my ninth grade home-room and social studies teacher was

Miss Houston, a big woman with huge breasts and an abdomen held so tightly in place by her corset that she looked like some of my mother's aunts in our family album. Her red hair was done in a style straight out of the 1920s with not a hair out of place, so that she appeared to be wearing a wig. She never sat down but was always pacing back and forth about the classroom as she addressed us, her shrill voice adding to the intensity of her words. But not once did I think of her as anything but sincere because this Victorian-looking woman was a liberal thinker, and she was the first to expose me to the socio-political events that were affecting people's lives in other parts of the world.

Her lessons were relevant. She was passionately involved in the turmoil in China as well as the trouble brewing in Europe. And when Europeans began their exodus to escape the growing threat of the Nazis, she galvanized the students through her passionate and realistic description of what was really happening over there to innocent civilians. She taught us to recognize need and be willing to help all people in need, regardless of race, colour or religion. It was not enough, Miss Houston told us, to reach out to people in our immediate community. After a year with her, I was no longer able to think of my world as mostly Bruderheim and Edmonton.

I was one of the kids she drafted to meet trains bringing the Czechoslovakian refugees who would be homesteading land in the wilderness more than 500 miles due north of Edmonton in the Peace River country. I could understand and speak some German because of exposure to it in Bruderheim and because my multilingual parents spoke a fluent Yiddish, which is similar to German. Our meetings took place on the platform of the Canadian National Railway, right next to the train. It was an eery, black-and-white scene, illuminated only by the station lights in the background. But there is nothing quite so alive and powerful as an old-fashioned, coal-fueled, steam locomotive in the dead of winter, with huge puffs of steam belching out in clouds from beneath it, and smoke from the top of the engine puffing high into the air above the steam, eventually disappearing as delicate wisps into the black night that surrounded us.

A heavy blanket of frost and ice covered the train as if that and the steam would keep it warm, and in spite of an outside temperature of 40 degrees below zero, we knew that it would be warm and toasty inside the belly of the train. As each train arrived, we greeted the refugees with food, coffee and a warm personal welcome. I can still see the joy and gratitude on their faces as they embraced us children. Their warmth helped us to ignore the bitter winter cold on the platform.

After a short stop the refugees boarded the train and were on their way again up to the frozen north. I worried about how they would thrive under such frigid conditions, but within a few short years they all prospered as they had been settled on some of the richest farm land in Canada. Many also profited from oil discovered on their acreage.

It was also during 9th grade at Oliver School, that I got into my last schoolyard fight. Billy Bushel, the school bully, began picking on my brother Howard, and by the time I came along, Billy was taunting him and pushing him to the ground. I pulled him off and challenged him to a fight in the basement of the school, well out of sight of teachers who might stop the brawl, but word got around and we were soon surrounded by a mob of boys.

It was a great fight, but after about twenty minutes of slugging, I hit his head so hard I fractured the fifth metacarpal in my right hand. He came out of it with one eye swollen shut—it stayed black and blue for a couple of weeks—but his bullying stopped, and he actually turned out to be a nice kid. I never told my mother about the fight nor did I go to a doctor to have him set the fracture, although the hand was badly swollen and the bone grossly misshapen.

It was after this that I joined a boxing class at the YMCA. What a wonderful change from all those years of fierce schoolyard brawling! But after only a couple of weeks, while sparring with an excellent boxer, he hit me with a sound right hook that really rattled my brain. I decided then and there to give up this sport because of the very real danger of permanent brain injury. It was finally dawning on me that brain power was going to get me further than muscle power.

My interest in canoeing began that same spring when my good friend Ralph Allman and I were hiking along the North Saskatchewan River, enjoying the break-up of the winter ice. The river was very high and moving fast with thick chunks of winter ice smashing into each other. It was an exciting scene to witness, and one I never tired of.

Suddenly a lovely red canoe appeared on a large chunk of ice floating past us near the shoreline. To our amazement the canoe seemed to be in good shape, so we followed until the ice butted against the shoreline. I jumped on, grabbed the canoe and was off again within a few seconds. Other than a few tears in the canvas covering, it was in good shape. There was no way that the owner could be identified, so we carried it back to Ralph's home about a mile and a half away.

His Dad was handy with fixing things so he told us how to repair it, then as favor he painted the head of a wolf on both sides of the prow. We bought two paddles and were in business. Since neither of us had ever canoed before, we were lucky to have Dave Kushner, Ralph's cousin and my friend, to teach us. He was an expert, having learned the craft by paddling canoes to his father's trading post in northern Alberta.

Mother was always telling me to not to hang around by the river. Of course I promised not to. What I did not tell her was that we were spending most of our time right out on the river. We would paddle upstream, have a picnic, do some exploring and then drift back to where we stored the canoe on racks built by the city on the first ravine. We even left our paddles in the canoe where they remained safe.

Sometimes on these canoe trips I would pull into shore to chat with a man hiking along the riverbank, looking for wild flowers. Much later I learned that this amateur botanist was Dr. Herb Rawlinson, a professor of anatomy at the University of Alberta.

In tenth grade, my teacher was Mr. Shortliffe. A pot-bellied little man, he stood only five foot four; he was almost bald and had a W.C. Fields red nose and twinkly little eyes that could make a student cringe in fear or laugh with delight. He was the best algebra teacher in the province.

On the first day of his class he announced that algebra could be learned with ease once we understood how to communicate! So we talked. I cannot recall the details of those few months, but it was all about observing, clarifying and responding without fear of being thrown out of the classroom. I do know that the class trembled when he would demand something like, "George, what is the eleventh commandment?" George, a very religious boy, naturally came up with a religious response. "No, George," said Mr. Shortliffe. "The eleventh commandment is that you can't divide by zero!"

During one early math class I responded in such a fuzzy way that he raised his yard stick and shouted, "Dlin, you make me so angry I'm tempted to throw you straight through the keyhole of that door! And don't you think I can't do it!" For a brief moment I thought he could. After class he saw me in the hall, gave me his merry chuckle and was on his way. About two months into the term, he announced that we were ready to do some math.

Mr. Shortliffe's passion was to to get our brains free of clutter, bias, and the fear of saying what we thought. He demonstrated that in all learning it was essential to make clear and precise observations and communicate exactly what was observed, a fundamental principle of the scientific process. He proved the value of his method year after year in the results he achieved with a group of both bright and average students. As long as he continued to teach, his students always led the province in the algebra finals.

It was also in 10th grade that I learned about the first aid courses offered by the St. Johns' Ambulance and taught by a physician who worked with the city health department. I could not wait to enroll and saved money to pay for training in both his beginners and advanced courses. A year later I took the advanced correspondence course offered by the British Columbia's St. Johns' Ambulance as they were reputed to be the best. I did well in all of them.

Ben Dlin, age 16, a tenth grade student in Edmonton, Alberta

Towards the end of the first year of World War II, at the age of sixteen, I also joined the medical branch of the reserve army corps. Here I did basic training and learned more first aid, casualty evacuation and field hospital operation. Our C.O. was Dr. Ernie Watts, head of the anaesthetic department at the university hospital, and his second in command was Dr. John McGregor, a pathologist also on the university faculty.

At school, the head of our army cadet corps was Mr. Walter Stewart who also taught physics. He was tall and trim with sandy hair and deep blue eyes. A man without guile, he was kind, supportive and a master at making each student feel comfortable in his presence. He did that by being fair, and because we respected him in the classroom and on the field, we wanted to please him, and so he brought out the best in us.

Although I was only average in physics, I played on all school teams and was the ranking officer in cadets. When Mr. Stewart relaxed outside of these activities, we would often meet in the basement office of Mr. Davidson, the school janitor, to play chess and just talk. He was Walter at those times. Our friendship continued until he died.

In spite of my wonderful teacher role models, I somehow managed, through the three years of high school, to remain near the bottom of the class. I had, however, excelled in all sports, held offices in student government, the school paper, drama club, chess and checker clubs. I had lots of good friends and a handful of best friends. School was such a blast that I shared my enthusiasm with everyone, and when I became a senior, I was voted the student with the best personality. So aside from not doing well academically, I felt that I had achieved an A-plus for all my extracurricular activities.

I had studied what I wanted, spending many an hour in a boring class secretly reading a book on medicine or science from the public library. One of my favorites was *The Microbe Hunters*. I read the *Books of Knowledge* from cover to cover and devoured volumes on Greek mythology. I read some romantic books, too, mostly because friends would tell me the page number of the "dirty" parts. Sexual descriptions interested me; the story mattered little.

Another source of information were the medical books of my friend Allen Spaner's older brother, Sid, who was overseas as a medical officer with the Canadian Air Force at that time. Together Allen and I would get out Sid's text books, especially those on obstetrics and gynecology, to look for sexually-revealing pictures. I recall puzzling over the vagina because it was always presented in some weird cross-sectional anatomical diagram. I was expecting something a little more exciting, as in *Playboy*.

During high school, I never shared my intention to go to medical school with anyone. I think that was because I did not want people to think I was daydreaming. As well, I didn't want to reveal my ambition, then fail in my attempt to even get into university. However, toward the end of my high school years I announced to my parents that I planned to go to university to study medicine. They were very pleased. There was no discussion of how I would pay for it. Mother simply responded by saying that I could have a room all to myself and that she would do all she could to keep the house quiet while I studied. Then she added, "You know that you will have to develop a good "tuchas" (rear end) if you plan to sit and study!"

Their reaction was about what I expected. If something had to be faced or a job had to be done, they had always dealt with it without complaint. Mother tended to be more rational in her approach to problems. Dad always relied more on his physical strength, but both exuded confidence in their ability to get the job done. And from my earliest childhood they communicated that confidence to me, so that now I fully believed that I could accomplish what I planned to do.

Of course, I still had two big problems: my grades were so poor I could not apply for admission to a university and I didn't have the money for either tuition or books. Obviously, playtime was over. I must settle down to a year of intense study in order to raise my grades to an acceptable level while at the same time earning enough money to pay for my university education.

I approached old Charley who ran the skating rink in the winter and the Westend swimming pool in the summer. He remembered me as the eager kid who had begged to push the scraper over the ice for him and he gave me a job working as a lifeguard. Then, in the middle of August, I left Edmonton to work on a farm owned by the Dewarts, a lovely English family who lived near the town of Vegreville, about sixty miles east of Edmonton. Their section of land was planted mostly with wheat and barley. The farm itself was typical of the times—a small wooden house with a few sheds, a big red barn, a pig pen, chicken-coop, large vegetable garden, wood pile, outdoor well, and outdoor privy. Before I arrived, they cleaned out an old 10-by-15-foot chicken shed, put in a bed, a chair, a small bureau for my clothes and a pot-bellied stove to provide heat for the harsh months ahead.

Work began before daybreak and ended at dark. My first chore was to muck out the stables, then feed and water the horses and get them harnessed. When that was done it was time for breakfast. I'd pump some cold water from the well into an enamel basin and quickly wash up, eager to satisfy my hunger. To get into the kitchen, one entered through a mud-room where dirty boots and jackets were left. The kitchen itself was just big enough for a huge old-fashioned, wood-burning, cast-iron stove and a large table laden with food. I never had so much consistently good food—an endless supply of oatmeal, bacon, eggs, potatoes, bread, butter, jams, milk, and coffee. The talk was animated, all about farm chores and preparations for harvesting the crops.

Weather conditions were perfect that fall, dry and warm during the day with no evidence of rain, hail, or frost in the near future, but there was a sense of urgency to get the crops in that was familiar to me. The window of time from the ripe crop to the grain elevators was a matter of a few weeks, and the whole year's plans and hopes focused entirely on that critical period. First thing each day, everyone would sniff the air and check the sky, hoping for good weather and dreading the emergence of a sudden fierce fall storm that could destroy the crop in a matter of minutes. Because of the flat prairie terrain, one could see black storm clouds roll in like huge locomotives, belting out thunder and lightning instead of steam and smoke.

I remember as a child running for shelter for fear of being drenched by rain, pelted with ice or struck by lightning when these storms rolled down from the prairie skies. And yet, as much as this was in the back of everyone's mind, on the Dewart farm weather forecasting was limited to *The Farmer's Almanac.* No one ever spoke of the omnipresent danger. Rather they would say, "Well, it sure looks like another beautiful day," or "We should get the back forty cut and stooked before nightfall!"

After breakfast my job was to get the horses hitched up to the binder, a machine that would cut the stalks of grain about six inches from the ground, bundle them together, tie the bundle with twine and drop it to the ground. I would then join the crew of young field hands from the local area who followed the binder, picking up the stooks and piling them up into a teepee arrangement to hasten drying and prevent rot.

On my first day on the job, the binder driven by Mr. Dewart had just got well out of sight when all four of the field hands lined up in front of me, and the biggest guy announced, "We're going to fight you!" There was no reason given. I figured it must be their stupid way of establishing dominance. The choice was to give in and be bullied or take the challenge. I'd never lost a fistfight in my life, and I was not about to lose my first to this lot.

I pointed to the leader of the group, a stocky muscular young man who easily outweighed me by forty pounds, and said, "You first." He attacked with sudden fury. I stood my ground, then just as he reached me, I sprang into action. I grabbed his shirt and, using his momentum, threw myself backward while holding onto him. At the same time I thrust my feet into his belly, assisting him on his forward path as he hurtled through the air. He landed in the dirt with the wind knocked out of him. Before he could move, I was on top of him with my hands around his throat, squeezing his windpipe firmly. Very quietly I said, "If you don't give up now, I will kill you!" He figured I meant it and gave up. I then turned and challenged the rest; they all backed away. I was disappointed because I was ready to thrash the lot of them. We went back to work. The bullies were no further threat to me.

That night as I lay in bed, tired from the day's work, my door suddenly burst open, and the room was flooded by the headlights of a car outlining a female silhouette in the doorway. "Get up and get dressed!" she said. "We're going partying!" Talk about comic relief: a fight earlier in the day and now this! It turned out that she was the girl from the farm next door, and the Dewarts had put her up to it. I threw on some clothes and asked, "Where are we going?"

"First we're going to one of our neighbors for some cream," she explained, "and then to another neighbor for some ice. We have an ice cream maker at home." It was past 11 pm, but we drove around waking everyone up to get what she wanted, and to my amazement no one seemed to mind. Then we made ice cream. We became good friends for the short time she was home before going off to school. There was never anything romantic between us. We were just two kids having a good time.

A short time after I arrived on the farm, Harold—a tall, quiet kid who was part of our social group in Edmonton—called to ask if I could get him hired by my boss. A city kid who played a great game of basketball, he knew nothing of farm life but wanted the experience of working on one. My boss was gracious about taking him on. Early the first morning we went into the barn, mucked it out, and then I brought out a team of horses for Harold to hold. Gingerly he took the bridles just as the huge workhorses reared up on their hind legs. Petrified, Harold let go of the bridles and ran out of the barn. Shortly afterwards, we sat down to our wonderful breakfast and I noticed that Harold was uncomfortable with all the flies buzzing about, although he was trying to hide it. But at the exact moment he took his first swig of milk, two flies locked in a nuptial embrace flew directly into his glass, and he swallowed them. That did it! He rose from the table and said in a strong voice, "I've had all I can take!" and left without even saying farewell. Afterwards he never mentioned his life as a farmer.

One Sunday, city friends of the Dewarts visited the farm. It was a first for their very attractive daughter, a girl about the same age as myself. She'd never seen a cow being milked before, so I was quick to volunteer as her guide. It was a perfect way for me to show off. The act of milking is rather seductive by the very nature of rhythmically pulling the cow's teats. However, this particular cow was a kicker so her hind legs needed to be shackled. As I bent down to apply the shackles she suddenly let fly a huge, loose, green bowel movement that splattered all over me. The young lady was horrified and ran to the house, while I ran for the horse trough and jumped in. I never saw her again, but that did not stop me from the joy of showing off whenever I had the chance.

I left the farm in November because of a severe staph infection in my right hand. After the abscess was incised, I returned home to recuperate and then do odd jobs in the city to continue building up my savings for school as well as contributing to the household expenses. At the same time I worked hard to prepare myself for the high school supplemental exams held each year near the end of summer vacation. I had a constant battle to overcome my feelings of reluctance and avoidance to sit and study Latin, mathematics, chemistry, physics and English.

Although I was determined to take the exams again and again if I failed, I passed on my first try in all my subjects, just making the minimal requirements for pre-med by one one-hundredth of a percent. When I met with the director of admissions, his only comment was, "Dlin, you sure know how to make it under the wire!"

A few days after I was accepted, dad came home and told mother, "One of the managers at the Hudson Bay Company tells me he has a sales job for Ben." He knew that I wanted to go to university, but the family's need for money to pay the bills drove him to make this suggestion. Mother's answer was, "Save your breath, Bill. It's out of the question!" She never lectured us on what we should do with our lives but she was a staunch believer in education.

Although Howard's educational opportunities had been sabotaged by his undiagnosed hearing impairment, Sarah had already left home at the age of 16 to study nursery school education in Chicago. Rita would later enter nursing, and Norman, after a delayed start, became a geography professor.

I knew what the odds were for getting through Pre-Med. It was definitely a long shot, since I would be competing against the best high school students from the three western provinces. Like an addict going cold turkey to cut his habit, I gave up sports, clubs, social life, Jewish holidays and free reading. From now on, my fighting would be directed to staying the course and beating out my competition; brain power would take the place of muscle power. My exercise would be limited to the walks to and from the university and the push-ups I would use to force myself to stay awake. My textbooks would take the place of romance. Even though I agonized over the task ahead, I never panicked nor did I lose sleep over it. I derived a little comfort from the thought that if I didn't make it, I could always study agriculture.

IN SEPTEMBER 1943, WORLD WAR II WAS IN ITS FOURTH YEAR. Although men were needed to fill the fighting ranks of the armed forces, I didn't even consider volunteering because my poor eyesight would have excluded me from active duty. There was, however, a major effort underway to train physicians as rapidly as possible to fill the ranks of the military medical corps.

To do this, universities had reduced pre-med and medicine from a seven-year program to six years by instituting longer school hours and shorter vacations. Courses not essential to the medical curriculum were omitted. We would receive a B.Sc. degree after completing the two years of pre-med and the first two years of medicine, and our degrees as medical doctors after our fourth year of medicine. In retrospect, I regret not having the time to enjoy culturally enriching courses such as philosophy and the history of art, but at the time I was happy to become a doctor that much sooner.

Of the ninety students accepted for pre-med at the University of Alberta, most were poor and had been tops in their high school classes around western Canada. Only the small group to which I belonged had been poor academic achievers. However, these ninety students would spend the next two years competing for just fifteen places in the first year of medical school, with the balance of that student body being made up of returning veterans and out-of-province students, to bring the total number in the class to thirty-six. As a result, the pressure to perform well was tremendous, not only for entry into medical school, but also because a failure in just one subject meant being asked to leave the university and get involved in the war effort. No student would be given the luxury of "goofing off."

With a war on, all university males were required to enter officers' training (ROTC). Our commanding officer, Major Towers, had left my high school at the beginning of the war to run the university army training program. We were issued uniforms and started on the drills associated with basic training, but as a result of my background in first aid, I was immediately promoted to the rank of sergeant and posted to the medical corps, commanded by Major E. Watts and Captain J. McGregor, both professors in the medical school.

The great perk of this promotion was that whenever we went on maneuvers at Camp Sarcee located just west of Calgary, I was excused from infantry duty to be in charge of administering the field hospital and assisting the medical officer during his rounds. That medical officer was Dr. Bob McBeth, who had been my cub master and later an opponent in handball at the YMCA.

However, running cross-country with a pack on my back in army training was a piece of cake compared to the job of becoming a good student. For me sitting for long hours and studying was sheer torture. But if I was to have a chance of making it, I would have to discipline my mind and body to learn, memorize and understand the massive amount of material pushed at us each day. I did have one advantage over some of my fellow students: from the moment I went farming after high school, I had become determined to settle down and focus on becoming a doctor. So by now all my energy and drive were effectively geared toward achieving my goal in life.

Howard, who had quit school at sixteen and had his own early morning milk delivery route with Woodland Dairy, still lived at home, as did Norman and Rita; Sarah, however, was living in Chicago. This made it possible for me to have a room of my own for the first time in my life. It was barely big enough for a single bed, a small table and chair and a place to stack my books and notes, but I was grateful for the luxury of it.

I insisted on complete silence within the house because the slightest noise served as a major distraction to my as yet undisciplined mind. I even had to put my alarm clock under the pillow to shut out the sound of its ticking. My mother backed me up and enforced the family's silence. To this day my siblings remind me of what torture it was for them to walk softly, whisper quietly and listen to our only radio with an ear pressed to the speaker. The only exception was my little sister Rita's piano practice. When I arrived home from school each day, she would practice while I took a power nap on the sofa next to her. As soon as she started her scales, I would fall sound asleep.

In spite of all the complaints from Howard, Norman and Rita, they did understand my needs and supported me in my struggle to study. And my folks never complained. My going to university was the beginning of a major shift for our family from a life of turmoil and struggle to the life of education and professional opportunity that they valued so highly. In the early evening they sat at the kitchen table and played cards, and when I needed a brief break there was always some hot tea ready for me and a chance to share with them some of what I was studying. This pattern gradually became a ritual that I followed day after day, month after month.

My need to escape from the overwhelming task of studying was almost constant. I would sit on a straight-backed wooden chair next to my little table and fall asleep as soon as I started reading my notes or books. My brain was exhausted even before I opened a text. I drank gallons of coffee to stay awake, and when that didn't work, I would chew coffee beans by the mouthful. I'd do sit-ups and push-ups in the narrow space next to my bed until my muscles ached. Since I refused to leave my desk until my work was done, many an hour was spent with my head lying on the desk with my mouth open and saliva drooling onto my notes as I slept.

For the better part of my freshman year, I felt constantly frustrated; apprehensive that I couldn't learn it all in time therefore paying the price for avoiding my high school studies by not making it. There were huge gaps in my knowledge in every subject, and I drove myself to grasp work that was totally foreign to me. At the same time I had to master the vast amount of new material presented in class each day. There were times when I felt like a drowning man trying to swim against the tide, but when doubts or fatigue would threaten to overwhelm me, I'd close my eyes, lean back and think about how it had felt shoveling manure on the Dewarts' farm. Then I'd open my eyes and contrast the comfort of our warm fam-

Ben as a Premed Student at the University of Alberta.

ily home in Edmonton with the cold quarters of the converted chicken coop that had been my home for three months. Better medicine than agriculture, I decided.

At the same time I discovered that my rebellion against discipline was slipping away. After a few months, I was putting in two hours of study for each hour of class time. I discovered that all I needed was about five hours of sleep; I no longer needed coffee. Drooling stopped and exercise became more tolerable. The light in my window was a signal to the neighbors that I was at my desk. Everyone encouraged me with lots of praise and support.

No matter what time I went to sleep, I'd be up and out of bed by 5 am to review what I'd ploughed through the night before, making summaries that served as essential outlines around which I could paste on the related new materials. Each weekend was used to catch up and to review the work of the past week. Gradually, a format for study began to develop. Learning began to be fun, taking me back to the highs that had come to me as a country boy making discoveries in my own little world.

Pre-medical courses were standard for us all. They included English, German or French, medical Latin and Greek, as well as organic, inorganic and analytic chemistries, biochemistry, genetics, zoology, physics, and other practical courses such as statistics. Lectures lasted an hour, while the labs in the chemistries, zoology and physics took two to three hours. Together classes and labs totaled about forty hours a week.

The three-to-four mile walk to and from the university on the south side of the city saved the cost of streetcar travel and provided fresh air and exercise. Two of my classmates, Len Maher and Eli Shector, who lived nearby, joined in the walk so that we had the additional opportunity of quizzing each other on subjects we shared. On the walk back we mostly used our time to unwind, talking about the day's events or just things in general.

We all delighted in the beauty of the vast expanse of the North Saskatchewan River as it wound through the city and the surrounding wilderness, though it sure got cold walking over the Highlevel Bridge when a combination of fierce winds and low temperatures drove the thermometer to 30 and 40 degrees below zero. And it was fun to spit over the side of the bridge and watch the spit float in the air to the water below. I guess that's a little like boys having a pissing contest. We'd take the streetcar only if it was raining hard, for then it was just too difficult to keep books and notes dry.

In spring, the most dramatic scene was the breakup of the river ice. Large chunks would crash into each other as the water from the melting snow rose and picked up speed. But I think I loved it best when the stands of white alder and birch trees slowly came to life along the river, first with a subtle display of green buds, then suddenly one day bursting into a solid mat of green as the leaves fully opened.

In spite of my improved study habits, throughout that first year of pre-med each examination and assignment filled me with the dread of failure because I had very little confidence in my mastery of the course work. I felt like a big klutz walking on thin ice. I couldn't forget that just one failure in one course meant eviction from university. This fear drove me to work even harder, but fear, as opposed to anxiety, is a normal response to a real danger, so it was both my enemy and my friend. However, looking around, I could see anxiety and panic taking hold of many of my classmates. Some of them tended towards paralysis of thought, others had breakdowns.

As the months went on, students began to drop out, and I realized that some of the brightest stars of high school had long passed their potential. My reaction to their failure was mixed: it was sad to see good students fail, but it was a relief to know that there were fewer students to compete against. On the other hand, others had already developed self-discipline. I was amazed when—at the beginning of both years of pre-med—two of my classmates, Dave Klassen and Jack Peck, left school in late fall to go home to harvest their farm crops. They missed several weeks of class, yet they survived the course. I could not imagine my doing the same and getting through unscathed.

I soon became aware that I had developed an interesting defense mechanism. Each time I took an exam, mother would ask how it went. I always would play things down. "Oh Ma, I don't think I passed," or "It really didn't go well at all." I could not allow myself to express my confidence for fear that I would diminish my drive.

Grades were posted on a bulletin board so that everyone knew exactly where he or she stood, and when the first academic year was drawing to a close, I discovered that my grade in English was just above the margin of failure. I met with my English teacher, Professor F.M. Salter, and said with all sincerity, "Doctor Salter, I want more than anything to become a physician. I will do anything you ask of me in order to prepare for the supplemental examination." Doctor Salter listened patiently, then suggested, "You can read all of Shakespeare's plays and Chaucer's stories. Write an essay on each play and story and send them to me." If that was what it would take, I was willing.

In the meantime I needed a summer job. The Americans were building an airbase in the north end of Edmonton, so a bunch of university students lined up for jobs hauling bags of cement. It only paid 90 cents an hour, but that was very good money in those days, considering that tuition for pre-med school was just $200 a year.

As I stood waiting my turn in that long line of applicants, I noticed a sign to my right saying that they also wanted to hire a certified first aid man. For me, it was a message from the Lord. I stepped out of line, went directly to the other window and was hired immediately. The pay was a dollar an hour. My certification in advanced first aid courses in both Alberta and British Columbia was paying off once more.

My first station was a one-room shack located in the midst of the airport construction site where work went on around the clock. Huge dirt-moving equipment tore up the ground, while thousands of men bustled to complete the job. My working hours ranged from eight to twelve hours a day, which meant eight to twelve hours of getting a sun tan while sitting

on my butt reading Shakespeare and Chaucer; my tranquillity only interrupted periodically by a casualty needing first aid. While I sat there reading, every once in a while I would spot one of my university friends lug-
ging bags of cement from trucks to building sites.

I wrote essay after essay and mailed them on to Doctor Salter. He corrected each with scathing though constructive comments, all in red ink.
From the first exchange I felt challenged to do better to avoid looking at
all that red ink, and it got so I really enjoyed the work. I began to learn
something about those two great writers, but of more importance, I
developed admiration and respect for Professor Salter.

After three weeks I was asked to take on a first aid station ten miles
north of Edmonton. This was Namao, which served as the staging area for
the northward push of the Alaska Highway. Thousands of miles long, this
highway would eventually travel northwest through a vast Canadian
wilderness to end in Alaska. Thousands of U.S. Army engineers were
being re-deployed from Namao to conquer the forest, muskeg, rivers and
mountains to lay a path for the highway. On top of that, they had to deal
with swarms of blackflies and mosquitos, as well as the harsh storms and
brutal cold of a northern winter. As the airport there was already complete, I was told the place would be quiet and clean, and the United States
Army would provide me with transportation between Edmonton and
Namao so that I could still live at home. It was an offer I could not refuse.

The activity at this new location was quite different from my previous
assignment. Here I had the emergency medical station all to myself. It had
a small waiting room, a treatment room that included a couch and a desk,
and a small attached bathroom. I took care of a few injuries each day and
ran the morning sick-call for the medical officers from the American
Military Hospital in Edmonton. These doctors were friendly, open and
good about teaching me some medicine.

Although the very sick were transported to the American Hospital in
Edmonton, because I was a pre-med student I was given responsibility for
the follow-up on most patient care. I loved the challenge, and my judgment and management skills increased daily. Injuries I tended to included fractures, cuts, burns, splinters and foreign bodies in the eye. I even had
one man who had a major axe wound on the buttock inflicted by an angry
fellow soldier. Medical problems included everything from skin rashes to

seizures, allergies, diarrhea, colds, pneumonia, insomnia and even hepatitis brought on by handling toxic chemicals.

It was very quiet on the base with only the arrival of the occasional plane to break the silence. I loved the quiet, but for a lot of boys from New York, Chicago and other busy cities, the silence was a source of stress; it drove them nuts. They needed city noise for comfort; it stabilized them. They also had trouble adjusting to the long hours of summer daylight, from 4 am to 10 pm. Many came in complaining of sleep disturbances, anxiety attacks and even depression.

I remember one young officer who grew up on a farm in Nebraska and especially loved being in Alberta. While reminiscing about his home, he told me, "I loved the farm so much that horse shit smelled like perfume to me."

Although I was on duty for anything from twelve to twenty-four hours a day, most of the time I would actually work two to four hours, which allowed me a tremendous amount of free time to read and write. If I wanted a break in my routine I would get clearance from the control tower and take the ambulance for a spin around the runways. With no traffic or police I could speed as fast as the ambulance could go.

Towards the latter part of the summer I sat for the supplemental examination. I felt confident and actually looked forward to the test, and I passed with a decent grade. I remain forever grateful to that generous teacher for the time and effort he invested in me.

The second year of pre-med went much more smoothly than the first. I worked just as hard but did not suffer from the fear and pain that had come from not knowing how to study. When the final results of our accelerated two-year pre-medical program were posted, I felt a great sense of relief and elation. I was one of the fifteen admitted into medical school, while all the others had either dropped out along the way or failed. I accomplished what many had thought would be next to impossible.

THE COMPETITION FOR THE FEW PLACES WAS OVER. WE fifteen from pre-med, together with nine returning veterans and sixteen students from the provinces of British Columbia and Saskatchewan, would become the University of Alberta School of Medicine's Class of '49. Because of the unspoken quota system in effect at that time, there was a limit of four women and four Jews to each class. Though this was never proclaimed or defended, it was something everyone simply understood. Alberta was not alone in its policy of limiting the number of Jews admitted into medical schools; all medical schools in Canada were guilty of this bias at that time.

Nevertheless, all thirty-six of us were accepted as part of the most esteemed sector of academic society, made welcome by everyone from the dean on down to the senior medical students. Some of our professors even called us "doctor" as a sign of respect. The faculty wanted and expected us to do well and were prepared to do anything to help us complete the four years that lay ahead. All we had to do was learn enormous amounts of material. We already knew that the hours and the workload would be at least three times what we had faced in undergraduate school.

Pre-medical school had been fiercely competitive and filled with uncertainty. Medical school was more secure and a lot more fun. And although still competitive, competition was no longer associated with being "in" or "out," but with just doing the best we could at learning medicine. By now my study habits were good, and my confidence in my academic performance had fallen into place for the first time in my life. I felt my fears and the need for never letting up melting away. I could focus all my energy on learning the basics of medicine.

Our class started out with four female and thirty-two male students. Our ages ranged from a very young group of four—Mamie Bailey, Harold Bell, Patrick Doyle and Ron Nattress—who were just eighteen when they entered med school to an older group of returning veterans who were in the early to mid-thirties. However, the class senior was actually Al Wright who had been a high school principal before he entered medical school.

Most of them were outgoing, enthusiastic, hard working, caring, competitive, and fun loving. Some of us had friendships that dated back to grade school. I had known Bill Lindsay since we were in fourth grade and Bob Paradney since fifth grade in Oliver School. When I went to Victoria High School I met four other future classmates: Don Colter, George Gibson, John Ragan and Eli Shecter. But the record for longest friendship went to Neil Duncan and Margaret Hunter, who had shared schools since they were in kindergarten.

The general attitude among my classmates was a mix of commitment to very hard work and a willingness for a good amount of friendly bonding—like relaxing at lunchtime by playing bridge and singing. We did have a few class members who remained aloof in spite of efforts to engage

Doctors or rock stars? Ben (far left) and classmates harmonize to relieve stress.

them. At the start, I thought it was a matter of age since the spread was about twenty years from the youngest in our class to the oldest. However, as time went on it became clear that they had chosen to isolate themselves. One particular classmate, a returning vet, remained distant from everyone. He was very bright but his profound isolation could not allow him to fulfill his potential. Years later he was found dead in his apartment. Alone.

Our medical school was in a handsome, dark reddish brick building with white marble trim; it matched the other university buildings in design, but for me it was the most prestigious. It housed all of the medical and dental faculty offices, laboratories, lecture rooms and research facilities. When I stepped out the front door, I could see the university hospital where we would begin our clinical training. Though it was just a hundred yards distant from where I stood, it was two years away in time.

Our class was issued lockers in the hall outside the anatomy lab, and we were given the privilege of using the private lounge reserved for medical students. It was a place to sit and read, play cards or just hang up a coat. We even had our own small co-ed washroom, more evidence of being part of the medical inner sanctum and a luxury that no one else had in our university of 3500 students. We were distinguished from other students by the white coats we wore, and I loved it when some naïve freshmen called me "doctor" all because of my white coat. I never corrected or shattered the illusion. We all felt very good about ourselves, a little smug and perhaps even conceited.

The building blocks of our medical education stood on a base of gross and microscopic anatomy. To this was added physiology to tell us how things worked, and body chemistry to inform us about the mysteries of the interaction of chemicals, hormones and endocrines with each other and on different systems of the body. We learned about body fluids and how to examine them.

We learned how to elicit signs and symptoms and arrive at a diagnosis. We learned what could go wrong with the body and how to recognize pathology, whatever the origin. After all of this, we learned about treatment when the clinical sciences of medicine, surgery, and sub-specialties like pediatrics, dermatology, urology, and ear, nose and throat were added onto the hard sciences.

When we were examining our own blood and urine, my partner Eli

Shecter, had his urine sample in a beaker sitting on the lab table. For fun, when he wasn't looking, I threw in a piece of a chiclet so that when he tested for sugar he got a very strong plus-four response. He was in shock, convinced that he had a severe case of diabetes. After he had endured a few moments of hysteria, I took pity on him and told him what I had done. We all had a good laugh.

Of all my experiences during my entire four years of medical school the one with the greatest impact occurred in my first year on the day we were introduced to the dissecting room, otherwise known as the anatomy lab. I could never bring myself to call it by the common jargon name of the "stiff lab." That just seemed a bit too disrespectful.

Dr. Herb Rawlinson was our anatomy professor. He was the man I had seen searching for wild flowers on the banks of the North Saskatchewan when I was canoeing, and though we'd exchanged some words as nature lovers do, I never guessed that this amateur botanist would become one of my teachers. A man in his early fifties, he was gentle and soft-spoken. He met us in the anatomy lecture room located on the same floor as the lab. It was a quiet place permeated with the smells of formaldehyde and whatever else was used to preserve and embalm the human cadavers that awaited us. I immediately flashed back to my childhood, remembering how I had stood in Dr. Boulanger's office with its antiseptic smell and its sharp odour of formaldehyde and stared into his bottled collection of body parts. Now here I was about to have my first hands-on experience of studying and cutting up a once living person myself.

Dr. Rawlinson began by setting the stage for our conduct in the treatment of patients. I do not remember all that he said, but I do recall his sincerity and the sober manner in which he addressed us." We are privileged," he told us, "to be able to work on someone whose body was donated to medical science or someone who is here because they were without family or friend and as a result became a ward of the province. I expect you to respect your cadaver and treat it with the dignity that it deserves. Nothing of the person is to be taken home or discarded." To make the point even clearer, we learned something about the personal life of each cadaver, which added to our resolve to respect that person and all of his or her body parts.

When our year was over, explained Dr. Rawlinson, all of those parts were to be collected and properly buried and a memorial held by all of us. And that is what happened. Not all classes were as respectful as ours. Two students in the class behind ours were caught playing catch with body parts. Such behavior was unacceptable and so both were thrown out of medical school. One of the culprits had a mental breakdown which ended in suicide.

I vividly recall the first time we entered the large dissecting room. We gazed in awe at table after table lined up in two straight rows: a dead body covered by a black tarp on each cold stainless steel surface. Silent and unmoving, they lay waiting patiently to make their last contribution to life, just as if they had been expecting this visit by the student dissectors. The effect on the entire class was electrifying. No one talked. No one moved. It was with a mixture of curiosity, anticipation, respect and even fear that we finally moved into the room to meet our cadavers.

It was traditional for each first year medical student to choose a working partner, then to draw lots for the table that would be that partnership's work place. Four students, two to each side of the table, shared each body. Eli Shecter was my partner while Len Maher worked with Jim Weslowsky on the opposite side. However, since no two cadavers were the same, during the year we would become familiar with all nine of them. Those with well-defined muscles were the easiest to dissect; the most difficult cadavers were the ones that had an overabundance of fat.

When Len, Jim, Eli and I uncovered our cadaver, we learned that he was a man in his mid-sixties who had been a long-time patient of the Oliver Mental Hospital where he died of natural causes. He was without any known living relative or friend. A slim man about five and half feet tall with good muscles, he had a pleasant face and a full head of hair. He seemed at peace as he lay on the dissecting table, and in some strange way we felt very close to Floyd, for that was his first name. I always greeted him each day and silently thanked him for what he was doing for all of us. We spent every morning for a full year learning how to dissect, expose, and identify all his body parts and their relationship to each other. This included skin, blood vessels, nerves, brain, muscle, fascia (the tough fibrous sheath that surrounds the muscle), bone, tendon, joints, and all internal organs.

We spent so much time in the anatomy lab that we began to feel it was home. We would sit on high stools next to the table reading from our textbooks as we carefully proceeded with the dissection. Our tools consisted of some sharp scalpels, a probe and forceps. At first it was strange to cut into human tissue that did not bleed, but that feeling left within a few days. We dissected cautiously so as not to destroy important landmarks. Our teachers (the three full-time members of the anatomy department(would circulate to offer assistance and to help us with complex anatomical parts that often seemed like a bewildering maze of muscles, nerves, tendons, fat, and blood vessels. In addition, there was a flow of practicing surgeons and surgical residents who would check our work and spend time at each table to chat about what we were doing.

For a short time, I used my own body as a point of reference for anatomical parts. I liked to think that all I learned in the lab on Floyd's body could be identified on my own. Then my kid brother Norman, who has been my partner in just about everything from cradle to old age, volunteered as a practice subject, and I began identifying and marking in ink the various anatomical landmarks on his excellent body. For one full year he went around looking like a tattoo freak.

I was also very fortunate to be able to borrow a fully intact skeleton from a local family doctor. For two years it hung from a stand next to my desk at home, so that at night during my long hours of study my skeleton and I became a neighborhood fixture as everyone could see us from the street below. Having the skeleton beside me as I studied was extremely helpful in keeping the gross anatomy in perspective, for the bones make up the scaffolding that supports all the other structures. I could look at a limb or the chest and visualize the soft tissues that lay within, through and around the bones.

That first year I spent a great deal of time with Eli and Len because, in addition to our lab time together, we walked back and forth to school each day as we had the previous two years. As we walked, we quizzed each other on anatomy. "Describe the brachial plexus," or "Name the muscles of the forearm and give their origin, insertion, blood and nerve supply." Day after day we reviewed with each other our gross anatomy until it was so deeply ingrained that I still remember most of it to this day.

Our cadaver Floyd, my borrowed skeleton, my brother, and our daily quizzes on the way to and from school served as teaching and practice aids to help me become very sure of my knowledge of anatomy. This must have been apparent to Dr. Rawlinson, for when it came time for the oral final examination, he handed me a set of anklebones. I thought, *This is going to be a piece of cake. I know each and everyone of these bones blindfolded.*

But the professor said, "Now, Ben, I want you to tell me the periods of ossification of the ankle bones in utero." In layman's terms that meant "Tell me when calcium begins to be deposited in the various ankle bones during the development of the human embryo." All I could visualize were four lines of tiny print in my text with that piece of trivial information. I recalled thinking, *I don't need to learn something like that.* I sat silent for my entire final. Dr. Rawlinson did not speak or ask me anything else. At length he said, "Thank you, Ben. The time is up." I was stunned, but I knew exactly what he was up to. I could almost hear him saying, "Gotcha!" but I didn't believe that he would actually fail me, and I was right. He gave me an 'A' for my final grade, but he taught me an important lesson in humility.

I used a mnemonic (memory aid) to organize my answers to medical questions. It was "DIE but Please Say Something Diagnostic and Therapeutic Please." The letters of the first word and the first letter of each succeeding word stood for Definition, Incidence, Etiology, Bacteriology, Pathology, Signs, Symptoms, Diagnosis, Treatment, and Prognosis. It was a simple technique that worked for me in organizing my answers for written or oral quizzes. If the question was to describe rheumatic heart disease, I would just follow the outline to be sure that I'd covered everything relevant.

During my second year of medicine, the Dean of the Medical School, Dr. John Orr, who was also chief of pathology, summoned the three Jewish boys in the class—Eli Shecter, Bob Paradny and myself—as well as Dave Klassen to his office. Not once in the rambling lecture that he then delivered did Dr. Orr mention the fact that we were Jewish, but the gist of his remarks was that it didn't look good for "our kind" to work so hard and do so well. He suggested that we let up and stop performing to the best of our abilities. He was perfectly serious. I felt I was facing a little Cossack disguised in a white coat; though he wasn't threatening to kill me, his words had a similar impact.

As he continued in this vein and it became obvious what he meant by "our kind," Dave Klassen suddenly spoke up and said, "There must be a mistake, sir. I am not Jewish!" whereupon he was immediately excused. Dave went directly to the rest of class and reported the incident.

Throughout this entire humiliating experience, the three of us who remained did not utter a single word, but I was boiling with inner rage and defiance. I became determined to work even harder, saying to myself, "To hell with this outrageously bigoted man!" Once outside Orr's office, Bob and Eli agreed with me. We would all continue to do our best.

That second year seemed to blend into the third year with smooth continuity as more and more basic information was added to prepare us to work directly with patients. By our third year our teachers were schooling us to take a thorough history and do a complete physical examination using the British clinical diagnosis approach. We discovered that the more we got into clinical work the more we felt like doctors.

We began this work by examining each other to make physical diagnoses. Then one day our instructor announced, "You are now ready to go into hospitals and do a complete history and physical examination on a real patient." I reacted with a mixture of joy and apprehension. *Was I ready?* I asked myself. *Do I need a little more time to prepare?*

My first patient was in a mid-sized general hospital, not too far from my parents' home. He had been admitted with symptoms of Meniere's disease, a condition characterized by ringing in the ears, vertigo and reduced hearing. He had been in hospital for two weeks and had made no progress in the treatment of his illness.

Eager to look professional for this first call, I arrived at the hospital dressed in my only good pair of trousers, a clean shirt and a tie. After examining his chart at the nurses' station, I marched into his room armed with the tools of a well-prepared doctor: white coat, stethoscope, percussion hammer, tuning fork, and a box containing instruments to check out his eyes, ears, nose, and throat. I had pen and paper and had rehearsed well-memorized steps to get a full and detailed systematic history before proceeding with the details of a complete physical examination.

I was psyched. I was ready. I knocked on the door of my first live patient, entered the private room, and saw a man about forty years old lying quietly on his bed. I had assumed that my patient would be an intelligent, articulate Caucasian who would be able to make this first clinical experience easier for me. I was taken aback to find that instead he was a Chinese immigrant. My heart fell. Most adult Chinese that I knew had trouble with the English language.

He looked well, but he didn't say a word. I introduced myself as "Doctor Dlin" even though I was still a green medical student. "I'm here to examine you," I said. Mr. Chan gazed at me thoughtfully, and after what seemed to be an interminable length of time, he began to talk in understandable but broken English. Two hours later I still hadn't asked my first question.

Once started, Mr. Chan had launched into a lengthy and passionate story of how he came to Canada without his wife and four children. The Canadian government would not allow them to enter the country, and as a result, he had not seen them in fifteen years. No longer able to bear the suffering from this prolonged separation, he had become profoundly sad, trapped by his need to be with his loved ones and the difficulty of supporting them long-distance. He told me about his village in China, his life there, how he came to Canada, and how hard he worked to send money home to help out his immediate and extended families. I learned about his wife and each child. He went on endlessly. As I found no way to interrupt, I listened.

It was obvious that his depression had its roots in political economics and bigotry. Chinese labor in Canada was good and cheap. Men were needed but not the women for fear their presence would result in Chinese children, which simply would not do. I remembered that my 9th grade school teacher had told us about this unfair treatment and how she raised hell over this discrimination. I could do nothing except commiserate with Mr. Chan.

The same thing happened on my second visit: he talked and I listened. And although I was desperate to get a complete medical history of Mr. Chan and do the physical, I simply could not interrupt him. Finally, on my third visit, I was able to complete my examination.

After it was over, Mr. Chan announced that he was better, and he attributed his recovery to our discussions. I really did not know what to say or think. I'd done nothing to help his symptoms. It wasn't until years later when I participated in a study on vertigo that I became fully aware how emotions play an important part in the treatment of these patients, and my experience with Mr. Chan helped me to understand. In hindsight, I am pleased that as a student I had the good sense to just sit and let Mr. Chan talk about what was boiling inside him. I did not know it then, but this was my first clinical demonstration of the power of listening and the therapeutic value of unburdening oneself of pent-up feelings. Mr. Chan was so grateful he invited me to come and eat at his restaurant free of charge. I accepted his offer two or three times.

During one of our early surgical classes in the Edmonton Veterans' Hospital, a small group of us attended a clinic on hernias. One of the three women in our class, Marge Fraser, who was a very attractive and shy blonde, was part of this group. On the examination table was a 20-year-old nude army veteran, a small white linen towel neatly folded to cover his penis and scrotum, giving the young man some sense of privacy.

Dr. Jack Bridges, our capable surgical instructor, explained that our job would be to push a finger through the scrotal sac into the inguinal ring (situated in the groin) and feel what happened when the young man coughed. We were feeling for a bulge in the canal which would indicate a weakness through which some intestine presented itself. The defect and the bulge are the hernia. When it came to Marge's turn to insert her index finger through the ring the towel began slowly to rise straight up supported by a hidden, yet powerful, erection. Our fast-thinking and resourceful instructor quickly turned the vet on his side. Directing our attention to his anus, he calmly said, "We'll now have a clinic on hemorrhoids!"

About a week later, a group of seven of us were honored by having Dr. John Scott as our instructor for one of our early teaching rounds. Head of the Department of Medicine, he was a brilliant physician, an outstanding internist at the University Hospital, and a serious man who commanded awe and respect. We joined him in a large ward that housed about thirty male patients. After greeting us, Dr. Scott took us to the far end of the room and paused in front of an elderly man sitting rigidly in a chair. He was stooped forward, with elbows on his knees and both hands shaking in a pill-rolling manner as he drooled saliva. This tremor is one that can be demonstrated by shaking some pills held loosely in one's hand. His rigidity, tremor and drooling were classical symptoms of advanced Parkinson's disease.

We gathered around and observed the obvious. Dr. Scott looked at our small group and asked in a soft voice, "Does anyone notice anything unusual?" No one responded. We were afraid of being wrong in front of the distinguished professor. As our awkward silence continued, he finally looked at me and said "Well, Dr. Dlin, don't you think the man looks happy?"

"Oh yes, sir, he looks very happy," I said, wishing only to please Dr. Scott. At which point he fired back, "Dlin, this man is so frozen he couldn't smile if he tried!" But he was good-natured and amused over our paralysis at our first ward experience, and it didn't take too long before we spoke up without prodding or fear.

Once a week we would travel to the Royal Alexander Hospital for a clinical pathological seminar. Our instructor there was the hospital pathologist, Dr. John Sturdy. Immediately before each conference, he would distribute a print-out of the essential clinical and the pathologic findings on a patient who had died from an unusual illness. Our task after hearing more about the case was to come up with a diagnosis, but each case was so difficult that it was rare for anyone to come with the correct answer. This was very frustrating. We knew that our class was bright, so it seemed unreasonable that even three or four of us couldn't come up with a correct response. I don't recall how our plot got started, but I think it was Tim Cameron who suggested that a number of us collaborate on the creation of a fictitious syndrome called "Wonk's Disease."

Word of our plot spread to most of the class so when all the answers were reviewed, it was Dr. Sturdy who was stumped, and he wondered out loud how so many of us had come up with such a diagnosis. No one said a word. We just sat quietly watching our bewildered instructor. After the seminar he asked us what this disease was. One of our classmates explained that it was a rare condition that occurred when a faecolith (a dry, hard piece of faeces) got trapped in the Circle of Willis (a group of blood vessels in the brain that are connected to each other to form a circle). Each time the faecolith passed the speech center, the patient would say "shit." Dr. Sturdy was a little embarrassed, but he got the message and eased up from then on. Unfortunately, he became convinced that I was the culprit who had hatched the plot and never forgave me.

The most inadequate course being taught then was psychiatry. In fact, I'm sure the course material was identical to what had been presented to students a century earlier, reflecting the traditional attitudes toward mental illness. I even recall reading in one of our psychiatric textbooks that much mental illness was due to excessive masturbation, a concept popular in the 1800s. I did some rapid calculations and figured that there was something was radically wrong with this theory because I should have been either dead or crazy by the time I was twelve.

Each lecture was conducted by one of the state hospital psychiatrists and consisted of a description of the symptoms of one of the types of insanity such as schizophrenia, paranoia or mania. All three lecturers were a little strange. Dr. McL. would hold his head to one side, look at the ceiling and giggle as he lectured. Dr. M. looked and carried himself like Boris Karloff playing Frankenstein, rambling on without any expression whatsoever. The third, a cadaver-like man, would describe and then physically imitate the "crazy" patients. Between them, they left us with the notion that all mentally ill patients should be closely confined within the wards of an insane asylum with caretakers who were just a shade away from joining them. Nothing in our lectures or clinics was related to the inner workings of the mind. Fortunately, in our senior year, our thinking was brought into the modern era with a few lectures on psychodynamics by Dr. Sid Spaner who was now on the staff of the Veterans' Administration Hospital, which was attached to the university. Sid was the first of my teachers to explain why people behaved as they did.

But while I was learning all this, I still carried the ongoing burden of earning money to pay for tuition and books. I refused to take loans, and I rejected offers from well-meaning Jewish parents who approached my folks with offers to put me through school if I would agree to marry their daughters. After the third such offer, I asked my parents to politely say, "Thanks, but I am not interested." I had no doubt at all that I'd continue to find other ways to cover my expenses.

The summer after my first year of medicine I earned money by writing a set of notes that provided answers for the questions that would be asked on the physiology final. By studying past final exams, I discovered that Dr. Ardrey Downs simply rotated the same series of questions year

Ben at the Leduc oil field in 1948, where he was the only attendant at the emergency burn unit.

after year. I summarized the questions together with the answers and sold the notes with the assurance to buyers, "Learn these and you will pass the final." That venture took care of my second year's tuition fees.

In the summer of '48 I got a job manning the first aid unit at an emergency burn station at the Leduc oil field, about twenty miles southwest of Edmonton. I lived in the unit and was on call twenty-four hours a day. That summer, one of the wells went wild, and a geyser of oil mixed with gas spouted over a hundred feet into the air. Experts were brought in from Texas and Oklahoma, and they worked around the clock, drilling at an angle from a safe distance to cap the flow under the ground. I think they called it "whipstalking."

Two aspects of this event left indelible memories. The first was watching a group of our local riggers smoking cigarettes in and around the area. This act of defiance was suicidal, a case of extreme denial that anything catastrophic could happen. When I confronted them they laughed and said, "Hell, Doc, nothing ain't gonna happen. I was even smoking while I was on top of the rig." Fortunately for all of them, fire did not break out.

The other lasting memory was the result of a drive I took in the ambulance around the perimeter of the huge dammed-up lake of oil. The wind was blowing from the west, carrying with it oil spray from the wild well. It fell like a soft summer rain. The farmer on whose land this was happening lived nearby in a three-room wooden shack, and I watched him standing in his back yard scattering chicken feed from a bucket. Every so often he would stop, take out his red handkerchief and wipe the oil from his face.

That farmer didn't own the mineral rights to his land. He stood there feeding his chickens so that he could sell their eggs for a pittance while being doused by rich oil taken from his land. Most of the early settlers and homesteaders, like my dad, knew nothing about mineral rights, and even if they had known, they did not have the money to acquire them. It was the oil companies, railroads, and big business which bought the rights and gained legal right to explore and work the area under the soil surface. Around 1940 when the search for oil was on in Alberta, I discovered that the mineral rights under dad's farm were owned by the Canadian Pacific Railroad. Ironically, large oil deposits were discovered in that entire area, but when dad sold his farm he got less than 50 dollars an acre.

As we approached our senior year, we had to decide where we would apply for internship. A disturbing problem confronted me. Although a few Jewish doctors and interns taught at the University of Alberta through the Veterans' Administration system, none served on the faculty. This fact coupled with the memory of our humiliating interview with Dr. Orr in our second year was probably the reason, in part, that Bob Paradny went to Mt. Sinai in New York to intern and Eli Shecter to Cedars of Lebanon in California, both top-notch Jewish-supported institution.

However, I was determined to remain in Alberta, so I decided to apply to the University Hospital and take my chances. I had two motives. One was that I thought it was the best place to train and the other was to challenge the racially biased system. Much to my surprise, I was accepted without any problem, probably because Dr. Orr had been replaced as Dean of Medicine by Dr. John Scott. I never ran into any more racial bigotry, and soon after this, Jews became members of the University faculty. I'm sure that this was due to Dr. Scott's influence as well as a change in attitude throughout all medical schools as a result of the war.

Our graduation from medical school took place at McDougal Church on 106th Street, and it was just for our class and the university's graduating class of nurses. It was a lovely June day with not a cloud in the sky. I borrowed a suit from Eli's older brother Morris and drove with my parents to the church, where we students decked ourselves out in caps and gowns and wore the colorful stripes that signified the University of Alberta, our B.Sc. and M.D. degrees. Of the original thirty-six who had started medicine together, we were now only thirty-two(three women and twenty-nine men). We had lost a few students on the way.

During our first year, Judah Bushakin, a brilliant young man, developed a severe case of malignant hypertension, a disease for which there was no remedy at that time. By mid-year he was confined to bed and died shortly after. Two others could not meet the workload and the required standards; they dropped out in the second year. Another classmate, a veteran with a family, was having trouble keeping up and was asked to repeat the third year. This was a wise decision by the faculty because he went on to finish medical school and become an excellent country doctor. All the rest of us completed the course.

We marched down the aisle to the front rows and faced the stage where Dean Scott and the other dignitaries of the university and medical

faculty were seated. After the opening speeches(of which I have no memory(we were called to the stage in alphabetical order to receive our diplomas. I do recall the warm handshake and the words of congratulation.

That same afternoon there was a party at our home for friends and relatives. My parents were beamed with joy and pride. This was a family first. No one on either

Benjamin Dlin, M.D.
Graduation class of 1949 of
the University of Alberta

side of the family had ever before graduated from university.

Chaim Satanove, who had come over to this country with my Dad, addressed me as "doctor."

"Chaim," I said, "please call me Bennie. It's what you have called me all my life!" The tall handsome man responded, "But you are a doctor now, Bennie, so I will call you doctor. You've earned it." I did not need any more celebrating.

Our internships were to start July 1. With a little more than a month at our disposal, a number of us took interim jobs at two of the provincial hospitals. It was easy money and good hours, plus it gave us a chance to play in our off hours. A few went to work at Oliver Mental Hospital, where our old dean, John Orr, became a patient during the last years of his life. I know that he had some Jewish psychiatrists taking care of him during that time, but I am sure that he did not realize it because of his dementia.

I went to Ponoka, also a hospital for the insane, a little more than sixty miles from Edmonton. Except for the fact that there were no bars, armed guards, or walls, the old red brick buildings looked much like a prison. The large gardens and farms that surrounded the buildings were worked by the patients, with the produce used to feed both staff and patients. These were the good old days when it was considered healthy for inmates to work the gardens, clean, cook, serve and do other chores. And it was good for them, both for their self-esteem and sense of personal efficacy, to be kept busy and occupied.

However, at Ponoka at that time a large percentage of the patients remained in locked wards or were secluded in locked cells. The only units not locked were the two where those well enough were preparing for discharge. All windows had stainless steel mesh screens in place inside the glass for safety and security reasons. But the entire hospital was very clean, polished, and free of odours, thanks to the obsessive-compulsive patients. With their various germ phobias and other compulsions, they went about endlessly scrubbing and polishing brass, glass, floors and bathrooms.

Severely depressed patients, laden with guilt, willingly accepted the job of scrubbing filthy toilet bowls in the locked units. It helped to assuage their profound feelings of guilt and offered them a way to make restitution. Withdrawn schizophrenics, living in another world, did simple repetitive chores from morning till night, totally oblivious to the outside world, often just mumbling incoherently or responding to their hallucinations. The hospital also had its "bedlam" wards, much like that portrayed in the classic movie *One Flew over the Cuckoo's Nest.*

Most of the staff members were somewhat weird themselves; many of them could, in fact, be easily mistaken for patients, and since the patients could sense illness, it affected their trust in their caregivers. One of the younger staff doctors, an overtly effeminate homosexual, was severely beaten one day for no obvious reason when he went to his assigned job in the closed, disturbed female ward.

Although the most violent and uncontrolled patients, some with and some without clothes, remained locked in padded cells, this one ward housed more than a hundred psychotic women ranging from manic-depressives to catatonic schizophrenics. Many were dangerous. They wandered barefoot in drab, shapeless cotton dresses; mumbling, screaming, begging, pleading, masturbating, rocking, or just standing or sitting like statues in one fixed position. When it was time for bed they would be herded to their locked sleeping quarters down the hall.

It was this unit of suicidal, homicidal patients and other psychotics that I was assigned to take over. Naïvely, I unlocked the door and stepped into a world of bedlam. Almost immediately a huge woman about six inches taller than I and weighing at least 280 pounds walked up to me and said in a heavy, authoritative German accent, "I take care of you!" Whereupon she reached over and picked me up with one arm and began carrying me around the unit. I was safe. I had the protection of the toughest woman I'd ever met in my life. "Vee go here," or "Vee go dare," she would say.

When I felt comfortable enough with her, I'd say, "Take me over dare," or "Vud you please pud me down und vate for me here," and she would comply. For the whole time I was in charge of the unit, she was my companion. I never read her chart because I was afraid that I might discover that she had killed her husband and her children. It seemed best just to carry on with the illusion that she was my protector. There was just not enough time to read all the charts, anyway. The focus instead was on handling each crisis as it arose and in dispensing medication.

Most of my chores were directed to dispensing medication for the epileptics, sedatives for the agitated, and electroshock for the depressed.

During these rounds I would also be on the lookout for physical illness or injury. Many women refused to eat, and without daily tube feedings most of them would have certainly died of starvation.

It was interesting to note that open, compulsive masturbation was far more common in the female than in the male units. I wondered if that had to do with the taboo at that time against masturbation. It came to me that the authors of those old textbooks on descriptive psychiatry must have assumed that since crazy people masturbated excessively, it was therefore a part of the reason for their being sick.

From time to time I noticed a thin older woman with a greatly distended abdomen as she slunk around the ward. She looked nine months pregnant. I thought that she might have a gigantic tumor, but when I finally examined her, I discovered that the cause of the swelling was a massive faecal impaction. The nurse on duty had no idea that she had stopped having bowel movements. There was nothing to be done but to begin removing the faeces manually.

We got her onto a table and I proceeded to remove stool that was mixed with glass, stones and other foreign objects which she had either swallowed or inserted up her bum. I must have torn a dozen pairs of rubber gloves as I dug and dug, filling buckets with her bowel products. I would have preferred using a shovel. All the while this was being done the patient screamed. When I was finished and she was cleaned up, she leaped from the table and disappeared into the crowd like a wild animal running for shelter into the forest.

Three times a week I administered electroshock treatments. Though rather primitive at that time, it was still one of best tools available to help those who suffered from depression, agitation and mania. Unfortunately, it was useless for most other conditions.

Food was not allowed prior to the shock treatment in order to avoid aspirating stomach contents and to decrease bladder incontinence. The patient would lie on a table with two attendants on either side, two holding arms and shoulders while the other two held onto shins and thighs. A fifth attendant would place a roll of gauze into the mouth for the patient to clamp down on, then support the chin and head. This way the body was given some protection when the patient went into the post-electroshock grand-mal seizure, but they were given nothing to alleviate the terrible physical trauma that the body had to endure.

My job was to administer the shock. I felt like some mad scientist from a Frankenstein movie as I set the voltage on the control box so that when the button was depressed an electric impulse would travel through wires that connected to the ice-tong-like instrument that I held. The ends of the tong were wrapped in gauze pads that had been soaked in a saline solution to improve conductivity. I would apply these wet ends to the patient's right and left temple, and we were all set for "blast off." I'd say, "Ready," and all five people would bear down with all their strength. Instantly the entire body went into severe continuous protracted spasm, which was followed by a series of powerful convulsions that lasted about a full minute. The force was so great that the convulsions often caused compression fractures of the patient's spine.

On one occasion the nurse forgot to wring out the excess solution from the gauze ends, and some of the brine leaked onto my hands and onto the hands of the nurse supporting the patient's head and chin. When I depressed the button the patient had a seizure and both the nurse and I followed along with seizures of our arms. It was a crazy morning. I told the nurse that it might well result in our having subsequent personality changes!

Most patients came willingly and without fuss for their shock treatments, waiting in line as if it were a dental appointment. After the treatment they would go into a recovery area, sleep for a while and then be taken back to their wards. Amnesia was both a complication and a blessing of shock therapy. On the one hand, it helped to erase the frightening memory of the event, but it often led to a profound confusion that could last weeks and even months.

There were two other forms of treatment for severely disturbed patients. One was very tricky to manage: insulin shock therapy. Patients were given a dose of insulin to produce severe hypoglycemia or a fall in blood sugar, resulting in profound sweating and stupor. Occasionally, they would have a seizure. Then we would administer intravenous glucose, thereby satisfying the excess insulin circulating through the body. The patient would wake up drenched in sweat, sleep for a while, eat, and then be returned to his or her unit. Other than sedating the patient and providing a lot of attention, I saw little if any benefit from this treatment.

The final form of treatment for the severely disturbed, a very ancient one, was to wrap the patient in woolen blankets soaked in ice-cold water. Within a short time, the body heat of the patient would rise and be kept constant by the wool swaddling. The patient would become calm, perspire profusely and usually fall into a restful sleep. Later he or she would be toweled off, and then indulged with food and fluids. This treatment provided the same temporary effect in tension reduction that one might get by sitting in a hot tub or a Turkish steam bath.

Years later, when I attended a meeting of the American Psychosomatic Society, I heard a very interesting paper dealing with the therapeutic effects of regressive psychotherapy. As I listened, it occurred to me that this is what had been taking place with our swaddled psychotic patients in Ponoka. The technique apparently took the patient back to feeling like a completely dependent child, his entire needs anticipated in such a manner that he was, for all practical purposes, reduced to the emotional age of one or two.

An entirely new process, the prefrontal lobotomy, was done on patients with severe obsessive-compulsive disease and on patients whose violence could not be controlled. Our chief of neurosurgery at the university, Dr. H H Hepburn, would drive down from Edmonton to do the surgery, and I was pleased whenever he requested that I assist him. One of the approaches he used was to burr holes through both temples; the other was to approach the brain through the thin bony orbit of the eyes. In both procedures a thin stainless steel probe was inserted into the brain and then the surgeon would sweep the probe in such a manner as to sever each frontal lobe from the rest of the brain.

After surgery it was necessary to re-educate these patients in almost everything. They had become docile little children. However, after all this tedious retraining, they would revert to the way they were before surgery, the crippling mental illness returning with no hope of ever getting better. All was for naught. This "ice pick" operation was a brutal one that illustrates the extent to which frustrated neuropsychiatrists would go to find the "cure" for mental illness. Today, we use simple medications to deal with the same sorts of illnesses.

It always amazed me when some woman approached me in the midst of this bedlam and said in the most rational tone of voice, "Doctor, I am okay now." After spending time with her, I would move her gradually through the various gates to healthier and healthier units until she was discharged. I had no idea why, or how, these patients got better.

There were also a few young women in their late teens or early twenties who had been admitted to the bedlam wards because of the sudden onset of insanity. I spent hours with these young inmates looking for some way to reach them. I recall taking one young woman for long walks in the garden and around the grounds. A university student, she chatted at first about the things around us, then finally began talking about her family. I felt this was important progress in someone who was diagnosed as having "simple schizophrenia" because schizophrenics are characteristically void of emotion and so withdrawn they have nothing to say. But when I reported my observations at the next staff conference, I was told by the senior staff, "Don't waste your time. She is a hopeless simple schizophrenic!"

Many years later, when I was on the faculty of medicine at Temple University Health Science Center, one of my post graduate students observed that most young girls with a first time admission to a mental hospital had their psychotic break because of an incestuous relationship with their fathers. I thought back to that young university student and wondered if she had been such a victim.

Our regular staff meetings were held in a large conference chamber that looked like a courtroom, with the jury of doctors and nurses sitting in a semi-circle. Patients were brought in one at a time and seated on a straight-backed chair in the center of this courtroom to be questioned like prisoners. The interrogation was brief, and after the patient was excused, decisions would be made as to diagnosis and disposition. It was medieval, and I realized that Ponoka was simply a cleaner version of insane asylums that had existed a hundred years earlier.

One evening while on general hospital duty I was making rounds in the chronically ill male unit when I noticed a young man leaping up and down on his bed and making noises like a one-year-old. He looked familiar. I went over to get a closer look, and to my horror I recognized Kasa, a Japanese boy who had been my high school classmate. A bright and studious kid, he had sat in front of me in algebra class. When I read his record, I learned that he and his sister had contracted congenital syphilis in utero because both parents were silent carriers of the deadly disease. Kasa would not live long because he was suffering from general paresis of the insane, a late stage of syphilis that destroys the brain.

My time at the hospital was not all work. Dances and other social events were held for the open unit patients, who had the freedom to do as they wished, and the younger staff members were encouraged to attend. I found it really fun dancing and chatting sensibly with women whom I knew and cared for, who had been psychotic only a week or two before.

I also became very good friends with Gladys, a terrific girl who had come from Edmonton with another nurse to earn a few extra bucks and get away from home. We had a great time together and, as was usual for me, I had a major problem controlling my passions. She did too, so we "suffered" the joys of passionate love-making without guilt or regret.

All in all, Ponoka was a fascinating experience. I had seen a slice of medicine that I hoped I'd never witness again. For many of us that spring, our brief jobs marked the end of having to grub for money. I had completed and paid in full for an intensive, accelerated, six-year pre-medical and medical program. Soon we would all be entering a twelve-month hospital training program. As interns each of us would have our own small room with maid service, meals and a salary of twenty-five dollars a month. White uniforms were included. Now that's what I call living!

THERE WERE SIX OF US INTERNING AT THE UNIVERSITY Hospital in Edmonton: one female, Margaret Hunter, and five guys(David Klassen, Lloyd MacLean, Jack Peck, John Skene, and myself)all but one of us intending to become general practitioners. Each of us were assigned a small room on the interns' floor of the hospital. It contained a hospital-style bed, a desk and chair, a bureau and a tiny closet—all very spartan but adequate since it was merely a place for sleep and to study and catch up on journals. We were supervised by the chief house physician, Dr. Floyd Rodman, whose first words to us were, "No women are allowed in your quarters nor is any alcohol to be on the premises!" He might just as well have been addressing a group of first graders. We were polite but agreed among ourselves that he was being an old fuddy-duddy. Consequently, despite his orders, booze and women were regularly smuggled into our quarters.

Our work contract was for twelve months without any designated vacation time. Our only time off came when the day's work was done or an occasional weekend away when one of the other interns covered for us. No one complained, though, as we were completely absorbed in the desire to get as much experience as possible to prepare us for practice.

Essentially, the two major services at University Hospital were medicine and surgery. Minor services included pediatrics, obstetrics and gynecology, orthopedics, and a few others. We rotated through all the services, although we spent most time in internal medicine and general surgery. A rotating internship is vital to preparing for general medicine, as opposed to a straight internship which is a direct path towards specialization. At that time, the former was preferred because the general philosophy was to expose graduates to the total field of medicine as we were all expected to do some general practice before selecting a specialty. Ironically, there were no general practitioners on staff, a failing in university hospitals throughout Canada at that time.

The model for us at the University Hospital was that no one person could do it all and the patient could be best served by a team of specialists. The authorities seemed to believe that the general practitioner was somehow not as capable as the specialist to heal and teach. However, in spite of this deficiency, the rotating internship did expose young doctors to the realities of practice and also served as another step in the maturation process. Just as anatomy and the other basic sciences had formed the foundation for learning medicine, the rotating internship served as a platform on which to practice holistic medicine.

As interns, our basic duties were much the same no matter to which service we were assigned: we served all the needs of the attending staff. The intern gave every new patient admitted to hospital a complete examination which included a detailed history and a physical. Naturally, the length of time it took to do this varied with the service and the type of patient we attended. For example, for the young, healthy high school boy who had broken his wrist in a hockey game, the exami-

The uniform of an intern. Ben at the University Hospital c. 1949-50

nation would take less than thirty minutes. Much more time was spent on the fifty-year-old businessman suffering crushing chest pains that had come on while he was attending a stressful meeting. That examination could take a minimum of an hour, with follow-up blood studies and cardiogram, plus all the steps necessary in taking preventive action in case he was experiencing a heart attack.

After each history we would establish a tentative diagnosis and a differential diagnosis (which includes a list of other possibilities) followed by a treatment plan. Not all cases were simple or clear-cut. In fact, the majority of patients admitted to a specialist's service presented complex issues. After the evaluation we would check in with the resident in charge and report our findings. He in turn would check the patient out, critique our evaluations and then report to the attending physician. Laboratory studies would be ordered and eventually a treatment program outlined.

We made regular rounds, seeing every one of our patients at about 6 a.m. and in the early evening shortly after supper. We also rounded with the attending physicians whenever they arrived. It was customary for the intern to present the facts, and then each new case would be thoroughly discussed with the attending physician and his resident. Whenever I was faced with a unique case, I would review the case material in text books and journals to learn more and also to help in my preparation for the Dominion Council exams which would license us to practice medicine in Canada. Studying and keeping up with new information became constants as long as I practiced general medicine, then became a life long habit.

I tackled internship with zeal, ready to soak up everything I imagined would stand me in good stead as a country doctor. I already knew that a country practitioner located in an isolated or remote place would of necessity have to do things that he would never do in a city, from pulling teeth to caring for a sick cow. In addition, the burden and responsibilities increased dramatically if the doctor worked alone with little if any access to anyone else with medical training. As a result, I took it upon myself to learn some extras to improve myself for country practice.

The first person I approached was Doctor Sid Spaner, the only dynamic psychiatrist in the city. I had first met Sid when he visited my friend Dave Kushner's dad, Sam, who was dying of heart failure. Sid was still in his air force uniform, looking quite handsome as he stood at the bedside calmly chatting with Sam in a manner that conveyed comfort and compassion. Slender in build, fair-skinned with dark hair and dark eyes, he talked in a soft voice with his head cocked to the right side. When introduced, he knew who I was and knew my family. In the few seconds that we chatted he was completely focused on me.

About one year later, he spent some time taking psychosomatic courses in Philadelphia. When I went to see him, I asked if, in return for my working with his inpatients and covering for him for the duration of my internship, he would teach me something about psychiatry. He was delighted with the idea; I would be his first intern. He was a generous teacher, adding many insights into techniques of psychotherapy and the inner workings of the mind. I had already figured out that a large chunk of family medicine was psychosomatic; now I began to understand something of the unconscious and how it could manifest itself in thought, action, feelings and bodily symptoms.

Sid Spaner was in great demand and worked very long hours. Once, on returning to the hospital at two in the morning, I noticed that his office light was on. I stopped in, thinking that I could be of some assistance. He was sitting at his desk absorbed with paper work, his ashtray filled with cigarette butts. "Sid, what the hell are you working on at this late hour?" I exclaimed. He smiled as he looked up from his work, and with total innocence said, "I've got to place my bets for tomorrow's horse race." He was nuts about horse racing.

My mother got a big kick out of Sid. She loved feeding him. If he was in our old neighborhood, he would drop in at our house and announce, "Hi, Mrs. Dlin, I haven't had a bite to eat all day," as he marched directly into the kitchen to see what was in the refrigerator. On the other hand, I recall visiting his home once when his wife Sylvia was out of town. I said, "Sid, I'm really hungry." I opened his refrigerator to find that all it contained was a tube of toothpaste.

At the end of my internship, just before I was to leave for country practice, I heard that Sid was critically ill, having suffered a severe heart attack. I immediately went to see him. He was very despondent and said, "I guess this is it, Ben!" He was most concerned for his young wife and their little daughter. "How will they manage without me?" he cried. The next day when I visited, Sid was getting dressed to head for the racetrack. It seems his cardiogram had been inadvertently mixed up with someone else's. Sid's tracing was perfectly normal. His chest pains were due to his heavy cigarette smoking.

As well as learning everything I could about psychiatry, I spent additional time working in radiology to learn how to take and read x-rays. I also worked in the clinical laboratories to learn simple procedures for examining blood and urine. After that, I struck a deal with the dean of dentistry, Dr. Scott Hamilton, who was a maxifacial surgeon. This specialty dealt with complex reconstructive surgery of the upper and lower jaws that were deformed either development-ally or by trauma. I told him that I would be happy to assist him and attend to his hospitalized patients if he would give me a crash course in tooth extraction because I knew that in the remote areas of Alberta, dental emergencies are common and demanded immediate attention. He readily agreed and immediately set up four patients who needed all their teeth pulled.

He coached me on how to inject specific nerves of the jaw in order to anaesthetize various parts of the mouth. He then taught me to use the specialized forceps for removing different types of teeth and how to chip bone from the jaw and to suture open bleeding gums. It was great training because he had me do the whole thing myself! All of these clinicians shared their knowledge and time with willingness and enthusiasm. The extra time that it cost me was worth it all; I still know how to extract an impacted molar, interpret a slide of blood and read an x-ray.

When I knew for sure that I was going into country practice, I asked a number of our faculty whom they considered the top notch GP in Alberta. The consensus was a certain Dr. Frank Coppock, who had a solo practice in the small town of Eckville in the western part of central Alberta. When I called him, I explained that he had been recommended and I broached the possibility of our working together. He was gracious and pleasant in response. "I'm planning a trip to Edmonton within the next few weeks," he said. "I'd be delighted to get together with you and talk."

Our first meeting is still fresh in my mind. He came to our home on a Sunday because he wanted to meet me with my folks. What I saw impressed me immediately. He stood about 6 feet 2 inches tall. Although only in his mid-fifties, he had a full head of silver-white hair above a red face with pale blue eyes. Vital, open and dynamic, he was well muscled and quite fit. He wore a white shirt and red tie that I later learned was his standard dress.

He greeted us warmly and joined us at the kitchen table where we had some tea and mother's pastries as we chatted. Then dad got out his bottle of Johnny Walker Black Label, and we had a few drinks, neat. It was another year before it occurred to me that dad and Frank must have known that each was a Mason from the moment they shook hands and said some secret words. Totally at ease and open, Frank took charge as the discussion became more personal about both our families and our work. The more we talked, the more I got to respect this rugged man. After about an hour, he said, "Why don't you come and visit me in Eckville, Ben? Let's spend a week working together and really get to know each other. Then our decision can be based on seeing how we get along."

It all made perfect sense to me. I liked the man and it was obvious that my parents were very pleased with what they saw and heard. Here was a bright, charismatic man who oozed confidence based on his inner strength and 25 years of successful solo practice. Frank Coppock would be an excellent role model. After he got into his big black Chrysler and drove off, my Dad said, "I like him. He's a real 'Mensch.'" And my Mother added, "He will be a good man to work with."

Frank had been smart in meeting us all together because he could see how I got along with my family and get some idea how I would fit in with his own. Whether we

Dr. Frank Coppock, 1949,
Eckville, Alberta

could work together would be left to our meeting in Eckville.

I wanted this issue settled as soon as possible, so at the first opportunity, I planned a week's leave, negotiating with the other interns to cover for me. It was early fall, and I took Dad's car to drive the hundred miles south to Red Deer, then straight west about 30 miles to the two-mile corner leading to Eckville. The weather was warm, the crops were being harvested, and I was filled with hope and high expectations.

I met Frank and his wife, Marjorie, at his office It was lunchtime so we crossed the dirt road to their bungalow. Marjorie had advanced rheumatoid arthritis involving most of her body, and walked as if the ground was littered with shards of glass. Her hands were badly deformed, and for her every day was filled with pain, yet she maintained a positive attitude towards her family and home and office duties. It did not take long for me to recognize that she wanted me to work with her husband, and I learned later that he relied a great deal on her judgment. She was an amazing and courageous woman.

While Frank showed me around the office and hospital, he filled me in on some of his background in medicine and something about his practice philosophy. When he was 10 years old, his family had left Winnipeg and moved to Saskatchewan where he finished his schooling. After serving as a pilot in the latter part of the First World War, he had entered medical school, graduating in 1925. I thought, *My God, I was just a year old when he graduated medicine!* A year's internship was followed by country practice in the small town of Rosthern, Saskatchewan. In 1936, when the small hospital in Rosthern was closed for financial reasons, Frank, who was by then married and had two young daughters, moved to Eckville. Although his new practice took in all the surrounding farm country and more than 10,000 people, the town itself had a population of only 159, just about the size of Bruderheim when I was a child. He never explained why he chose this place.

"When I got here, the local hospital—what is now the Jenkins house—had been shut down for about a year. I re-opened it but it was terribly inefficient. I'd deliver babies and do surgery on the ground floor and then carry the patient up a flight of stairs to one of the converted bedrooms." That went on until 1944 when the community, with Frank's leadership, built an efficient new hospital on the outskirts of the town. He

The Eckville Hospital, designed by Frank Coppock, 1946

delighted in telling me how he had planned it and of his intention to build a care facility for older people adjacent to it.

Wherever we went, I saw the respect and intimacy that existed between Frank and the community. He was Dr. Coppock to the nurses, "Doc" to most of the town folks, and just Frank to his closer friends. Although by nature a "man's man," he was equally comfortable being loving, tender, and compassionate with all adults and children. It was obvious that he was the most respected and well-liked person in the community and surrounding farmland, revered because of his dedication to the well-being of the people and his excellence as a physician. They knew him as a totally reliable, honest, hard worker; a straight shooter who spoke his mind and commanded the respect due a natural leader.

"I am totally dedicated to the prevention of illness and the early detection of problems," he told me. "The territory that I cover is so great that I've had to teach my patients to come in when symptoms are in the early stages. I've got them to understand that it is better to prevent complications by coming in for regular check-ups even if they feel well. One unnecessary rural home visit can waste a half a day, and that makes running a solo practice totally impractical because I still have to tend to my office patients and those in the hospital."

In the first few days with Frank, he told me about his management of obstetrical patients, his routine examination of breasts and the annual pap smear for the early detection of cancer. His immunization program for children was up-to-date, and his concept of the hospital nursery was well ahead of the times. There mothers participated in the care of their infants from the first day of delivery.

There was a very high incidence of tuberculosis among the Estonian and Finnish population in the area. "I bring these patients in for frequent check-ups including X-ray examination. I also bring in the healthy members of the family and check them as well. If they are going to get TB, I want to catch it quickly." Once a week he drove to Red Deer where Bill Parsons and his older brother, Mac, ran the Parsons Clinic. Bill, a radiologist, went over Frank's x-rays to be sure he wasn't missing something.

"When I have major surgery, like the removal of a gall bladder, a thyroid gland or a uterus," Frank explained, "I call on Mac, who's a highly qualified surgeon, to do the operation and I act as his assistant. If the case is too risky or complicated, then I ship the patient out to the University Hospital in Edmonton." A great piece of advice that he volunteered was said very simply. "Ben, if you are not sure of something or the patient does not seem satisfied, then recommend a consultation and send them to the most qualified person you know. It works well for everyone involved. Patients are pleased and will respect you more for your willingness to say 'I'm not sure' or 'I do not know'."

He was the master of a myriad of sensible and practical techniques gained from years of experience. His examining rooms were set up so that he could use both hands. "When you're practicing alone, the only assistant you have is your other hand. Learn to make good use of it." I was amazed at the way he did surgery. A nurse would prepare the patient while Frank scrubbed up. He would come in and start the anesthetic, scrub again and get gowned and gloved. After draping the patient, he would operate with decisive moves that wasted little time, all the while keeping tabs on the patient's vital signs and level of anesthesia.

During my week with Frank, I'm quite certain that we did some surgery every day, and each day was a learning experience. He had scheduled two appendectomies, one hernia repair, about six tonsillectomies, one caesarian section and a number of teeth to pull. He had me do the surgery while he assisted and taught me how to work as if I was alone. He had me give all sorts of anesthetics; ether was the safest of them all if you were working alone, he explained, while chloroform was the most dangerous. Both were administered by dripping the contents onto a mask that covered the patient's nose and mouth. He also had me use intravenous pentathal, spinal and caudal blocks as well as a variety of nerve blocks using novocaine by injection.

Just as important as the techniques for administering the anesthetics was monitoring the patient's vital signs while one performed the surgery. While Frank always had some assistance from the nurses on duty, if he was short-handed, he would call in Larry Knudson, the local garage mechanic, to assist. All of this experiences in Eckville made me think even more about how I should enhance my training when I returned to Edmonton.

After being with Frank one day, my mind had been made up. Everything I'd heard about him was true. I'd work with this man in a heartbeat! And before the week was over, we sat down and struck a deal. I would start work immediately after completing my internship. My pay would be $400 a month plus room and board, sixteen times what I was making as an intern! "One other thing, Ben," he said, "you will treat the neurotics and the fat women. They drive me nuts." That suited me just fine. I'd already been preparing myself to deal better with people afflicted with emotional problems. I left Eckville after that week filled with enthusiasm and with the knowledge that my professors and parents were right in advising me to seek work with Dr. Frank Coppock.

It was no more than two weeks after my return from Eckville that I got an urgent call from Frank. "Ben, I've got a young man here who was pinned under his tractor. He's sustained multiple fractures, most notably a compound fracture of his left femur and tibia, and I'm sure he has multiple internal injuries as well. I've sedated him with morphine, and I've got intravenous fluids and oxygen going, but that's all I can do here to minimize further shock. He will surely die if he doesn't get immediate expert help." Air ambulances did not exist in those days. His only choice was to load the young man into his big Chrysler and get him to Edmonton as quickly as possible. "I want you to meet me at the hospital and have a crisis team in place when I get there."

The patient, a 30-year-old man, had been plowing a hilly portion of his farm, driving his heavy tractor across a sidehill when it toppled over, pinning him to the ground before he had a chance to jump out of its way.

The old tractor had no mercy. Its tremendous weight crushed both his pelvis and legs. Frank had started treatment for shock as soon as he got to the accident site, while others were still pulling the tractor off the young farmer. There had been no way to evaluate the extent of his internal injuries.

I located Doctor Max Geisinger, a competent surgeon who was in the hospital at the time, and together we lined up an anesthesiologist, the chief orthopedic resident, a surgical resident, nurses and an operating room, all in readiness for the emergency. The moment Frank arrived with his patient, he was rushed to the operating room where the team was all scrubbed and ready to work. The man's injuries were horrendous, much worse than I expected. His body had been impaled on the sharp metal parts of the tractor as he lay in the dirt. Bones contaminated with dirt and bits of clothing protruded through the skin in a half dozen places. His limbs were a mangled mess of skin, muscle, bones, blood and dirt, and he was by now in profound shock. While the surgeon, two residents and myself worked to tie off the bleeders, the anesthetist tried desperately to deal with the massive loss of blood pressure, but it was hopeless. He died fifteen minutes after entering the operating room. He never came out of shock nor regained consciousness.

I caught my new boss's eye. He looked very old and haggard, like a warrior defeated in battle. Exhausted. Demoralized. Bewildered. This tragedy had taken more out of his spirit than just the rush to the city with a dying young man. It seemed to puncture his soul; this proud, extremely capable man who could do just about everything he tackled had failed. He blamed himself, and even though he understood when his colleagues said it had been hopeless from the beginning, he still felt responsible.

I took him home to help him get settled. He told us he had delivered both of the victim's children. How could he go back and tell the family that he had failed to save his life? His grieving and doubts were painful to witness. I assured him that he had done everything humanly possible. There was no way the young farmer could have made it.

The next day after Frank had returned to Eckville, I attended the young farmer's autopsy and saw the massive amount of internal damage that had resulted from the crushing weight of the tractor. His liver had extensive tears, as did a good portion of his intestines, and there was evidence of massive bleeding that had filled the abdominal cavity. It confirmed what we already knew: the man could not have been saved. I then called Frank to tell him about the autopsy findings. I sensed some relief, but I knew by his tone and his comments that he still felt that he should have saved the young man.

This experience bothered me. I could see that there was a vulnerability in Frank Coppock that I had not expected. And the whole incident remained in the back of my mind festering as if it had more to it than I yet understood. I chose instead to ignore it.

During my internship, I found internal medicine the most intellectually challenging discipline. This service was the area of medicine that dealt with difficulties in both diagnosis and management. A patient might come in with a variety of seemingly strange and unrelated complaints and be suffering from a metabolic disorder, an incipient blood disorder, or a developing malignancy. As interns, it was our job to come up with preliminary answers.

The medical and surgical wards, each with about thirty beds, were the domain where interns and residents practiced on patients. In some ways these patients were lucky because they got a lot more individual attention than those in private rooms did. But wards also produced problems for the patients. Privacy was achieved by a thin white curtain, which essentially meant no privacy at all. When a patient cried out in pain or had a stinky bowel movement, it was heard, or smelled through the entire ward.

I found it most distressing to attend to a patient who was in some crisis, such as hemorrhaging or a cardiac arrest, with the other patients witnessing what was happening. It was even worse when the patient died. On one occasion I was paged over the loud-speakers with "Doctor Dlin, ward B, code emergency!" which meant that a crisis on my ward needed immediate response. When I got there, I found that a patient had collapsed on the floor and appeared to be dead. He was in cardiac arrest.

There was no time for privacy protocol: if a patient isn't resuscitated within four minutes of cardiac arrest, the brain will be permanently damaged. Today the response to a "code alert" results in a rush to the patient by trained teams and whoever is nearby, but back in 1949 I was on my own. The most I could do to try and stimulate the heart into action was cardio-pulmonary-resuscitation (CPR) by breathing into his mouth to fill the lungs, pump the chest, then plunge a long needle through the chest wall to inject adrenaline directly into the heart. All the while I was dimly aware of the patients nearby. They remained perfectly quiet. My success rate for reviving an arrested patient was zero, but I still had a terrible feeling of sadness and defeat when I had to give up on him, and I sensed the anguish of those watching.

I had the nurses and aides cover the body and pull the drapes so that the other patients would not have to suffer the further emotional trauma of witnessing the deceased being wheeled out. Of course, this did not protect them from viewing the empty bed when the drapes were reopened. They watched in silence, suffering with their private thoughts.

Another stressful event for ward patients was the arrival of an attending chief doing bedside rounds with an entourage of residents, interns, medical students and the ward nurse in his wake. We would circle the patient and listen, probe, discuss among ourselves or ask the patient questions. Sometimes everyone's attention would just be focused on the patient's chart, with the patient ignored as his or her case was being discussed, evoking even more anxiety in an already apprehensive person. As our group moved on, we left a bunch of stressed-out folks to stew about what they had just heard.

The wards that amazed me were the isolated polio wards which, despite the seriousness of the disease, were permeated with optimism. The beds were filled with the young victims struck down during the latest of our recurring epidemics, but all we had to help them with was Sister Kenny's method of hot packs for the painful affected limbs and monstrous iron lung machines that went on day and night without a stop, pumping the paralyzed chests of those who could not breathe on their own. The sound of those pumps could be heard throughout the ward.

The hot packs consisted of long strips of wool cloth soaked in hot water. They were squeezed out and carefully wrapped around the limbs. This eased the pain and seemed to have some beneficial effect. The procedure reminded me of the poultices that mother used to apply to our chests or backs when we suffered from pulmonary distress or when there was an abscess to be brought to a head.

These wards were also the places that evoked the most fear in me. I felt like the kid who still believed in camphor and garlic, hoping to somehow be protected from this unknown pathogen. How did it spread? Would those of us who looked after these kids get infected? It took a while before denial and a sense of invulnerability dissipated my fears, allowing me to care for this stricken group of young people who, if they survived, would suffer some degree of muscle paralysis for the rest of their lives. It is interesting, however, that not one nurse, ward aid or physician on our staff came down with the disease during this particular epidemic.

This sense of physician denial would also surface when we cared for patients who suffered from infections such as tuberculosis, syphilis, streptococcus or other contagious diseases. We did, however, maintain good judgment in using precautions: wearing masks, gowns, and gloves and washing before and after contact with the contagious patient. The only difference from my Mother's techniques was that she did not wear the gown, mask or gloves.

During the time of my internship, the newly discovered sulfa drugs and penicillin were in great use. I recall giving a teenage boy a dose of cortisone which had just been introduced into the marketplace. It was still experimental and each dose was valued at $400. The boy had been admitted in crisis just the evening before, dying of an inflammation of the lining of his heart. His skin was blue, his breathing laboured, and his fluttering heartbeat could be seen pounding against his thin, frail chest wall. But it was his eyes that I remember the most. They conveyed terror, desperation and pleading all at the same time. He knew that he was dying and wanted ever so much to live.

I told him that this experimental drug had great promise and that he was lucky to be selected to receive some of it. Resigned to the hopelessness of his situation, he tried but was unable to smile. It was a last-hope shot in the dark that failed. He died that evening. I don't remember his name or anything else about him. I share this experience because it illustrates how little we understood the new miracle drugs and how desperate we doctors were for the help they could bring.

The great Canadian physician, Sir William Osler, believed that the last part of the patient examination was at the autopsy table, so whenever one of our patients died, we were urged to watch and often assist in the autopsy. This was the final chance to get answers. This is where one learned a tremendous amount about illness, gathering information so we might better understand the pathophysiology of disease and face the next patient who exhibited those symptoms with more knowledge. Autopsies also showed up the mistakes made through ignorance, negligence or stupidity. Should a particular case be of special interest, we would present it at a meeting of the entire staff. Comments and discussion by learned and experienced clinicians were always instructive.

The surgical service was by far the most dramatic of the various rotations; here patients were admitted who needed a cutting out, cutting off or just repairing. The diagnosis and work-up was much easier than that of the medically ill, and it was very satisfying to take someone who needed a repair and, after a short period of cutting and stitching, send him or her home as good as new. Little wonder that the surgeon stands at the top of the list of omnipotent and revered doctors.

I vividly recall the day I performed my first abdominal operation. I was new to the surgical service. My boss was our chief of surgery, Dr. Walter McKenzie, a brilliant Mayo Clinic-trained surgeon, a superb teacher and researcher, respected throughout the surgical world. (Much later I learned that he was also on my Dad's list of respected surgeons to whom he had referred many Bruderheim farmers.) We were all scrubbed and set for surgery. The patient was anaesthetized and ready to be operated on by the chief surgical resident. "What is the patient's hemoglobin?" Dr. Mckenzie asked him. Shamefaced, the resident mumbled, "I'm sorry sir, but I don't know. I didn't check the patient's chart."

Without a moment's hesitation, Dr. McKenzie turned to me and asked, "Dr. Dlin, what is the patient's hemoglobin?" When I told him, he said, "Then you will do the surgery and your assistant will be Dr. Chief Resident!" I took the scalpel, checked my landmarks and proceeded to cut through the skin just as I'd practiced so often by cutting through the skin of an orange. It went well in spite of my initial apprehension. I learned four valuable lessons from this experience: never take short cuts, stick to basics, be thorough, know everything about your patient. In that way you'll not be caught short because of neglect or plain stupidity.

There was one surgeon on our faculty, however, who was totally incompetent. Everyone in the OR knew of Dr. A's problem, and it was a mystery to us all how he ever practiced. When any of us scrubbed with him, we usually had to take over because he would be overcome with anxiety. I recall once when we were in the midst of gall bladder surgery, he completely lost it. "Would you like me to complete the operation?" I asked. He immediately switched places with me and I completed the task. I really had no right to, but I was convinced that something terrible could have happened to the patient.

For reasons that I do not understand, once in a while an incompetent physician like Dr. A is protected by others in the profession, but I thought it was not only disgraceful to the profession to protect him but a terrible disservice to the innocent patients. In Dr. A's case the protector was a senior staff surgeon, the same senior surgeon who had told our medical class, "Don't mess around with nurses because you have to work with them the next day." By the time I was an intern, he had modified this advice to "Don't shit where you have to eat!" We did not heed his advice. Actually I found that the nurses with whom I socialized seemed more willing to cooperate in the management of patients.

One of the most difficult operations I ever performed was on my father. He called and asked me to check out a small growth on his forearm. I said it should come off and that it really was a simple procedure. He insisted that I be the one to do it. It was then that I understood what Hypocrites meant when he wrote that the physician should not treat members of his family. My dad just wanted to take pride in seeing his son, The Doctor, do an operation. I did it to please him but suffered terribly throughout the entire procedure. Dad went home feeling proud; I went to my room a nervous wreck.

One evening when I was on call, I went to the emergency room to examine an outpatient who was suffering from acute abdominal pain. It didn't take a rocket scientist to figure out that he had an acute gall bladder with stones lodged in the bile duct, but as soon as I looked at the man lying on the table, I thought, *Well, I'll be damned if it isn't Dr. George Meisner, my old high school Latin teacher!* I'd rated last in his classes for the better part of three years. On one occasion, this scholar of Latin and Greek was so exasperated with me that he asked, "Dlin, why are you taking Latin?" When I told him with all sincerity that I intended to be a doctor, he laughed and said, "Dlin, not only will you not get through Latin, but you will never get through high school!"

As I approached him now, he recognized me immediately, and he was delighted with the knowledge that I would be assisting the chief of surgery in removing the diseased organ. Taking care of him during his recovery was sheer pleasure. He recalled with affection the time that my buddy Art Hiller and I had every student in school bring him an apple for his birthday. This became an annual tradition and from then on he was called "Uncle George," a name that students continued to call him until he retired. I did confess, "You know, Dr. Meisner, you really did have every reason to believe that I would never pass Latin."

Another night while on-call for emergency room duty, I was roused to attend to one of two men brought in after their car had crashed at 80 miles per hour into a cement wall. My patient was lying unconscious under a sheet with one foot pointing up toward the ceiling and the other pointing down toward the floor. I thought, Oh my God, the man's leg is so badly busted up that it's completely turned around. When I removed the drape, however, I discovered that one was an artificial leg. He died within five minutes of my arrival, and at the autopsy I was amazed to see that every internal organ in his body had been ripped by the sheer force of the bodies continuing forward at 80 mph after the car had smacked into that cement wall. Heart, lungs, brain, intestine, and bones were all torn, broken and bleeding. Death had been inevitable.

Another time, a husky logger was admitted to emergency with a compound fracture of his right thighbone and of both long bones of the lower part of the leg. A huge tree he was falling had rolled onto his leg. In spite of the tremendous damage he had suffered, this large, muscular man showed no evidence of shock, although he was moaning and writhing with pain. A pretty first-year nurse, trying to be sympathetic and supportive, softly asked, "Does it hurt very much?"

The logger stopped his groaning, turned his head toward the nurse and asked in a calm voice, "Do you know what a logging chain is?"

"Yes," she said.

He responded, "Good. Then try imagining what it would feel like to have a logging chain pulled through your asshole!" He then proceeded to moan and groan until I gave him some intravenous morphine. The young nurse reacted with shock and tears. I comforted her as best I could while getting on with the job at hand.

On another occasion while I was attached to the orthopedic service, I had been working for about forty-eight hours without rest. Finally I was able to flop into bed and collapse into a deep sleep. Shortly thereafter, the phone rang and a nurse from the orthopedic ward said, "Dr. Wilson's patient is complaining of a very tight cast. He is asking for some painkillers. Could you come and see him?"

"I'll be up in a few minutes," I said, but instead I fell back to sleep.

One or two hours later, Dr. Gordon Wilson came to my room, shook me gently and asked me to get dressed and come with him to the operating room. "I have to operate on that young man who was complaining of a tight cast. We have to be sure that shutting off his blood supply will not result in a Volkmann's ischemic contracture." I was horrified. What he meant was that the boy might end up with a permanent claw-like deformity of the hand due to impaired circulation and the resultant damage to the nerves beyond the obstructed area.

The cast was removed and much to our relief his circulation gradually returned. The doctor then told me in a most gentle way, "No matter how tired you are, you must force yourself to get up and attend to something that has the potential of ending in a catastrophe." I never forgot the lesson. Dr. Wilson understood the meaning of responsibility and empathy, and I was grateful to this man for the kind manner in which he handled me.

While on the neurosurgical service, I recall attending a man in his twenties who was dying of an inoperable cancer at the base of his brain. He would scream and scream from the indescribable pain. The nurses on the unit were visibly upset with me for administering frequent large doses of narcotics because the patient then lost interest in eating and drinking. They wanted to prolong his life and I stood in their way. They could not accept my course of action, as the more narcotic I gave him, the less food he ate. Without enough food and nutrients, he would die sooner, but would feel very little pain.

With great reluctance I gave in, furious with the nurses but keeping my feelings to myself. As the analgesics wore off, the patient screamed so much without stopping that the nurses begged me to restart the narcotics. By catering to the nurses' denial of what was inevitable, that patient was put through a few hours of needless suffering. He died two days later.

Most interns loved obstetrics service because we got to deliver so many babies, though always under the watchful eye of the obstetrician in charge. We got practical experience at turning breach babies, applying forceps, repairing cuts and tears, as well as attending to the immediate needs of the newborn. Usually everything ran smoothly and without complications, and everyone enjoyed the excitement of this greatest of life's miracles. As soon as the delivery was over, the staff became all smiles and the banter was open and pleasant. A guiding principle in obstetrics that served me well in my own practice was to follow Dr. Roy "Shorty" Clark's dictum of "watchful expectancy and masterful inactivity," his way of saying, "Don't be too hasty in interfering with Mother Nature." I do not recall any deaths during this rotation.

Most male babies were circumcised by the house staff, among whom there was the tradition that if anyone accidentally took off too much foreskin and nicked the penis, it would cost that individual a case of beer. I only recall drinking beer once, and fortunately it was not because I was buying.

Christmas came around while I was on the obstetric service, and even though I'm Jewish, I asked for the day off in order to help my brother Howard. He had enlisted in the army in 1940 but been discharged for medical reasons and had returned to delivering milk with a horse and open wagon for Woodland Dairy. During our sub-zero winter days he would keep warm by running behind his wagon, but Christmas presented a special hazard because good old Howard could never turn down a drink from a well-meaning, grateful customer. By the time he had stopped at his eighth customer's house, he would be in a state of euphoria, completely unaware of the cold as he followed his wagon. So for many years on Christmas day, I would deliver both milk to his customers and my brother to safety.

On this particular freezing Christmas Day I walked up to the second floor apartment of a customer, knocked at the door and entered crying out, "Milkman!" A young woman seated at her kitchen table sipping tea looked up startled and started screaming. I was bewildered by this sudden outburst until she blurted, "A week ago you delivered my baby!" She didn't know whether the milkman was a doctor or the doctor who delivered her baby was a milkman.

"I'm really both," I told her. "I'm the milkman who happens to be the doctor who delivered your little girl." After I explained the situation, she laughed. I joined her for tea and left to continue my work. I bet she's told that story a hundred times since then.

In contrast to the joys of obstetrics there was the agony and despair that I felt for critically ill children while I was serving on the pediatric rotation. I just could not take the pain of helplessly standing by and watching children die from terminal illnesses such as leukemia, cancer, congenital organ abnormalities or some other fatal illness. They seemed to understand that something was terribly wrong, and like sick animals, would lie quietly with sorrowful eyes, totally dependent on the caregivers. They never seemed to complain. I prayed that in general practice this would be something I would never have to face. In those days my focus was more on the child, but after having children of my own, I can better imagine the agony of the parents.

For me, facing death with grownups was much easier for they at least had experienced some life, and I soon learned that there was much that I could do to help the dying. Even back then I realized that death was only the final stage of the life process, and with that as my perspective, I found that one of the most important things I could do was sit with the dying person to listen and talk. Our discussions were always very personal and meaningful. The patient welcomed and appreciated the comfort and closeness I offered. Most were not afraid of dying but of suffering and of losing control of bodily functions. They wanted to die with dignity, love, and freedom from pain.

I think that a doctor's only way to shut out the pain of his patients is to be oblivious to human suffering or be so emotionally insulated that one goes through life with little capacity to feel. I still cry every day of my life over the suffering of my patients.

One night toward the end of my internship I had the evening off and dropped in for a visit with my family. I discovered my parents playing gin rummy with Morris, the Fish King, and his wife.

Morris's name was well earned for he bought huge amounts of white fish from the lakes of northern Alberta to ship to markets in Chicago. While they played, Morris sat there, a hundred pounds overweight and smoking a huge cigar while pontificating about politics. Suddenly he became very pale and sweaty. "I feel weak," he said. "I have to lie down." I accompanied him to the bedroom and asked him to tell me the whole story.

He said that this was a recurring event that seemed to improve with lying down. I checked his pulse and listened to his heart by placing my ear to his chest, and I knew immediately that he had a serious irregular heartbeat (auricular fibrillation) that was causing interference with proper heart function. It was life-threatening. I suggested a meeting with Dr. Ken Hamilton, a competent cardiologist at the University Hospital. Ken confirmed the diagnosis and was able to correct the Fish King's problem with medication, prolonging his life for years.

Unfortunately, Ken himself had developed a complete heart block for which there was no treatment. Crude, life-saving pacemakers were invented just a few years later, but too late to save him.

In gratitude for my diagnosing his cardiac arrhythmia, the Fish King offered me an interest-free loan upon completion of my internship. This offer allowed me to order a two-tone green, Pontiac sedan from Detroit so that I could be independent in my new job. The car came with sunshield, tinted glass, radio, electrical windows and a rack on the roof. Since I wanted to have the car as soon as I got to Eckville, my kid brother Norm, who was between sessions at school, agreed to pick it up and deliver it to me. As I did not like to be in debt, I resolved that I'd repay the Fish King as fast as possible.

Our lives as interns were not without relaxation. We would party with the nurses and a few of the female physicians, sometimes in the female quarters of the hospital and sometimes in apartments outside the hospital grounds. Once in a while, we would sneak girls into our quarters unbeknownst to our chief resident. Not being able to afford whiskey, we could always get a small amount of 100-proof grain alcohol from the pharmacy for "medicinal purposes," mix it with fruit juice and ice and after a few drinks feel relaxed, buzzed and rapidly uninhibited. No pot, cocaine, or hallucinogens were used; we had fun without all that stuff.

Often these parties would end up with passionate lovemaking, but to my knowledge, no one ever got pregnant or contracted any sexually transmitted disease. Our party partners were a fine group of women who were just as horny as the guys were. We were all single and had little thought of marriage for some time to come, although some of my classmates did end up marrying the girls with whom they fell in love before or during internship. Those marriages have all lasted a lifetime.

Those twelve months of internship did more for us than we could have hoped. The experiences of our early years of growing up, the gradual accumulation of knowledge and putting it into practice all came together in that one year. Observation and information obtained through intimate interaction with patients and their families led to even greater insights into the family. Each new patient was a challenge, a mystery, and a new adventure that left me wondering at the immense complexity and inseparability of body and soul. But I also discovered that everything I had previously learned would be open to challenge and change.

At the end of our internship, everyone got through the Dominion Council exams. We exuded confidence and couldn't wait to enter the next phase of our medical careers. Lloyd MacLean went into a surgical residency in Minneapolis while the rest of us went straight into general practice in Alberta. Marg Hunter went to the mountain town of Canmore prior to studying pediatrics in England and practicing in Montreal. Dave Klassen practiced in Mayerthorpe and then specialized in the surgical subspecialty of ear, nose and throat and settled in Chilliwack, British Columbia. Jack Peck practiced in Barhead and then went on to Trail, British Columbia, before entering into the specialty of obstetrics and gynecology and practicing in New Westminster. John Skene started out in Red Deer and then joined our classmate Ron Nattress to work as general practitioners in Lloydminster. And I packed my few belonging and went home to prepare for the next phase of my life in Eckville.

MOM, DAD AND I LOADED UP THE OLD DODGE WITH MY ONE
suitcase of clothes, four cartons of books and a basket of mother's pastries
and headed for Eckville. I don't think my parents would have missed the
opportunity to share in this joyful journey. I was about to fulfill the most
significant dream of my life, and I was going to this new beginning with
the two people who had been key players in making it happen, although I
don't think they perceived their influence as keenly as I did.

The miles flew by quickly as we talked. My folks seemed young to me.
I had just turned twenty-five and they were in their late fifties, but it was
as if we were much closer in age. During the years I was in university, they
had both confided in me more of their concerns and their personal feelings, and I had come to understand that I was becoming the child designated to take on the family responsibilities. On this trip I realized that the
baton was subtly being passed on to me. They talked about some of their
concerns for the future.

Although they didn't go into details, I knew that Howard was at the
top of their list. They also briefly talked about matters having to do with
their aging; they made it clear they did not want to be a burden on their
children, and should the need arise, they would prefer to reside in the
Jewish Old Folks Home in Winnipeg which was, at that time, the only
such facility in western Canada. And they wanted me to be executor of
their respective wills. It was a beginning of a dialogue that was to be ongoing. I felt a mixture of emotions: honored, proud and a little sad. It was
tough enough dealing with the social problems of being one of God's
chosen people and now to this were added the issues of family responsibility.

When we turned off the highway and drove down the short stretch of road to Eckville, the town gradually unfolded before us. It was situated in the midst of rich farming land just below the foothills of the Rockies. The town seemed tranquil and lazy, the way western towns generally strike one on first viewing. It was a lot like Bruderheim without the hitching posts and horse and buggies. In both towns, most of the townspeople ran the stores and various service facilities, but some were retired farmers who enjoyed living near other people and using the services offered by the community. The major difference was the presence of a doctor and a hospital.

We drove straight to the Presbyterian manse for it had been arranged that I would live with the minister. Newly arrived, Kingsley King, a pleasant-looking guy about my age, was as delighted as I was at the idea of sharing living quarters as well as the religious and medical needs of the area. The manse was a three-bedroom wooden bungalow furnished with the essentials, as befitted the simple needs of a bachelor minister. My room faced the front of the house which suited me because of the erratic hours I'd be keeping. His was the back bedroom.

After we unloaded my belongings, my folks and I drove around to check out the town and meet with Dr. Coppock. When I entered his office, Ida Knudson, the young receptionist, handed me a sealed envelope. Inside was a note from Frank.

"Welcome, Ben. Hope you are settled in with Kingsley. Marjorie and I are off to Saskatchewan for a little vacation. We'll be back in a month. You'll do just fine."

What a way to start! I was to be on my own serving a population of approximately 10,000 people scattered over about 2,500 square miles of farm, bush and foothills! I could just visualize the impish grin on Frank's face as he prepared that introduction to country practice for me, but I really appreciated his show of trust and confidence in me. Meeting a challenge and testing myself had always been a part of my life, and it came naturally to me to be confident and believe that I could accomplish what I considered to be realistic goals. I hadn't even a twinge of anxiety about having this awesome responsibility thrust upon me; instead, I felt the same self-assurance as when I ran first aid posts. I was eager to get started, and I was elated to have the use of Frank's oversized, specially equipped black Chrysler. It looked a lot like Batman's batmobile because Ida Knudson's mechanic father, Larry, had welded a thick steel plate along the entire length of the undercarriage so the car would skim over any road obstacles. It was like driving an amphibious tank.

Mom and dad were openly amused at this new development. As far as they were concerned, Frank's actions were perfectly reasonable: he needed a rest, I was available to take over, so he had gone. I found it instructive that they simply took it as a case of one just did what one had to do. And I thought how different my fresh beginnings were to theirs when first dad, and later mom, came to Bruderheim to start their new lives. I had electricity, running water, indoor plumbing, a telephone and an income of $400 a month, more money than I had ever before held at one time. My life was wonderful.

We went back to the manse, had a little snack, and said our farewells. It was just about noon when my parents got into the old Dodge and headed back to Edmonton. A straight walk of 500 yards took me from the manse to the hospital, over wooden sidewalks well elevated above the dirt road. The weather was warm and the air was permeated with the remembered aroma of fields, barnyards and wood fires. I walked past the main street, past simple wooden homes and stores, most of which needed painting, and arrived at the Eckville Municipal Hospital.

A road led to the front door and then circled around an area of uncut prairie grass growing in the center of the driveway loop. I was taken back to my childhood and the dirt road I had walked to our four-room school; both were one-story structures standing alone in a large open field of prairie grasses. Only here there was no playing field with two outhouses, and I was not barefoot.

The setting was perfect for a prairie hospital. It was a well-planned simple wooden structure with wide polished corridors and high ceilings. From the top of a short wide stairway inside the building, the interior fanned out in three directions. The work area, which was straight ahead of this central entrance, included a room for the critically ill, a spacious delivery room with a newly designed delivery table, complete with stirrups that Frank had installed as a favor to me. I had not been trained in the Sim's position, the technique he used which gave the doctor much more control when working alone. The woman would lie on her side with one leg over the doctor's back, allowing him free use of both hands to guide the baby through the birth canal.

A separate scrub area was next to a large operating room. Nearby was an X-ray room that also served as a place to set and cast broken bones. A small doctors' lounge was furnished with a writing table and a chair and sofa for napping. We even had our own little dressing room equipped with a shower, toilet and sink.

The corridor to the left of the entrance area led to rooms for post-operative care and medical patients. To the immediate right of the work area was the nurses' station, beside it the rooms for new mothers, and across the hall from it the nursery with six bassinets designed so that mothers could tend to their own newborns—a concept far ahead of its time. The staff took over when it was time for mothers to rest. Frank's philosophy was that this was natural and fostered bonding in a relaxed atmosphere. "I also want mothers to be well rested," he explained, "before they return to farm work as well as taking care of their newborns."

The entire facility showed remarkable planning and thought, with everything laid out to provide maximum efficiency with minimal effort. All twelve patient rooms were spacious with windows that could be opened and each was provided with a good light to read by. The two rooms at the end of each corridor were reserved for the chronically ill or the dying to give maximum privacy and quiet.

Two nurses were on duty during the day assisted by one or two aides who helped with patient care; one nurse was on night duty. With a few exceptions, most of the staff were young, single local women. Family participation in hospital care was also encouraged to provide additional comfort to the patient. Mothers were always given a bed when a child was admitted for one or two nights. To provide extra comfort and security for First Nations patients, a cot or mattress would be placed in the patient's room for a family member to sleep on. A tent was usually pitched in the circle in front of the hospital for others in the family should they wish to be around.

Downstairs there were rooms for nurses and the caretaker, including separate toilet and shower facilities, a kitchen and a small staff dining room. The hospital was heated with an oil-burning furnace with hot water pipes running to radiators in all the rooms. It had plenty of storage space and a separate back entranceway. It was all that one could ask for in a rural hospital.

It was only a matter of weeks before I discovered that as soon as I set foot into that small, spotlessly clean hospital, my senses automatically tuned in to the feelings of both staff and patients. I could actually tell when all was or was not well. If there was a patient crisis, a strange quietness would prevail throughout the hospital. Patients' doors would be shut and the usual bantering and corridor strolls ceased. It was as if everyone understood that it was best to remain unobtrusive.

Superficially, the hospital routines which Frank had set up did not give the appearance of structure, but they underlay everything that happened there. On the other hand, I had come to Eckville with rituals of my own, learned as an intern; fortunately, I could easily fit them into and around what he had already established. My routine began with a visit to the nurses' station where the charge nurse would give her report, after which we discussed each patient. It was very important to hear how the nurses perceived patient progress and what other input they could offer because their judgment was usually accurate.

Following the report and my review of each chart, I made rounds. Time spent with each patient was totally dependent on the need of the moment, which varied from day to day, but the extra time spent dealing with their issues was not only reassuring for them, but in the long run saved time because things went smoother and patient cooperation was better. This format relieved me of needless worry that I might miss important matters. If I fretted about a patient, I would go back and clear matters up as soon as possible. All of this helped me sleep better at night.

My first task on my first day on the job was to check on the in-patients. I made rounds, met all the patients and then had coffee with the nurse on desk duty. Our relationship was cordial and comfortable since we had met during my introductory week some months earlier, but I knew that she, like everyone else, must be wondering how I would handle that whole month alone. I would have to earn their trust and confidence.

While we stood chatting, a telephone call came for me from a man who introduced himself as Ray Sestrap. "I know you've just arrived in town, doctor," he said, "but my daughter Sandy's horse is bleeding to death from a bad leg cut." I took directions, grabbed my doctor bag and drove out to his farm on the edge of town. I was greeted by a friendly man about ten years my senior who took me immediately to my first Eckville patient.

The animal had a severed artery in its right hind leg and was in shock from blood loss. The cut was ragged and deep, and blood was squirting out about ten feet. Five farmers were standing helplessly around it, obviously unsuccessful in their attempts to stop the bleeding. Another man, a skinny blond Swede named Freddi Molander, was lying on the ground nearby, passed out from the sight of all the blood. No one was paying any attention to him, not even his wife, for apparently everyone knew that Freddi was squeamish at the sight of blood and prone to fainting. It took me less than ten seconds to open my little black bag, take out a pair of forceps, and clamp the artery. The bleeding stopped.

Much to my relief, the horse behaved well and did not flinch as I went about my repairs. I cleaned the wound, sprinkled it with sulfa powder and then sutured the jagged edges together. I inserted a drain and sutured it in place, leaving an opening for drainage should the area become infected. After the wound was neatly dressed, I injected the horse with a large dose of prophylactic penicillin and then had him taken to a small corral. I told Sandy—a ten-year-old, freckle-faced blonde—and her folks to feed him well, provide plenty of fresh water and give him lots of tender loving care. The horse seemed comfortable, and Sarah was relieved and elated.

All the farmers shook my hand and congratulated me for a job well done. Then Ray and his wife, Myrle, invited us all into the house for a drink and a toast to the horse. By the time they had toasted me, I, too, was feeling no pain. My limit has always been two shots of Scotch, but there in the middle of the day as we talked and laughed and had a hell of a good time, I wasn't counting anymore. The Sestraps started calling me "Doctor Ben," and the name stuck.

When it was time for me to get back to work, Ray asked, "How much do I owe you, Doc?" I suggested that since it was Sandy's pet, in lieu of cash, she could deliver the horse to me whenever I wanted to go for a ride. We shook hands on the deal. From that day, I became close friends with the Sestraps.

Word spread quickly about the new Doc and his first house call, and

Ben checking up on his first patient, Sandy Sestraps horse. Beside him, Sandy and a Friend, 1950

I was immediately accepted into the community. They knew that it was okay to call me to attend to sick animals. Little did I realize that tending to animals would become a regular part of my routine work during my time in Eckville!

I got to know Freddi, the skinny Swede, a lot better. He really was a funny man. I recall his telling me how poor his family was after settling in Canada. He said, "Ve vass so poor that ven it came to Christmas, my momma vould cut holes in my pants pockets so dat I'd have something to play wid, by God!"

A hundred yards from the hospital stood Frank Coppock's office and across the street from it, his residence; together these buildings made up the medical center of the town. The office, a single storey wooden building painted a sort of battleship gray, sat behind a privet hedge. Four steps led up to the front door, which opened into a common waiting room on the left with a receptionist's desk on the right. A large bookcase filled with medical texts lined one wall; the rest of the wall housed file cabinets with all patient records in neat alphabetically arranged folders. All this was in full view of the waiting area. While Marjorie Coppock did all the bookkeeping, during office hours Ida Knudson helped with office procedures and kept the place neat and tidy. Patients were seen in the order that they came in—first come, first served—with emergencies the exception. I discovered that Frank usually saw from fifteen to twenty-five patients a day.

Frank Coppock's office and clinic, 1949

To the right of a center hall, leading to a back door and a stairway to the basement, was Frank's office, furnished with a large desk and comfortable chairs. It, too, had a bookcase filled with medical books. It was a warm, cozy room. The window behind his desk faced the open fields and the hospital. The room next to his was a fully-equipped examining room.

Across the hall on the left of the entrance was the women's examination room. The table had stirrups and the various instruments needed for pelvic examinations and minor surgical procedures. The room adjacent to it was used for minor outpatient surgery and emergencies; it contained a dental chair used for the removal of teeth, repair of eye injuries, and the taking of blood. A simple lab in one corner was used to examine urine, blood, sputum, and other body discharges. The microscope was a good one, so examination and identification of cells could be done with confidence.

There was also an EKG machine, rather primitive by today's standards but good enough for me to identify disturbances in heart rhythm, unusual extra beats and abnormalities of the heart muscle so that I could determine evidence of myocardial damage. A small bathroom on the right side of the hall was shared by all. All the examining rooms had sinks that were designed for scrub up.

My first few house calls to people were not as successful as my first call to the Sestraps' horse for in each case the patient was dead before I arrived. It was clear from what history I could gather from family members, each patient had suffered a fatal heart attack. I discovered that my boss, for some reason, had a blind spot when it came to the early detection of coronary disease, even when there was a history of shortness of breath or pressure pains in the chest. In spite of the fact that he knew much about coronary disease and that his office was equipped with an EKG machine, the block remained. This realization was especially disconcerting to me because in the early months of my time in Eckville I began picking up a number of cases of incipient heart disease. I assumed that Frank's blind spot came from the fact that he came from a long-lived family.

Both parents and his Uncle John were alive and in their mid-eighties. John was a six foot four, handsome, silver-haired retired farmer from Saskatchewan. He was endowed with wit and wisdom and could play one hell of a game of cribbage. His comment on the busy and frenzied activities of some young farmers across the road has always stayed with me: "Rushing about like they do won't make the crops grow faster." It was a simple observation, but I interpreted it as a statement on life itself.

I hadn't been settled in very long when one day during office hours, a middle-aged, short, stocky, pot-bellied man came to town because belly pains had become so intense that he was unable to continue with his farm chores. Until now he had always enjoyed good health. He said that the pain had started in the center of his belly and shifted to the lower right side of his abdomen. A review of his other systems did not reveal anything of concern. I drew some blood and had him give me a urine sample. His white blood count (WBC) was a little elevated with a shift to the left, indicating an inflammatory reaction, but his urinalysis was normal. So far it looked like a straightforward case of appendicitis.

While I was in the laboratory, he undressed and waited in the examining room for the physical examination. Unless faced with a crisis, I had already established the practice of giving all new patients a complete examination, starting at the top and going all the way down, head, neck, chest and so on, leaving the abdomen last for careful scrutiny. His potbelly seemed a little distended, although not enough to cause me concern, but he was tender in the lower right quadrant of the abdomen in the usual anatomical area of the appendix. By doing a rectal exam I could usually get close enough with the examining finger to actually feel the heat of the inflamed appendix radiating through the rectal wall. Touching the area also results in pain. However, this part of the examination was not conclusive; he was tender in the area, but I could feel no heat from the appendix site. I figured that the appendix was walled off by some omentum, a fatty apron that hangs from the intestine, thus giving it some insulation. I also thought his thick belly created another barrier to the probing finger. Adding it all up, I made a diagnosis of subacute appendicitis and booked him for surgery.

It happened that John Skene, a former classmate of mine, was visiting from Red Deer where he was working at the Parsons Clinic, and since he was kind enough to offer his help, we both scrubbed up to do the operation. When the patient was asleep, I incised him over the site of the appendix. To our amazement, the man's distended bowel pushed through the opening and spilled out and over his belly. His gas-filled guts looked like a long string of sausages. The endless loops of intestine reminded me of the silk scarf that the magician pulls and pulls out of someone's ear. It was a little frightening. Figuring that this was "paralytic ileus" (a paralysis of the bowel due to irritation), we struggled to contain the bowel as we searched for the man's illusive appendix. Under normal circumstances it is about the size of a woman's little finger, and when we found his, damned if it wasn't perfectly normal. We were stymied. I took the appendix out anyway as we were there and as it served no function other than to cause future trouble. Then while one of us was stuffing the distended bowel back into the abdominal cavity, the other sewed him up. This was one time I really did need four hands.

After getting the patient back to his room, I put a tube down his nose and into the bowel in order to suck out the gas that was pushing out his belly. This provided him some relief and it prevented pressure building up and rupturing the incision. Then John and I sat down to review everything about the case. My diagnosis was obviously wrong. It had to be kidney stones. I called Dr. Gordon Ellis, the chief of urology at the university and told him of my mistake and that my classmate and I figured it was a complication of one or more kidney stones. Then after leveling with the farmer and his family, I packed him up and shipped him off on the hundred-and-some mile trip back to my alma mater.

Dr. Ellis was nice enough to call and tell me that a stone was indeed the problem and that the patient was doing well. I felt great relief although I still felt a little like a fool for erring in my diagnosis. Had I been a little less hasty and observed him another 24 hours, the underlying pathology would have emerged and presented a more definitive picture of what was really wrong. This was clearly an error in my judgment. Thank God that John had chosen that day to visit me.

That same week a young lumberyard worker came to see me because of recurring sore throats. His tonsils were a mess, swollen, filled with crypts and exuding pus. During that era of medicine this simply meant get them out as soon as possible to prevent them becoming a source of infection for heart valves, kidneys and joints. I put the patient on antibiotics and suggested a tonsillectomy just as soon as the acute infection subsided. He readily agreed, then asked if he could be circumcised at the same time. His longer than usual foreskin was much too tight. Sheepishly, he said, "What really bothers me, Doc, is whenever I get a hard on, it really hurts! And it's embarrassing when I take a piss 'cause I never know in which direction it'll go." He was not the sort of person you'd like to be standing next to at a urinal so his request made good sense. It was agreed that when I put him to sleep I would remove his tonsils and snip off his foreskin. I reassured him that there would be no confusion on what happened to what.

Now these two procedures are rather simple in a child, and just as there is limited pain for a child who has his tonsils removed, there is a minimum of pain when a newborn is circumcised. A clamp is placed around the excessive loose foreskin. A simple cut and the skin is off. Bleeding is rare and evidence of discomfort is momentary. Not so for grown-ups because the skin is much thicker and more vascular. Removal of the tissue is by scalpel, and sutures are used to close the raw edges. As a result, when recovering from surgery, each time the adult has an erection or any penile engorgement it is accompanied by intense pain. Since during the normal sleep cycle erections occur about four times each night, our poor patient did not sleep too well, even with painkillers. Nor did he fare any better with his throat which caused him so much pain that for the first two post-op days he didn't eat and was even reluctant to take fluids.

The nurses and female aides gave him much TLC together with considerable teasing. They even took pleasure in acting just a little bit provocative so as to evoke a sexual response in our young man. In spite of his suffering, it really was comical to see him clutching at his throat with one hand and his penis with the other for the three days of hospitalization. He told me that had he known that eating, urinating and having erections would be so distressing, he would never have had the two operations at the same time.

Ours was a small town and word spread around quickly about our patient, and for a week he was something of a celebrity. By the time he was back on the street he seemed to enjoy laughing at himself as well. Some months later he told me that he was "eating well, pissing straight, and doing quite well with the ladies."

Living with the Reverend Kingsley King was a blast. We were both working hard, but sometime each week we would find the time to talk about his Sunday morning services. "Kingsley," I told him, "you have to liven up your sermons. You're putting everyone to sleep." I'd suggest topics ranging from "Sins of the Flesh" to "Living the Good Life without Guilt" or something like "Can One be a Good Christian and not Believe in God?" He was intrigued by my ideas, so every second Sunday he would use one of my suggestions, struggling to formulate his presentation without seeming too brash or threatening to his congregation.

Kingsley was good at his job. He looked like a preacher. He was about my height, five nine and a half, but very thin, and when dressed up in his preacher's black suit, he looked like a cross between a young Frank Sinatra and a starving Messenger of the Lord. If I was not busy at the hospital or tied up with an emergency, I would walk over to the small wood-framed church, take a seat in the back row and try to figure out ways to crack him up. It took a fair amount of control for him to avoid looking to where I sat. Once in a while I got lucky and watched with glee as he struggled to maintain his composure.

The congregation seemed pleased with the spirited, unusual sermons, and they enjoyed the idea that the young, newly arrived minister and the new doctor shared the manse. The women, indulging their motherly instincts, catered to our need to be fed; or maybe they just wanted to fatten up the emaciated-looking minister. Most mornings we found a pie, a cake, or a pot of stew on our front porch. It got so we were like Pavlov's dogs, becoming conditioned to goodies each morning.

Almost every evening Kingsley joined me in making hospital rounds. Patients looked forward to being visited by the healers of the soul-and-body together because our professions complemented each other and our enthusiasm was contagious. And it gave me a chance to teach Kingsley the finer points of bedside technique.

I particularly remember our visits to a critically ill man in his late sixties with advanced congestive heart failure. He knew that he was dying. His only hope of staying alive would have been to receive a new heart and that operation was still many years in the future. He had immigrated to western Canada from England about forty years earlier to settle on raw acreage given him under the Homestead Act. He was a fine gentleman with a great sense of self, and his intellect and knowledge reflected an excellent old-country education. He told us of the rich cultural life he had enjoyed in England as contrasted to his primitive life in Alberta, of making birch beer and doing woodcarving. One evening on rounds and in the midst of our discussion, he politely asked Kingsley, "Reverend, would you mind reciting the Lord's prayer with me?" They joined together in prayer, "Our Father, who art in heaven…," and when the prayer was finished he drew one last breath and died. We both broke down and sobbed. This was the most peaceful, serene death I have witnessed in my fifty years of practice.

Before many more days passed, my friend, the minister, became dissatisfied with just making rounds and bedside talk. He wanted to see a real operation and be present to observe the birth of a baby. I spoke to one of my maternity patients who was near term, explaining that it would help with his ministerial maturation and he would be observing from the doorway. She agreed willingly. It all went well and for the first time the miracle of new life was demonstrated to this awestruck preacher. He did well and kept talking about the event for many days. Within the course of one week we shared two major events, the end of a life and the beginning of one. The next task was to line him up with a surgical case.

I was working alone in the office when a husky, middle-aged farmer came in with a mass about the size of a grapefruit on his back. It was clearly a huge abscess, the largest I'd ever seen, and it was ripe for cutting and draining. This seemed like a simple case that would be perfect for my friend to witness. I called him and said, "Kingsley, get your butt over to the hospital. I've got a good surgical case for you to see." I showed him how to scrub up, put on a mask, cap and gown and stand behind me as I proceeded to put the patient rapidly to sleep with some IV pentobarbital. When he was nicely out, I turned him onto his abdomen and explained to Kingsley that the next task after cleaning up the area and draping the abscess was to drain it of its contents so that the lesion could heal from within.

My attention was focused on the job at hand, all the while explaining every step to my observant and curious friend. "Now that he is out, Kingsley, it is safe to incise the abscess. All I have to do is jab it with a scalpel and make two cross-cuts in order to create an ample opening for drainage." We had lots of gauze pads in place to soak up the pus that would come pouring out. Then I proceeded to do just what I said I would. Thick green and yellow pus erupted from the wound and poured freely onto the pads. As the pus poured out, I heard a low moan and turned just in time to see the nurse catch the preacher as he fell backwards in a dead faint. I asked the nurse to drag him to the back of the room and let him lie on the OR floor until he recovered or the patient was wheeled to his own bed. All Kingsley could say after his recovery was, "I was just fine until the pus started to pour out." That ended his interest in surgery.

One day Kingsley had a phone call from two female seminarians, women in their twenties, who were doing church work in a nearby town. Could the Reverend King house them for one night and then drive them to their place of work just 30 miles west of Eckville? The good minister assured them they were welcome to stay the night and asked them to join him for dinner that evening. He failed, however, to tell them that they would be sharing the manse with two lecherous 25-year-old bachelors. We discussed—or rather we plotted—our strategy to make the most of our arrangements. The spare bedroom, just next to Kingsley's, was tidied up. We shopped for food and made our preparations.

When the two ladies knocked at the door, they were visibly surprised to see that their hosts were two grinning young bachelors. But we were equally dismayed to discover two stern, uptight, unsmiling women in their mid-twenties, their hair clipped short and straight, their shapeless dresses cut high in the neck and hanging well below the calf. No makeup adorned their pale skin. From the expressions on their faces, I'm certain that they feared the loss of their innocence, which was about as likely as Eckville being invaded by Martians.

While Kinglsey and I prepared a lovely meal of steak, vegetables, and some good apple pie for dessert, the talk got around to issues of sin and innocence. And then somehow the subject of aphrodisiacs came up and how they could be given to innocent people by sprinkling cantharides (Spanish Fly) powder into their food and drink. Now all the food was prepared right in front of the ladies, the water we offered them was poured fresh from our pump, and they watched every move we made; but when we sat down to the table, they said a prayer but politely refused to eat, even turning down the apple pie. The Reverend and I ate with gusto.

The ladies went to bed early, locking their bedroom door. They looked exhausted in the morning when Kingsley drove them to their next stop. When he got back we reviewed the visit, priding ourselves on how well it went. Other than our verbal rascality, we had actually behaved like perfect gentlemen. We tried to imagine how they would function with a congregation, giving pre-marital counseling or dealing with the myriad of social problems that arise within any community.

This was the first time I had lived in a place where there no other Jews. I liked going to synagogue and sharing the service with family and friends, and as I grew older, taking some time for personal reflection. However, what I missed most was the warmth and comfort of celebrating with family on the special holidays such as Passover, Rosh Hashanah (New Year), Yom Kippur (Day of Atonement) and Chanukah (Festival of Lights). I missed all of this in Eckville, yet attending to the needs of the sick took precedence in my mind over religious obligations.

Strange as it may seem, I found that I could enjoy the services at Kingley's Presbyterian Church by sharing the peace and quiet there with others and taking the opportunity to reflect, just as I had back home. The issue of God did not trouble me in either place because I was never able to accept the concept of God as an all-powerful and all-knowing being. From the time I was about twelve years old, I had thought of God as being present in all living things and that each person had to be responsible for the principles of godliness. I felt that love, charity, honesty and all those good things were my responsibility; if I did wrong or failed, it was my job to make repairs.

Upon reflection, I believe that this is what mother also believed. Dad, on the other hand, did not question or challenge the concept of deity. He thought that belief in God was intimately tied up with the job of carrying out God's wishes.

As planned, Norman picked up my Pontiac in Detroit and delivered it to me during my first month in Eckville. That car was a beauty, and because of my discomfort with debt, I was able to repay Morris, the Fish King, the $2000 interest-free loan within six months. However, I was not about to risk my beautiful new car on the country roads in bad weather and so I continued to use Frank's batmobile on those occasions. Whenever I approached a section of the road that was flooded, had deep muddy ruts or big holes, I simply hit the accelerator and skidded across

Enjoying some time off with a friend, my first car (a pontiac) and my red canoe.

the obstacle at about 60+ mph. I never once got stuck or bogged down, though I'd hold my breath in fear of drowning or running off the road.

When I traveled on bush country roads that twisted and turned with the contours of the land, it was easy to become lost. I sure could have used one of the current navigational devices like Loran or the global positioning satellite. There were few landmarks to navigate by in daylight and only the moon and stars at night, so I found my way mostly by instinct, just letting myself wander the countryside as I had wandered through bush country and fields of grain in my childhood. I knew that if I was really lost, some good farmer would take care of me, just as when I was a kid.

At the time Norman delivered my car, he was training to be a precision toolmaker. He was cool, steady handed, and willing to try anything; so since I was working alone, I persuaded him to assist me in the OR. I began by teaching him how to scrub up and observe sterile techniques because I didn't want him to screw things up by contaminating the operating field. The first time, he got all scrubbed up, gowned, capped, and gloved. Then, without thinking, he adjusted his glasses. I pointed out this break in technique and had him repeat the entire pre-op scrub procedure. He never made that mistake again. I believe his first case was an inguinal hernia repair during which I showed him how to clamp small blood vessels that I would tie off to minimize wound bleeding. He was also instructed on snipping sutures that I tied and to hold a retractor to keep the operative wound exposed so that I could work in an open field with unobstructed visibility.

When I worked alone, the nurse was too busy getting instruments and doing a number of other tasks to assist me, but when Norman assisted, the work went much smoother and faster. He was meticulous, steady, and not a bit squeamish, all attributes of a good surgeon. We did a number of emergency appendectomies, elective hernia repairs, and other relatively simple surgical procedures, and he would have done more, but I just didn't have the courage to give him full rein. It was always fun to introduce the patient to my brother, the machinist, who helped with the operation. He was every bit as good as Larry Knudson, the local garageman who Frank often drafted to help with operations when he needed an extra pair of hands. No one ever complained or protested.

After I was confident that the kid brother was comfortable in the operating theater and was totally reliable in following orders, I trained him to use the liquid anesthetic, ether. I would either induce the patients with ether, which took time, or induce them rapidly with a few whiffs of chloroform. The latter was very tricky, but when used carefully and with a sound knowledge of the problems involved, it was great. As soon as the patient was anaesthetized and back on ether, I instructed Norman how to keep the mask over the patient's nose and mouth and drip ether from the can onto the mask. Then I taught him how to read and report the state of the patient's pupils so I could determine the depth and stages of anesthesia. I also had him report frequently and regularly on the patient's vital signs by monitoring pulse, respiration, and blood pressure and give me a reading on the patient's skin color and report on any evidence of cyanosis, the blue color which can be seen in the nail bed of the fingers.

Norman left Eckville by bus after a few weeks of a memorable stay to enter the school of precision mechanics at the Calgary Institute of Technology and Art.

FRANK AND MARJORIE SEEMED WELL RESTED AFTER THEIR lengthy vacation, but I could see that Frank was eager to get back to work. I gave him a full report on my month alone and it was obvious he was genuinely pleased. Over dinner that night they talked about their trip and the relatives they visited. They had also gone into the States where Frank had spent a week at a continuing education seminar on surgery.

After that, Marjorie insisted that I join her family each evening for one of her delicious dinners; there was always plenty of meat, potatoes, vegetables and some great homemade desserts. I loved being part of that family. We'd start with drinks before the meal to give us a little time to unwind and talk, mostly about work, though occasionally about some local gossip. I would have one shot of scotch, neat. Frank would pour about six ounces of gin over some ice and never seem to get drunk. What he didn't know was that his wife had diluted the gin in his bottle with water on a one-to-one ratio because she worried about his drinking. What she couldn't control were all the friends around town who happily indulged "Doc" with scotch or gin. They sought to please him because they loved and admired him and because he really was the most important and charismatic man in town.

I don't believe they ever admitted or even saw the wear and tear that years of solo practice had taken on him. They just saw him as a man with limitless energy who carried on without need for sleep or rest. In any case, I never saw him drunk or unable to function in his work as a result of his drinking.

During my time in Eckville I gave little thought to the fact that most rural medicine was practiced by men like Frank. A large percentage of them worked alone or with one associate and were on call twenty-four hours a day, seven days a week, with a little time off for a vacation or attending a post-graduate course. Most worked until they retired, were too sick to continue, or died. They worked with little of the support available to those in the large towns or cities. Yet it was no accident that most patients did very well under the care of doctors like Frank because they took both the time and interest necessary to do their very best.

There had, of course, been many changes in the practice of medicine since the days when I had visited Dr. Boulanger, our old family doctor in Edmonton. Sulfa drugs had been developed, then penicillin, and the war had brought new medical techniques and surgical procedures. And there was less formality. Our office had no jars of surgical or pathological specimens or trays of weird looking knives and other surgical tools. Dr. B. had always worn a white coat or a jacket and tie; Frank's uniform was a red tie and a white shirt buttoned at the wrist. I wore a white shirt with sleeves rolled up, no tie. And for me, the sense of mystery was not the same as when I was a little boy either, for now I was the one who sat with patients behind the closed door.

With Frank back, the office got busier with those who preferred waiting until he returned. I was careful to keep him up to date on all previous examinations. With new patients I would go over the data so that he would know the situation and comment on my management plan. Occasionally, he would check the patient out himself. When there was anything unusual or special we would consult with each other. Often he would call me and say, "Ben, come and have a look at this," or "Here's something that you should see," or "What's your impression of this?" Frank was a natural teacher, constantly giving me bits of advice and practical suggestions that came from his rich background. It was like having a private tutor in the daily practice of medicine.

I particularly remember him calling me into the examining room one busy office day that September. He looked quite serious and I assumed that he wanted my opinion or that he had something interesting to show me. Lying on the table was a woman I had examined in July while he was away. She was a 48 years old and a grandmother, whose children were all married, and she had asked me to give her a check-up because her periods had stopped. Since her mother's periods had stopped at that age, she felt she had reached menopause. She was a good spirited woman who was well prepared emotionally to accept the changes that come with aging. I had taken a history and given her a complete physical including a pelvic examination and a Pap smear. I told her that everything looked healthy and that she was obviously entering her change of life.

Now Frank asked me to perform another pelvic examination, which I did, and darned if the uterus wasn't enlarged to about the size of a grapefruit. She was about three months pregnant. My boss laughingly explained that not all women with cessation of menses were necessarily menopausal even if they were close to fifty. He and the patient giggled, enjoying my embarrassment for missing the obvious. It brought to mind the old saying that "To assume, makes an 'ass' out of 'u' and 'me.'"

Six months later, I was fortunate to be the one on call when she gave birth to a healthy little girl who started out life with half a dozen older nieces and nephews and four siblings who were already parents. All the kids celebrated the event, delighting in the fact that Dad and Mom could still do it at their age, but they also enjoyed teasing me about my diagnosis.

On other occasions I was the one with something to show Frank in the examining room. I remember a very healthy, robust, pink-cheeked young farm woman, about twenty years old, who came in for a consultation. She was in perfect health except for a strange rash on the palms of both hands. It consisted of rather large, discrete, circumscribed lesions, reminding me of pictures of smallpox that I had seen in medical texts, but when I asked if she had ever been vaccinated for smallpox, her answer was no. I was surprised so I took my time examining her shoulders and thighs for evidence of the scars so typical of smallpox vaccination, but there was no sign of her ever having been immunized. I was amazed to find such a rare person, someone who had somehow slipped through the cracks of preventive medicine.

I dove into the medical books and found a picture that was identical to the lesions on my patient's palms. Then I called Frank to examine the lesions. He had never seen anything like this before either. My diagnosis was cowpox and he agreed. Now we were both excited because what we were seeing was exactly what Dr. Edward Jenner had seen when he discovered how to prevent smallpox, the plague that for centuries had killed millions throughout the world. We were looking at the very clue that had led him to develop the serum that became the greatest public health achievement ever.

We told our young milkmaid that she was blessed with a natural immunity to the smallpox virus because of antibody resistance that she had acquired through milking a cow whose udder and teats were infected with the pox virus. I said, "The great Dr. Jenner observed that milkmaids with cowpox, like you, did not die during lethal smallpox epidemics. Just go home and stop being concerned! Your hands will heal nicely. You are a very lucky and unusual woman."

Frank was always hungry to update his general knowledge of medicine and loved to pick my brains. "So Ben," he would ask, "what did they teach you about the current treatment of diabetes?" He had been working hard for years to keep up with the long and short-term management of each of his diabetic patients, but when I joined him in practice we were in many ways no different from doctors who practiced medicine a hundred years before us. Reliance on a detailed history and a thorough physical examination served as the mainstays to uncover the mysteries of the patient's complaints.

When a patient presented symptoms of diabetes, all we could do were a few simple lab tests like checking the urine for sugar and ketones. Thus the mainstay of management depended mostly on clinical judgment. Some of the questions might include, "How do you feel? Did you notice any changes in drowsiness, thirst, weight, perspiration, energy, urination, healing of wounds?" and so on. But by the time we were finished with a detailed history and physical examination, which usually took an hour, we had at least ninety percent of all we needed to know to treat the patient adequately.

At that time we adhered to the management profile for diabetes suggested by Boston's famous Joslyn Clinic. We had two kinds of injectable insulin: one longacting and one short. We did not have all the classifications of diabetes that we see today, but our concerns then were much the same, namely good daily management and a program to prevent complications. We kept our diabetics walking the tight rope of good balance through education and prevention.

The payoff for me was that during my tenure in Eckville none of my patients died or lost a limb or suffered from such diabetic complications as kidney or nerve disease. This, however, does not mean things went smoothly. I spent many anxious days and nights sweating it out with patients who developed diabetic acidosis, hypoglycemia, stupor or fell into a coma when they slipped out of control. The young and the very old diabetics were the most vulnerable to these complications; the young because of bravado and denial and the old because of diminishing mental capacity coupled with poor judgment and forgetting their therapeutic guidelines.

While diabetes is silent and its symptoms are hidden, the heart is the organ associated with sudden death and is anything but silent. When it malfunctions, a host of signs and symptoms appear that are difficult to deny or ignore. In 1950, we had crude digitalis (an excellent drug), and a good substitute called digoxin, which strengthened the heart muscle, helping it to pump more efficiently. Quinidine was great for regulating altered heart rhythms and mercury diuretics for ridding the body of accumulated fluid. These were remedies that Frank had great knowledge of and decades of experience with. Since all the rest was dependent on prevention, I spent time educating my cardiac patients on proper diet, exercise, avoidance of tobacco and the reduction of emotional stress.

There were, however, always some who looked for an easier way to control their heart problems.

Bill was a sweetheart of a man and a superb fly fisherman. Only 35, he was being treated successfully for a severe disturbance of his heart rhythm and high blood pressure complicated by thyroid gland dysfunction. All of these issues were under control with medication, but the balance was delicate and needed frequent monitoring. He was on digitalis to strengthen his heart muscle, quinidine to help with the irregular heartbeat and some thyroid to control its malfunction. Late one afternoon shortly after Frank returned, when the weather was warm and I was in a great mood, the phone rang with bad news. Bill's wife called to say that he'd had a massive stroke.

A few weeks before this upsetting call, I had examined him and found everything under control. I was pleased with myself, feeling good that even with our crude set-up I was able to manage a very complex medical problem. Afterwards, in high spirits, Bill had given me a lesson on fly-casting. We'd set a bucket of water on the road in front of the office and used it as the target for the fly. Now I was at a loss to explain what could have gone wrong so soon after his appointment. Doubt and uncertainty replaced my previous smug feeling.

His wife gave me detailed directions on how to reach their farm. She would leave a lantern on the gatepost to serve as a guide as it would be dark before I reached their place, and their home was in an area unfamiliar area to me. The Coppock's older daughter Audrey, who was home for a brief visit, volunteered to ride along and direct me. It was a beautiful evening, the stars were bright and there was a full moon, so having Audrey along suited me just fine; she kept me from obsessing about what might have gone wrong with my management program.

The farm was about 20 miles from town and we drove on and on through hilly and heavily forested areas. After a dozen miles or so I became certain that I could see the lantern twinkling in the distance; it was a while before it dawned on me that I was following a bright star that was just above the horizon. We stopped at a farmer's house, got our bearings again, made a course correction and finally reached Bill's place. There was the glowing lantern on a front fence post.

Bill was in bed with a total paralysis of his left side, which meant that the damage must be on the right side of his brain. Because the speech center is on the left side of the brain, his speech was preserved, and he was able to tell me that a self-taught local "healer" had persuaded him to stop taking all my medicine and instead take the natural minerals which his body lacked. It had all seemed perfectly logical to Bill who longed to be cured and live a normal life once again.

"Sorry I let you and Doc down, Ben. Please don't be upset with me," he said.

I reassured Bill and told him to restart his medicine and we would see how he progressed. I figured that clots clinging to the wall of his heart had broken loose when his arrhythmia returned in full force. These clot fragments traveling through his blood vessels had jammed the small arteries nourishing a part of his brain, resulting in brain tissue destruction and paralysis. I knew his prognosis for life was bad and hopeless for recovery. I never found out the name of his evil healer, but had I known who it was,

I'd have been tempted to tear his heart out. Bill never fished again. He remained paralyzed for the rest of his brief life.

For some reason, multiple sclerosis, a chronic illness that targets young adults as its victims, was unusually common in our area. I don't know why this was so, but it caused me to feel helpless and frustrated because while the diagnosis was relatively easy, there was no treatment. The scary thing about MS is that it attacks any part of the brain and/or spinal cord in a totally random, helter-skelter way, leaving stricken patients feeling desperate and hopeless because of its destructive, unpredictable neurologic symptoms. Remission raised their hope of a cure, but when the illness struck again, the victims would once more sink into despair. We could only offer them the hope that with all the research going on, help was on the way sooner or later.

Gastrointestinal illnesses abounded in the town. Eating disorders, particularly overeating, were common yet I never saw a single patient who was anorexic or bulimic. Peptic ulcer was common and was treated with a strict, bland diet, antacids and stomach sedatives. Stomach surgery and vagotomy were reserved for those whose ulcer obstructed, perforated, hemorrhaged or caused intractable pain. Today, ulcer is treated with such ease medically that surgery is rarely performed. If we'd had such medication seventy-five years ago, the Mayo Clinic, which was built on the revenue from vagotomies, would likely not have become the medical mecca that it is today.

Overall, the most challenging patients were those in the medically ill group, particularly those with difficult diagnostic or management problems because management in these cases required greater reliance on careful clinical judgment rather than on our inadequate laboratory set up. However, primitive as it was, with minimal technology and the absence of experts, I found Frank's judgement to be excellent at most of the medical problems he tackled. And Eckville's medical problems were certainly varied. They involved every system of the body, and every kind of minor and major issue from hair loss and itching to disturbances of the endocrine glands or major organs of the body. But while these were the biggest challenges to our practice, surgical and orthopedic problems abounded as well, demanding skill and innovation.

Most surgery, such as the removal of a gall bladder or a fibroid, is elective, allowing us time to prepare. Dr. Mac Parsons would drive in from Red Deer to do most of this work for us with Frank and myself assisting. Emergency surgery, most of which involved immediate threats to life, required more prompt attention. I must admit that although I enjoyed the comfort of doing elective surgery, I much preferred the excitement, tension and drama of emergency surgery. And as Frank was often away, leaving me on my own at least 25% of the time, I discovered that working alone and coping successfully with something totally new were great for developing resourcefulness and increasing my confidence.

Minor surgery was a constant in our office practice. We took out fatty cysts and sewed up all sorts of lacerations. We had an emergency eye kit that was in constant use. I would dilate the pupil with atropine and stain it with a dye that highlighted foreign bodies imbedded in the cornea. Most of these objects were metal grindings that penetrated the vulnerable eye because farmers just did not bother with protective goggles. A few drops of pontocaine provided enough local anesthesia to allow me to remove the metal without it causing further damage.

I remember one farmer came in because of a recent onset of diminished hearing in both ears. When I looked in his ears all I could see was a smooth, shiny black object that completely blocked both of his ear canals. After a little puzzling and gentle probing it occurred to me that a tic had attached itself to each eardrum and was engorged with blood. I took out a large needle, heating it over a flame until it was red-hot, then touched each body. That got their attention. The tics let go, allowing me to pull them out, and the hearing problem cleared up immediately.

Farmers and loggers sure seemed to get a lot of broken bones. There was always someone being kicked or thrown from a horse or getting in the way of a heavy piece of equipment which fell on him and broke his leg or smashed a wrist. Once in a while it was a lot more serious, like the farmer pinned under his overturned tractor. I keep referring to "he," but it is true: men get broken bones, women get sprains and strains. During my tenure as a country doctor not one woman suffered from a fracture. The reason was simply that men working around heavy equipment, logs and animals were at more constant risk of injury.

A man would come in with a Colles' fracture, a common break at the end of both bones of the forearm at the wrist. The diagnosis could be made as the person walked into the office because he would be supporting his arm with a swollen wrist that resembled the letter 'S.' There was a standard procedure for this kind of injury. I would take an X-ray, show it to the patient, and explain in layman's language how I intended to fix it. That was enough to settle him for the next stage which was to give him a quick-acting anesthetic allowing me to reduce the fracture deformity by gripping the hand and firmly pulling the arm toward me while at the same time compressing and molding the broken parts into place.

Once the bones were set I applied a plaster cast extending from above the elbow to the palm of the hand to keep the broken ends from shifting about. There were exceptions to this routine, of course. Sometimes a wrist bone reduction would not hold in place, so with assistance from another person, I would go through the same procedure but have my helper hold the parts in place as I went about wrapping plaster.

In Eckville I fixed breaks of every long bone of the body, ranging from a simple break of a pinkie to the long bone of the leg, the femur. Simple break means a clean break, making it easy to set the bone straight, but medically the break is like a crack, leaving the bone clean without any displacement. Things get a little rougher when the bone is broken in more than one place, which is more frequent in the long bones of the leg. Before the limb is put into traction the X-ray may show the broken pieces of bone scattered about and seemingly far apart from each other. My first reaction was, "Oh my God, how in hell can I get these pieces lined up to eventually resemble the original bone?"

Fortunately for the physician, Mother Nature kicks in to help out. Muscles act like elastic splints which help to align the parts together, aided by immobility and traction. Then from around the bone ends, little precursor bone cells build bridges linking the fragments together. Like ants they seem to know what to do, working non-stop until the pieces are back in reasonable line again. Calcium deposited in the cells results in formation of bone or ossification, and over time, usually months, and aided by exercise and physical therapy, the bone gradually becomes straight again.

The really nasty breaks were the ones in which the sharp jagged edges of the broken bone had broken through the skin. With farmers the danger of infection to these jagged bone pieces is great because of ever-present animal feces. It isn't that you see the feces, but the invisible,

127

omnipresent micro-organisms of tetanus and e-coli are present. Extra care must be given to reduce the chances for osteomyelitis and the subsequent nightmare of having to deal with bone infection.

Sterile techniques are mandatory. All visible dirt and debris have to be removed and the part liberally irrigated with sterile cleansing solution like saline or Ringers solution, which resembles blood serum in its salt constituents. Then, we would dust the area with sulfonamides and give the patient large amounts of penicillin together with a tetanus shot. I shudder to think that less than a decade before, antibiotics did not exist and this sort of injury frequently resulted in a chronic oozing osteomyelitis, amputation or death.

We often needed to improvise orthopedic apparatus because our hospital was small and did not have the room or the money to keep a large appliance inventory on hand. I'd go to the hardware store, lumberyard and blacksmith to shop for the necessary parts and get ideas from these guys for putting together what I envisioned. They were always willing to help out and were very resourceful at improvising. All that was needed was a little creativity, a knowledge of carpentry, elementary physics, and an understanding of anatomy and physiology. It was one sub-specialty of medicine that was fun, rather like boys playing with hammers, pulleys, ropes, weights and Lincoln logs.

Frank, checking on the progress of one of these inventions, would say, "That's good, Ben. That should work just fine." Or when he had ideas that might make things better, he'd say, "Try adding a pulley here, Ben. I think it might improve the efficiency of the apparatus." He never reprimanded me for a mistake.

The best "Rube Goldberg" setup we worked out was for a farmer who had been run over by a truck and suffered a crushed pelvis and multiple breaks of his femur. His internal injuries, other than some bleeding from the bladder, were minor. What he needed was a frame that was firmly fixed to the bed so his pelvis could be supported in a sling. At the same time his leg, undergoing traction, was being stretched out by a series of pulleys and weights to facilitate bone realignment. My helpers on this job were Larry Knudson from the garage, the blacksmith, and the owner of the hardware store.

We met at the hospital and I told them what was needed and together we soon had the apparatus made and working. We even had some special pulleys rigged up so that the patient could be easily moved up, down, and sideways in order to give him proper nursing care, and making bowel movements, bathing, and skin care much easier. The patient was comfortable and healed rapidly. I visited my three technical consultants to keep them up-to-date on our patient's progress. That apparatus was as good or better than any I'd seen in the city.

Another time, I got the blacksmith to convert a wide-ended surgical clamp into sharply pointed needle-nose forceps to make it easier to do plastic surgery, and darned if he didn't shape that delicate instrument on the same forge and anvil that he used to make horseshoes. As I watched in awe of his skill, I felt just like a kid again, watching old man Schultz in Bruderheim. It's revealing to me how in my mind I literally superimposed the first blacksmith shop onto that Eckville one, a perfect example of how an emotional early childhood experience impacts on the present. Those forceps proved so practical when doing delicate reconstructive surgery that it inspired further inventiveness.

Dislocation of the shoulder was also common among the men. I found the treatment fascinating and a little comical. The patient would come in with his arm dangling uselessly at his side. I'd get him to the hospital, have him lie down, then I'd take off my shoe and place my heel in his armpit on the side of the dislocation. There was no need for an anesthetic, especially for those with recurrent dislocations. After assuming the heel-armpit position, I firmly grasped the man's hand and pulled it toward me as I pushed up with my heel. "Snap, pop" and the head of the humerus was back in its socket. The pain was brief and tolerable and the entire procedure was over in less than a minute. I would then put his arm in a shoulder sling and send him on his way with a simple list of instructions for the next few weeks.

The rest of the office visits dealt with pregnancy check-ups, immunization shots, prostatic massages for chronic prostatitis, shots for syphilis, nutritional check ups, and a host of other items, not to mention the removal of stitches, dressing changes, eye dressings, throat swabs, ear exams, tooth extractions, and so on.

Well-baby clinics and children visits were emphasized in our practice, so there would often be mothers sitting contently in the waiting room nursing their infants. I liked the scene because it seemed to give the waiting room an aura of serenity. Those who were more modest went downstairs for privacy. Both babies and young children were seen for regular check-ups, shots, vaccinations and other procedures dealing with disease prevention. The more common problems included rashes, earaches, colds and sore throats, fevers, tummy aches or just malaise.

Although we saw illnesses that involved every system of the body, 75% of the people who came into our offices were suffering from a significant level of emotional distress. No matter the condition that had brought them there, each of them reacted with concern that was realistic or inappropriate or more often a mix of both. Symptoms of apprehension, palpitation, insomnia, worry, sweating, tremors, headaches, and so on would emerge, but more often they would cloud the underlying problems, creating all sorts of red herrings.

Anxiety, however, was by far the most common symptom of unrealistic fears, but it is so elusive that it can express itself in the form of thought disturbances, physical symptoms, emotional disturbances and even acting out, such as stealing, drinking, and skipping work. Moreover, anxiety often involves more than one of these expressions. Suppressing the expression of anxiety in one area usually results in symptoms popping up elsewhere, like cutting off just one snake from the head of Medusa. As I began to understand all this, I realized these folks needed time and patience to expose and remove the source of their inner conflicts.

I also began to understand why Frank Coppock had said right out when I agreed to come and work for him, "Ben, I can't stand fat people or neurotics, so I would appreciate it if you take charge of them all." He never explained why he felt that way, but I gave him credit for admitting his bias and shifting those patients to me. Later I began to suspect that they took time that he just didn't have available to delve into the confusing maze of their emotional lives. Just like all doctors of his generation, he had no training in this area of medicine. And even with my year of working with a good psychiatrist like Sid Spaner, I still felt poorly equipped to cope with the emotional problems presented by this group of people.

We had no antidepressants or tranquilizers to ease the pain of people suffering from emotional ills. All we could offer was talk therapy, and for this kind of doctor-patient contract, time and patience were the essential ingredients because most of these talk patients had never revealed their inner thoughts and feelings to anyone before. If the problem did not go away with a few office visits or if it still exerted a negative influence on the patient's progress, I began setting aside whatever time it took after office hours to listen and talk without interruption. By getting into my patients' minds and inner feelings, I discovered an added dimension to the doctor-patient relationship that a doctor rarely gets when just attending to matters of the flesh, but pursuit of this added dimension added much more to my daily workload.

Talking helped in many cases, even if I didn't understand the underlying psychodynamic issues. While I welcomed the challenge and the rewards, I felt an increasing sense of frustration with my limitations. In some cases I tried some psychotherapy, but because I had no training in it, I soon found myself floundering, just as I might if I were faced with doing brain surgery. I really needed to know more about the inner workings of the mind and just how the brain interacts with the body to produce illness.

One of my early successes with a talk patient happened in that first summer of my practice. A young man—tall, slim, handsome and bright—complained of fierce, intermittent attacks of belly pain, often accompanied by frequent, loose, smelly bowel movements and endless amounts of embarrassing bowel rumbles, belching and flatus (farting). Newly arrived in the area, he had set himself up in business for the first time as an independent newspaper editor and publisher, and he wanted desperately to be successful. His place of business was on the main drag of town, and it had a large plate glass window through which people passing by could see him at work. Type was set by hand, locked into a press, inked, and then each sheet was cranked out manually. It was a tedious and demanding job, and he worked well into the wee hours of the morning, especially when approaching a deadline.

He had also been recently married, and while he laboured over his press, his bride, a lovely lass, longed for his attention. When I asked what impact his symptoms had on their relationship, he confided with great difficulty and shame that he was impotent. He simply could not get an erection, and it was driving both himself and his wife to distraction. She constantly reassured him, while he conjured up the image of sure failure each time he tried to make love. The more he pushed the press to do better, the worse was his performance at home. He wanted both his press and his penis to be perfect.

My clinical exam suggested that all physical symptoms were due to emotional stress. His central problem was mental, not physical. We set up a series of evening meetings, a few of which included his wife. It was soon clear that his poor sexual organ could never function with the sort of demand that he was making on it. On the one hand, he was demanding that he perform flawlessly; on the other hand, he was convinced that he would not be hard enough to penetrate his wife. His escape from his predicament was perfect: work harder in the shop, develop painful gut symptoms and then have fatigue and illness as his excuse for his sexual failure. When this notion was presented to him, he understood and agreed. He rallied with reassurance and began to improve. His progress was confirmed by the look of constant pleasure on his wife's face.

Worry about money and how to manage without it was a constant for those who lived off the land. So much depended on the unpredictability of nature. One hailstorm or an early frost could wipe out a crop within minutes. A wet summer and fall made it virtually impossible to harvest the crops before winter set in. Summer drought left the fields looking shriveled, stunted, and burned out. However, I was always amazed at the resilience of most farmers and the expectation they shared that "next year would be better."

I quickly adopted the routine Frank had established for new patients. This included a thorough history, physical, and lab checks of urine and blood. A chest X-ray was always part of the examination because of the high incidence of tuberculosis in the area. All this would take about an hour. If more time was needed, he would generally have the patient return for a second visit. The charge for all this was $5; follow-up visits were $2. An extra dollar was added if lab studies were done.

Maternity patients were seen every month of the pregnancy and every week during the last month prior to delivery. Those visits included a weigh-in, blood-pressure check, urinalysis, a cursory check on the progress of the pregnancy and a brief examination of the heart, lungs and whatever else was necessary. A charge of $75 included pre-natal visits, delivery, and the six week follow-up visits.

When a patient, usually a farmer, was not able to pay, Frank never pressed for money. He would simply ask, "So what have you got these days?" The response would usually be something like potatoes or cabbages or carrots or pigs or turkeys, to which Frank would reply, "Well, the hospital could sure use some! Why don't you drop some over the next time you're in town?" The farmer felt good, his dignity was maintained, and the hospital was supplied with a free supply of healthy food. It was a good balance of give and take for all parties concerned.

The charge for house calls was based on the procedures involved, not the time they took or the distance we had to cover. I particularly recall one house call that occurred that fall as the weather got cooler and the crops began turning to gold.

Frank was in Red Deer going over some X-rays with Dr. Bill Parsons. I was having a slow day in the office when an urgent call came in from a farmer who said that he was having terrible abdominal pain and that he had not been able to void for days. I threw an assortment of urethral catheters into my doctor bag and headed for his farm. On my way down, I automatically ran through a checklist of probable causal factors, everything from an enlargement of the prostate to cancer.

When I got there, the patient was lying in bed in obvious agony. I could see and feel that the top of his bladder was at the level of his belly button; he looked like he could be six months pregnant. The story was one of a gradually developing prostatic obstruction to one of total occlusion. He reported having difficulty starting his stream and would dribble after he was finished. The symptoms worsened but he managed to endure the discomfort for a few days, then became totally obstructed. When in spite of grunting and pushing he could not squeeze out one drop of urine he got desperate enough to call for help. Lord knows why he waited so long!

I took out a catheter and tried without success to thread it through the urethral tube of the penis only to be met by the firm resistance of an enlarged prostate. I then tried my thinnest catheter, and that, too, would not pass the obstruction. He was shut down tight! With such a blockage the urine backs up in the bladder, and when that is filled to capacity, it continues to back up all the way into the kidneys. Meanwhile, the kidneys go on putting out urine even as they are being compressed by the back flow. In time the kidneys begin to show damage and a diminished ability to function.

I decided to plunge a large needle through his abdominal wall into the bladder and remove a good percentage of the damned-up urine, a procedure that would provide relief for the few hours it would take to have him transported to a urologist. At the same time, I had to be careful not to relieve him of too much urine in case his bloated kidneys collapsed and completely shut down. I gambled, taking my time as I gradually removed about a bucket of urine. While that was going on, I had one of his sons get the car ready for a fast trip to Edmonton. I called Doctor Gordon Ellis, the chief of urology, and related the story.

Within a few hours of fast travel he was in the University Hospital where they prepared him for prostate surgery the next morning. Luckily my patient suffered no kidney damage and I got away with my rather risky emergency procedure. I remember that my charge for the house visit and the handling of the crisis was fifteen dollars. In those days even that amount seemed excessive.

I never regretted following Frank's advice to refer patients for consultation. In each such case the patient's confidence improved. Our admission of not knowing everything helped with our continuing education by feedback from the specialist and with the patient's respect for our candor. However, I didn't always refer patients when I should have done.

It all began one day when this lovely old woman came in for a consultation. She was a sweet-looking, silver-haired 75-year-old woman with a kindly manner who would have been totally content were it not for her progressively enlarging abdomen. Kiddingly she assured me that there was no way that she was pregnant for it was about 30 years since she'd had her last period, but the mass protruding in her belly was becoming increasingly uncomfortable and was causing concern to family and friends as well. They all thought it could be due to cancer or some other scary condition.

I took my time in giving her a complete and thorough examination. She was in excellent health except for a mass in her abdomen that was about as big as a basketball. It wasn't fixed to the surrounding tissues as I could move it with some degree of freedom, and it felt spongy, which is quite the opposite to the firm, fixed feeling of a malignant growth. I summed up my preliminary examination saying, "I believe this mass is not due to cancer but is a benign growth. It should be explored surgically and removed for two primary reasons: first, it is continuing to enlarge, and second, it might twist and cause complications." My prime concern was that the mass would cause a blockage of circulation to the bowel, resulting in intestinal gangrene. She agreed to go along with my recommendation. "Go ahead and take it out," she said.

It was amazing to me that a woman fifty years my senior and of sound mind, should trust me to do the job. She had to know that I was a brand new physician, and yet she said, "Do it." I know that patients vary a lot in their faith in the doctor, based on age and experience. Some prefer older physicians because they are "more experienced," while some prefer the younger doctors because they are recently trained and are "more up-to-date." This woman did not tell me her reason for trusting me nor did I ask.

I started the anesthetic and then turned it over to a nurse as I went to scrub up. Fortunately, that day I had the luxury of two reliable nurses to help me. The second nurse would be my assistant, handing me instruments and holding a retractor or cutting a suture when both my hands were fully occupied. The incision was a large one. I wanted plenty of room so that I would not be restricted when dealing with a mass that size. I was relieved to see it was a huge fatty tumor that was all wrapped in the greater omentum. This is an apron-like fold richly supplied with large, visible blood vessels that are attached to the bowel. But to make matters much more challenging, portions of both small and large bowel were also wrapped around the fatty tumor.

The good news was no evidence of cancer. The bad news was that I had to remove the huge mass without nicking the bowel. Any escape of fecal matter would quickly result in life-threatening peritonitis. The other great danger was gangrene of the bowel should the blood supply to the bowel be compromised. Thanks to my thorough background in anatomy, I was able to dissect away the tumor carefully and maintain bowel circulation. It was slow going, but the patient was doing fine, so time was not an issue. When I had it out, the mass weighed almost twenty-five pounds, more than the weight of three newborns.

She did well during the operation, loved her flat belly and was not at all concerned with the huge incision. I was a little worried about adhesions developing in the future because of my cutting and messing around with tissues directly connected to the bowel, so I kept a close watch on her bowel function and I urged her to come in for regular checkups. Fortunately, she did well during the remainder of my time in country practice.

In retrospect I saw that by operating on her, I took enormous risks. Many years later, as a result of my analytic training, I learned that when people are ill and face invalidism or death, transference feelings are much more intense. The doctor is looked upon as all-powerful and all-knowing, just the same as Mom and Dad were when the patient was a child. Whatever feelings are projected, it becomes vitally important for the physician to be aware of them and detached enough to separate out what is true.

To believe what is projected, such as omnipotence and omniscience, is dangerous. In this case I knew that this was an elective procedure and that it posed many potentially dangerous problems. She should have been referred to a specialist or I could have arranged to have Dr. Mac Parsons come from Red Deer to do it. The least I should have done was to consult with Frank, but he was away, so I had decided to go ahead and operate. Looking back, I see how stupid my decision was. I did not pay attention to the dangers that I knew lay ahead. Just four months into practice and I was behaving like a trained surgeon! Thankfully, this was another useful lesson that I learned without doing any damage.

One day as I stood in the reception room chatting with Ida, our receptionist, I looked out the front window at a man whom I had never seen before struggling to get out of the passenger seat of a car and then observed how he walked slowly towards the office. As he approached the steps, I was surprised to see him turn around and walk backwards, one slow step at a time, up the office steps. In a flashback to an article I had read in medical school, I knew instantly that he was suffering from an advanced case of diminished thyroid production—hypothyroidism. The article had described the wasting and subsequent weakness of the large powerful quadriceps muscles of the thigh. These muscles reach a point where, even though the person can walk on a flat surface, they do not have the strength to lift the body to climb upward, so the person simply turns around and uses the healthy, stronger gluteal (butt) muscles to lift the legs.

The patient's skin was very dry, scaly and yellowish in color. His face was puffy with thinning eyebrow hair. A careful and complete examination also revealed that all his bodily functions, such as bowel movements, speech and motor activity were slowed down. However, even though everything about his body and its functions was retarded, I could not detect anything unusual about his thyroid gland. I called Frank in and we went over the patient again. He agreed with my diagnoses and also with my suggestion that the man see an expert. I explained the situation to the patient by saying, "Look, Mr. T., this thyroid malfunction has been developing for a long time, so there is little harm to be done in putting treatment off for a few more days. We also want to be certain of our impressions." He greed.

Later that week Dr. John Scott at University Hospital in Edmonton confirmed the diagnosis. The patient's prognosis was excellent, as shown by his response to thyroid hormone replacement therapy, and he made a dramatic recovery. When the mask of illness disappeared, it was like the fairy tale when the handsome prince emerges from a wicked spell. The man actually became handsome, appearing 20 years younger as the yellow, dry, puffy mask of illness cleared up. His hair grew in, vibrant in texture, and his movements became brisk and strong. He did not look anything like the man who walked up the front steps backwards. Most cases, of course, are not that dramatic.

EVER SINCE I HAD REPAIRED SANDY SESTRAP'S HORSE ON MY first day of practice in Eckville, word had gone around the community that Doctor Ben fixes pets. Most of the pets requiring attention were small animals brought in by children; cats and dogs, as well as birds with broken legs wings. Usually one to four kids showed up at a time with one of them carrying the pet in a box or cradling it tenderly in his or her arms. The children, who ranged from six to fourteen years, never made appointments; they just came in telegraphing their expectations by the look of love and concern on their faces. Barring any adult emergency, kids and pets were always given number one priority. I would see them as quickly as possible, determine the needs and then arrange to care for the pet.

If a small animal needed surgery, I would perform it in the basement of the hospital in a room equipped with an old operating room table that was still in good condition. I sutured bad cuts, repaired broken bones and performed sterilizations. I always asked the pet's owner if he or she would like to assist me by holding and comforting the pet. I wanted them to feel a part of the healing process and to have first-hand experience of witnessing a surgical procedure. They accepted 100 percent of the time, their eyes bugging out with amazement as they stared intently at something that they had never witnessed before. Who knows, maybe one of them became a nurse or doctor when they grew up. I would have given anything to have had the same chance when I was their age.

It was easy to anesthetize the animal, and we could then comfortably go about preparing the area for whatever had to be done. If it was the repair of an open wound or the invasion of the abdomen for sterilization,

I'd shave and wash the area with soap and water, then paint it with merthiolate. I'd scrub up, put on some gloves, drape the area with a few sterile cloths, and proceed with the surgery. By using sterile instruments and techniques, I never ran into any complications such as infection. Broken bones were easy to fix especially when the fracture was a clean break. Dogs and cats do very well hobbling around on a cast because they are blessed with three other legs to navigate with.

Whenever a child came in with a box, I knew that there would be an injured bird inside. It was usually a wild bird or a pet pigeon with a broken wing or a broken leg. I'd strap the broken wing to the bird's body and just hope that it would heal. The biggest concern I had was to be sure that the bird took in water and food; wild birds need to be encouraged because they tend to just lie down in a corner and die.

While all this was going on, I would answer the kids' questions and explain the reasons behind everything I did. The kids loved it. I asked them to be responsible for home care and gave them instructions about returning for a checkup and the removal of sutures. It was very gratifying work, especially with the enthusiasm of the grateful young children. Frank took pleasure in the fact that I was having fun. We never charged a fee; both Frank and I looked on it as community service.

But not all my attempts to deal with broken legs were successful. Once when I was on duty at the clinic at Sylvan Lake, a nearby resort, a young couple brought their cat in with a badly fractured hind leg. I gave the animal a shot of morphine to ease the pain, figuring that if it worked for people it would do the same for cats. Not so, I discovered, as the cat leapt straight into the air, landed on the front of my chest, dug its claws into my shirt and ripped it off my body. It then leapt onto the floor and ran out of the office on three legs. The last I saw of it was watching it run down the street at full speed dangling its shattered hind leg and followed by its apprehensive owners. Morphine, it turns out, serves as a powerful stimulant for cats.

My most interesting animal case came up in mid-fall when my friend Ray called with an urgent request. "Can you come to my farm, Ben? My pigs are dying!" This was very serious since most of his winter income came from the sale of the hundred pigs he raised each year. I grabbed my bag and went over.

It must have been a little before 5 pm when I got there for it was just beginning to get dark. Ray took me directly to the pens. A few of the pigs were already dead; some others lay around in a lethargic state, their breathing laboured and shallow. My initial impression was that Ray was faced with a swine flu epidemic. If I was right, we could prevent droplet spread of the virus from one pig to another by separating the sick from the healthy ones. Pigs cough and sneeze, but unlike humans they don't cover their noses or mouths.

A number of neighbours had dropped in to help out, and I had them drag the dead pigs out of the pen to a place about 50 yards away. I suggested that all the healthy pigs be taken to the farthest end of the farm and those that seemed questionable be isolated in a clean pen some distance away. The very sick and dying pigs were left in the original pen.

I set about doing an autopsy on the dead pigs. After all, I would have done the same if I were confronted with a human epidemic. It took no more than five minutes to discover that they had died of pneumonia. Their lungs were engorged with blood, somewhat similar to hemorrhagic lobar pneumonia seen in humans. "We'll set up a crisis center for the sickest pigs a respectable distance from the pens," I told Ray. "Call everyone you know who has oxygen tanks and have them bring them to the sick bay." Back at the hospital I collected some old and new face masks, some tubing to carry the oxygen, and a number of bottles of glucose and water with IV tubing, needles, penicillin and even aspirin. I grabbed whatever I figured I would need if this had been a human epidemic.

By the time I returned with my materials, a number of women had also come to pitch in, some bringing coffee and sandwiches, and friends with industrial oxygen tanks stood by ready to help out. It was great to see how neighbors and friends rallied to the crisis. As it was now pitch black and the sick pigs could stand some warmth to minimize the effect of chill, I had the guys build some fires around the crisis center to provide heat and light, and to burn the dead pigs' carcasses. Within half an hour the emergency center was set up and I was ready to administer treatment. Farmers, mechanics, and others were transformed into totally-focussed medical assistants.

The sick pigs acted much like sick people. They seemed to sense that something was being done for them, reminding me of sick children who lie quietly without complaint as mother or doctor tend to their needs. We placed them parallel to each other with just enough room between them so that I could move quickly from one to the other. Because of their fever and profound weakness, they made no attempt to get away. One person was assigned to each pig. I plugged in the intravenous so that they could be hydrated with the glucose and water, and I injected penicillin into the tubing so that it could be delivered instantly to begin its attack on susceptible primary or secondary pathogens. As soon as that was underway, each patient was put on oxygen.

Just picture the scene! Bright bonfires lighting up a row of sick pigs, each with its own farmer-nurse, getting oxygen from industrial tanks and intravenous transfusion of fluids. It was a sight to be remembered and a night that no one who took part in it would ever forget.

Except for the light that came from the fires and flashlights, it was by now pitch black, but we worked without letup until late into the night. Every six hours I gave each pig more penicillin in its hindquarters. Between times, Ray and I made the rounds of the pens and immediately injected any pig that showed the slightest sign of an upper respiratory infection. By three in the morning I felt that all was under control. All the very sick pigs showed signs of rallying.

They breathed more easily and did not seem as listless. As soon as they started to get up on their feet, they were moved into clean pens that I still treated as areas of quarantine. Before leaving at four in the morning I left orders for Ray to continue giving injections of antibiotics every six hours to the sick ones. I was so jazzed up that it took me a while to fall asleep and be up for another day's work.

The next day we assessed the damage. It was gratifying to see that by separating the sick ones we had contained the epidemic; not one pig in the healthy pen became ill and not one of our sick pigs died. The crisis center was closed. Before the neighbours took their oxygen tanks home, I had Ray get them to help clean up the original pen and burn all the straw that was lying around. I wanted the pig's living area to be clean and free of contaminants as soon as possible, but I suggested that he wait a few weeks before using the pens again. No one got drunk as we did after the horse incident; we were all too tired.

Ray was not charged for anything; I just asked him to reimburse the hospital for the fluids, masks and medication at cost. How could I charge for something like that experience? How many times in my life would I take part in stopping a pig epidemic in consort with neighbors and friends? I felt that it was I who should pay Ray. However, once again he wanted to settle up with me, and finally he came up with an idea. "Ben, I'm going to give you the entire litter that comes from the next pregnant sow! They will be yours and you can take care of them until they are ready for market. Whatever they bring in dollars is yours."

"It's a deal," I said. We shook hands and said no more. Within two weeks I became the proud father of six piglets. They were adorable, pink, cuddly little babies that one could hold and even bottle-feed. They, however, much preferred to suckle at the real thing. Each evening that I could spare the time I'd go over to the farm and make sure that my litter was well fed and cared for. When Ray told me that they were ready for market, I accepted their fate and bid them a sad farewell. It is not good to become attached to animals that will end up in the slaughterhouse for table food. They were part of the food chain, and I was happy to get the money which came to about $70.00 a pig, more than a month's wages for me. I felt rich for the money I got and richer still for the experience I shared with the pigs and people of Eckville.

Gradually the rehashing of the pig epidemic petered out. Life returned to the routine of normal practice, allowing me the luxury of catching up on some reading and shmoozing with the town folk. One day I was sitting in Frank's office reading when he approached me and asked casually, "Ever been to a stampede, Ben?" When I said I hadn't, he announced, "Well, the Benalto Stampede's on tomorrow and I'm on call there every year in case there's an accident, so we're going. We'll close the office. We can make a few house calls in the town, but the rest of day is for us! It's going to be a fun day!" It was cowboy time and I responded immediately with an enthusiastic "Yes!"

Benalto, a small town just a few miles southeast of Eckville was known for only one thing: its annual stampede. While the biggest one in Alberta is the famous Calgary Stampede, at which hundreds of thousands of people congregate from all over the world to celebrate for an entire week, Benalto had a one-day event for the real cowboys who compete in rodeos. The fans, plus all the locals and contestants who drifted into town might have added up to a thousand people. It was in those days, however, the second largest, real honest-to-goodness, old-fashioned rodeo in the province. The cowboys who took part came from all over North America to compete in riding wild broncos and steers, calf roping, steer wrestling and horse and chuck wagon races. If they did well at Benalto, they went on to compete at other major rodeos in Canada and the USA. Unlike Calgary, there were no parades, square dancing on the street, Indian dances or sideshows. It was all business, except for the local beer parlor and a few vendors who were busily quenching the thirst of competitors and onlookers.

Frank and I took plenty of emergency equipment to sew up cuts and splint broken bones because getting thrown by an animal had a few risks, such as getting trampled or even being gored. It's a sport for the brave and the fearless, not the lighthearted or cowards like me. Brave as I might have been as a kid riding on the back of a pig, there was no way I'd take a chance on being thrown twenty feet or trampled by a 3000-pound steer.

We watched the proceedings for a while, then, since things were quiet medically, I left to make a few local house calls in order to check up on some young patients isolated because of scarlet fever. In those days we had to put a bright sign on the front of the house as a warning to others to stay away. Today the treatment is an antibiotic and a little caution to deal with what is essentially skin redness associated with a streptococcal infection. When I returned to the arena, Frank was nowhere to be seen, and I found myself a comfortable perch on the top railing of the high wooden fence that surrounded the arena. Suddenly, I felt a rush of adrenaline as, without any warning or announcement, a horse and rider catapulted out of a chute. One arm flailed as the man held onto the rope surrounding the horse's torso.

I was flabbergasted. The rider had silver hair and wore a white shirt with full-length sleeves and a red tie. It was my boss, Frank Coppock. He rode well for about a full minute and then was tossed straight up and forward as the bronco jumped, twisted, and spun about. He flew through the air to make a perfect three point landing on his hands and his face. I spent hours picking small stones and dirt out of his bleeding wounds; all Frank did was laugh and curse. He'd had a few snorts of Scotch and so was feeling little pain. The really crazy thing was that I had to restrain him from going back and doing it again!

Frank was fearless, a risk taker who loved challenge. Only a few weeks before, I had patched him up after the motorcycle he was riding wiped out on a dirt road. Same wardrobe, same injuries, and same type of treatment, just a different venue and a different mode of transportation. I knew that when he got home his wife would chastise him as she would a lovable boy who had merely done something naughty. Within a short while both of them would be laughing about his daredevil behavior. Frank was a little devilish and always had a merry twinkle in his eye that suggested something impish was about to happen. This was another trait that endeared him to all of us who knew him because the man we worshiped and respected was also a fun-loving, adventuresome big kid.

Frank was my only casualty that day.

Having two doctors running the practice meant that we could both afford a little time for recreation. At Marjorie's urging, Frank took more time off. Sometimes it was just a few days away to attend a conference or confer with a specialist, but there were also week-long vacations with Marjorie just to restore his energy. I made the most of the times when he was in town, especially when the practice was quiet, for my own recreation. I would call and ask Sandy if she could bring me her horse for a short time. She would ride him to the office and leave him all saddled up for me at the front steps.

I'd ride through the countryside, exhilarating in my freedom, a young man exploring, singing to his horse. Or I became a little boy again, imagining that I was a real cowboy. Sometimes we just galloped full speed or swam across the small nearby river, with me swinging my feet up on the horse's neck to keep dry and enjoying the wonderful feeling of floating over the water as the powerful horse took charge of keeping me safe. After about an hour's ride, I'd get back to the office and call Sandy to pick up her pet.

Sometimes I'd drive over to her father's farm, and Ray and I would unload my 10-year-old canvas-covered canoe from the top of the Pontiac and go fishing in the creek that meandered through his property. He was always ready to leave his chores to paddle with me, trolling for pike or trout. If we caught any, we would just let them go and paddle on. We'd top off the brief fishing expedition with some of his wife Myrle's coffee and cake.

Ray slept until 10 or 11 in the morning, by which time most farmers had half a day's work done. "Hell, Ben," he said, "why should I get myself up at 5 in the morning? It's my farm. Let the animals adjust to *my* clock." So Ray would start chores around noon and finish his milking near midnight. I didn't see any evidence of rebellion on the part of the cows, chickens or pigs. They seemed perfectly content.

Once in a while there would be a turkey shoot at someone's farm. This was a civilized event in which people paid to shoot at a fixed target with a regular bull's-eye in the center. The best score won a big turkey to take home. The first shoot I competed in was at a farm about ten miles from town. It was just before harvest time; the evenings were cool, and there was just enough light left to see the target. About thirty farmers and woodsmen, old and young, milled about with rifles in hand. A target was set up and the shooting took place after each participant paid a two-dollar entrance fee. Most would fire from a standing or kneeling position; I preferred the traditional army type of target shooting, lying prone, which gave me the best support and rifle control. I was a good shot so I'd usually win a turkey to bring back to the Coppocks' or to the hospital.

But the best escapes were to Ray's one-room log cabin located south of Nordegg and west of Rocky Mountain House. Julius Rodke had built it just about a mile from his own logging camp as a wedding gift for his son and daughter-in-law. When the kids moved away, Julius gave it to Ray for as long as he wanted it.

Just as soon as we got on the road and headed west, I could feel the relief of knowing that I'd have a few days of complete tranquility. Once off the Nordegg graveled highway, the few miles of dirt road became a rutted trail cut through a vast virgin forest. In a number of places where it was muddy from streams or creeks, logs had been laid parallel to each other across the road to serve as a primitive bridge to prevent cars bogging down in the mud. This kind of trail was called a corduroy road.

After driving for miles through pristine wilderness, we arrived at a large meadow on top of a hill. The cabin sat above a lake filled with trout that jumped from the water to snatch at insects hovering above it. Beyond the lake, small creeks that had been blocked by beaver dams over the centuries had created a series of smaller lakes, stretching into the distance.

The shallow parts were filled with tall marsh grasses in which majestic moose wandered leisurely, munching away like contented cows. On the slopes above them, the forest stretched as far as the eye could see in all directions, ending in mountains and sky. It was an area of unbelievable beauty. A pristine wilderness in its absolute raw state, filled with birds, deer, moose, elk, cougar, bear, and all sorts of small animals, just as God had created it.

The silence was wonderful. The ring of the office telephone was replaced by the chirping of birds, chipmunks and croaking frogs. The tensions and troubles of work were swept from my mind as if someone had taken a brush and wiped them away. Once again, I was as free as a child to wander in the fields, marshes and woods.

The cabin was about 300 square feet and built of thick pine logs taken from the surrounding forest. Everything in it had been made by hand. One window faced the vast series of beaver lakes; the other, next to the door, faced the trail that approached the cabin. All timbers were caulked with clay, keeping out wind and rain. A large fireplace made of local field-stone was used both for heating and cooking. A solid table and two chairs stood in the corner with the view. A double bunk bed was in the opposite corner.

On the wall next to the fireplace were a few shelves and a tiny cup-board for dishes and groceries. A few simple-cooking pots hung from the ceiling. A broom in the corner was used to sweep the wooden floors clean. There was an outhouse in the back, a stack of wood under a little shelter and a picnic table with benches in front of the cabin. We had a great bar-becue pit with a grill on top for outdoor cooking in warm weather. Ice cold drinking water came from a rapidly running mountain stream. We bathed in the lake below. No electricity. No phones.

We always kept a rifle handy just in case. Every once in a while there could be trouble with a hungry bear or an aggressive cougar, but as long as we made little noise as we walked through the woods and did not leave food lying about, there was no trouble. If I wanted to do some shooting it would be at a tin can that I'd place on a log. When we broke camp, we were sure to leave everything tidy and always leave food—canned milk, beans, sugar, salt and pepper—for anyone who might seek shelter there. The door was latched but never locked.

My old red canoe was perfect for paddling around the lakes and for portaging over the beaver dams. We could paddle silently as we explored mile after mile of the great series of lakes and marshes without disturbing the environment. We always made certain to keep a respectable distance from the munching moose even though it seemed as if they paid us no mind. Our best source of food was from the lake in front of the cabin, but even though we could see the trout jumping, it took a lot of patience and skill or luck to catch them.

I can still see the look of sheer joy on my brother Norman's face when he caught his first trout there; he got so excited he stood up and almost capsized the canoe. Just as soon as we caught a couple of rainbow trout we would head for shore, clean the fish and cook them on the grill together with bacon and onions. The fish were tender, sweet and juicy, bearing no relationship to the expensive trout served in fancy restaurants. We washed them down with freshly brewed coffee.

When fall came, we hunted. I recall walking down a game trail for the better part of two hours looking for a buck deer. This was to be my first kill since snaring gophers as a kid, but while I wanted to do it, I was really hoping that the opportunity would never present itself. Then as I tramped along, wrestling with my conscience, through the trees to one side of the trail about fifty yards ahead of me, I saw the mane of an animal. With thumping heart I took a bead on the area and waited. Then to my horror I saw that my quarry was a forest ranger on his horse. That was it! I lowered my rifle, turned and went back to the cabin, my conflict about hunting resolved forever.

The next day, though I accompanied Julius and Ray on their day of hunting, I did not carry a rifle. However, Julius asked me to follow a deer trail and keep alert. After about an hour two shots rang out just ahead of me. When I got to the spot, there was Julius, sitting on a stump as relaxed as could be, smoking his pipe. He had just bagged two big bucks. All he had done after giving me my trail-walking assignment was to wait patiently, knowing that the deer ahead of me would catch my scent and walk away from me, right into the sights of his rifle.

Later that evening Ray and I walked the mile back along the forest trail to Jasper's home camp to share in the ritual of eating the liver of the newly killed animals. I suppose this was associated with a primitive belief that by eating the liver one gained strength or fulfilled some other ancient hunter's myth. It was dark when we approached the camp. There were about five or six log cabins in the clearing for living quarters, equipment storage and for the gas generator that provided electricity. Wood smoke from the stoves and fireplaces hung over the camp, and the smells of roasted venison, oil from the generator and pipe tobacco filled the cool night air with a blend of sensual odors. That night as the talk ranged from stories of the hunt to my being set up by savvy old-timer Julius, I was aware of the great sense of intimacy in this small, tightly-knit group of woods-wise people.

TOWARD THE END OF OCTOBER, JUST BEFORE WINTER SET IN, a minister with a family arrived to replace the Reverend Kingsley King who was transferred to another parish. I knew he would be richer for the experience of sharing my medical work. I missed him a lot.

After he left, I moved into the living quarters in the basement of the office building. My new quarters—a nicely finished furnished room with adjoining bathroom—were always warm and comfortable. I found myself contrasting it to the tiny room at my old home, with its one bathroom shared by the seven of us. It was positively palatial compared to the con-verted chicken coop I had lived in when I was working on the Dewarts' farm to earn the two hundred dollars for my first year's university tuition.

On my occasional weekends off, I'd head back home to Edmonton to visit with family and friends. The trip was a little more than a hundred miles and a pleasant journey; quiet rural areas and small towns, endless prairie fields, fresh and green in spring and summer, and amazingly beau-tiful as the grain began to ripen in the early fall. But it was the light of the early morning or late afternoon sun that gave the ripe stands of wheat, oats, and barley that special deep shade of gold that I loved the most. Their colors grew darker and softer, much like the last rays of the setting or rising sun reflected on the clouds above. The wind flowing over the fields created soft undulating waves like the rhythmic motion of the ocean, yet the soft, rustling sound as the long stocks of grain brushed against each other was far more tranquilizing than the pounding of waves on the shore. All around was the delicate aroma of those thousands of acres of growing wheat mixed with clean, crisp country air.

As I entered Edmonton, my first stop was the home of my folks to catch up on news of friends and family and share some of my work experiences. Neighbours and friends would drop over as we sat around the kitchen table drinking tea and eating mother's light pastries. It was great to call old childhood playmates and go out with the 'gang,' sharing with them in a way that ensured the continuity of our friendship.

During our teen years a split had taken place in our crowd of peers. One group went off to work in businesses and marry early. The group I belonged to focused on education and professional development, delaying our settling down. Now I could see that our lives were changing—most of my old gang were seriously involved in relationships and committed to marriage—and inevitable breaks and separations would be coming as we moved into the next stages of our lives.

One early winter Sunday morning, as I headed back to Eckville, travelling about 30 miles an hour on my favorite back roads, it began to snow, coming down thick and heavy and showing all the signs of becoming the first blizzard of the winter. Landmarks disappeared within moments. The road and the deep ditches on either side were one solid white blanket of snow. The only markers left were fence posts. With limited visibility due to the heavy snow it became impossible to see through the windshield. In order to avoid ending up in a ditch, I drove with my door open, traveling mile after mile at a snail's pace, using the farmers' fence posts on my left as a guide to keep a straight course. Fortunately, the blizzard ended after about two hours, making the rest of the trip seem easy. As I approached Eckville, ruminating over my work and future, I thought back to my friends who were married and planning marriages as they settled down to enter family life. I envied them but knew that it would be years before I would be ready to settle down.

I had no assets except for an unpaid-for car and an uncertain future. I just could not commit to a serious relationship. I would continue to date and have fun and further sublimate my interest in women through my work as a physician. I must confess that I preferred working with women patients more than with men because I found them to be better communicators, both intellectually and emotionally. And my work with women was made easier after the coaching I got from Frank. Most women loved him because he was so sensitive, understanding and capable.

He was superb at obstetrics and gynecology, and these were busy items in our practice. We did Pap smears for uterine cancer on a routine basis. Breast examination drove me crazy, especially with women who had polycystic breasts. There were lumps of all sizes and texture, and I was filled with the dread that I might miss an early cancer; it was like examining an anatomical minefield. All I could do was have them come in for more frequent examinations and encourage them to become expert at knowing their own breasts.

Women also came in for regular check-ups, discharges, vaginal infections, abnormal blood flow, pregnancies, uterine tumors, prolapse of bladder and uterus, piles, and varicose veins. I saw so many of them that I began to understand better why the daily Morning Prayer of the Old Testament says, "I thank God that I was not born a woman." Men have it so much easier.

By the time I'd finished medical school and my internship, all discomfort from attending to naked men or women was gone. I never recall experiencing any sexual arousal with either sex, though many of the women I examined had beautiful bodies. My relaxed attitude helped patients feel comfortable during the examination, and by explaining what I was doing, I found that they would then be more absorbed and cooperative in what was going on. For example, if I were doing a breast examination, I'd say, "Now, Mrs. Jones, I'd like to teach you how to examine your own breasts. In this way you will be the first to detect anything different or unusual. Now this is how you go about it." Then I would show them the steps involved in self-examination. By sharing, teaching and explanation, anxieties were reduced and sensitivity to naked exposure was minimized, no matter if it were for the examination of a belly, hernia, vagina, rectum or any other body part.

Since my training had made me sensitive to women's need for privacy, when I began practice in Eckville, I followed the city practice protocol of asking the patient to undress and cover up with a white linen sheet while I went about other office business. I was therefore a little taken aback by one of the first women I examined, who stripped without the slightest hesitancy or modesty and lay down on the table before I was out of the room. As it turned out, that was what most of the women did. It made examinations a lot easier. There was no fussing with a sheet that was forever falling or slipping as the examination proceeded. And it meant less laundry for Marjorie.

Women were also very straightforward when it came to stating the reasons for their visits. I recall being struck by the delicate features and ladylike demeanour of one young lady as she entered the office. But although this was her first visit, she quickly got to the point. Without the slightest hesitation she stated, "I'm twenty-three and I've been married three years, but I'm having some inconvenience when my husband and I make love. Can you help me?" I decided to get to the point as quickly as she had, and rather than get into a detailed history, I asked her to prepare for a physical examination. She was not at all timid about undressing and getting onto the examining table.

When I looked at her genitals, I was amazed to see that her labia minora hung loosely down like a curtain, more like the ears of a Beagle or a Basset hound. They completely covered not only the entrance to the vagina (entroitis), but extended so far down that they almost covered her anal sphincter. When I pulled the labial folds apart they looked more like elephant's ears with a pink opening between them. Other than this defect, she was perfectly healthy and well put together. I suppose that the counterpart in an uncircumcised male would be a four-inch foreskin.

She explained that when her husband was prepared to enter her she would take hold of each labial fold and hold them aside. I pictured the scene and had a few private thoughts. The first was that this all seemed quite normal to the young woman and she was either in denial or was terribly naïve. The other thought was that sex for them must have been like theater: she pulled the curtains apart and her husband began his performance. She said that her difficulty was when the labial folds would get caught up and dragged into the vagina, making sex especially difficult for both of them. The solution was really quite simple, and I suggested a little plastic surgery to remove the excess tissue, indicating that not only would it solve her problem but it would also have a more pleasing cosmetic effect. She asked to have it done as soon as possible. When she was prepared for surgery, the two nurses on duty were amazed and fascinated by this remarkable genital anomaly, marveling at the fact that she had been able to manage sex for so long without seeking help.

I think I did a good job of snipping about 90% of the tissue off, leaving what seemed to be two normal sized folds of equal size and shape. Even though she seemed much relieved, I wondered how she truly felt giving up her folds, since it is a well-known fact in medicine that when an extremity is removed the patient is often left with phantom symptoms of the lost part. I never got to ask her that question. In any event, it was one of those unusual cases that had an easy solution and was stress-free for me.

When it came to the subject of intercourse, two central issues concerned most women. The first had to do with either conceiving or preventing conception and the second was her partner's ability to perform. Seldom did we run into problems of infertility; in fact, it was the exact opposite. It struck me that our patients were an extremely fertile bunch. Perhaps it had to do with the subtle psychobiological influences on the reproductive system of country women. People living in the country are surrounded by the naturalness of sex and reproduction. It's now well known that women are more likely to conceive when they are around babies or are on vacation. (Later when I was consultant to hospital nurses in Philadelphia, I discovered that they often reacted to time spent working on the maternity ward by missing a period. This also was the time that most nursing trainees lost their virginity, clearly the result of so closely identifying with the birthing mother and the wish to conceive.)

Life is demanding on the wife of a farmer, but the emotional stresses are somewhat different than her city counterpart. The surroundings seem to promote a mind-set far more receptive to the naturalness of sex and reproduction so the stresses in most instances are far easier to identify and to resolve. When these women came in for a check-up, it was "safe sex" that was first on their agenda. Much time was spent in sexual education and in the selection of birth control techniques.

In those days men preferred not to use condoms, leaving their wives to deal with the mechanics of birth control, so it was the exceptional man who would come in voluntarily and participate in such a discussion. I guess it was a male ego thing not to have anything interfere with his pleasure of enjoying naked penetration. There was little compassion shown to the wife with respect to the more complicated application of inserting a diaphragm smeared with spermacidal jelly, not to mention the business of douching and cleaning up after intercourse. When once in a while some woman would say quite directly to her husband, "Give me a break and use a condom once in a while!" I'd always support this sensible request. However, most wives did not complain and just seemed to think that the arrangement was perfectly natural. I did not try to impose my values on the balance they had agreed upon, and I must say that I got to be good at fitting patients with diaphragms.

The second problem for the women who came to our offices was the issue of having satisfactory sexual relations. In my routine inquiries as to health and bodily functions, I always asked about marital relationships, sex, and child rearing. My approach was to incorporate this subject into the general interview about all other systems of the body. In most instances, women seemed to be well adjusted. Occasionally, I'd run across someone who suffered from varying degrees of frigidity, or from the inability to climax, or painful sex, but few of our women patients had major mechanical problems.

Virginity was still a valued part of the cultural norm at that time in rural Alberta. When it came time for a young woman to marry I saw a number of virgins for their pre-marital examination, their concerns centering on being physically able to have intercourse. The common question was "Is everything O.K.?" or "Am I normal?"

Once in a while I'd discover a young virgin with a hymen that had only a small opening and with skin thick enough to present problems for sexual penetration. I would explain the situation to the bride and suggest a simple office procedure. Using local anesthesia, I would make a few radial cuts that would ensure comfort with initial penetration and still result in a little virginal bleeding when some of the hymen tore with sexual penetration. It always went well.

However, one young woman who visited the office after being married for more than six months had not been one of the virgin group who came in to be checked out before marriage. She was very upset as she recounted her complaint. Beginning with her bridal night, she explained, she and her husband had attempted to have sex almost every night without success. No matter how hard her amorous husband tried to penetrate her, he was unsuccessful, even though she was willing, helpful and passionate. Failure and frustration were having a negative effect on the marriage.

She was a husky, strong young woman who enjoyed excellent health.

She worked hard at all the farm chores and until this problem surfaced had always thought well of herself. Now she blamed herself, feeling that there must be something seriously wrong with her, while he felt that there must be something wrong with either his technique or with the strength of his erection. I was amazed that neither party had bothered to seek help before this. Had they talked to a parent or even another married person the problem would have been diagnosed instantly, without any physical examination.

When I attempted a pelvic examination, my fingers ran into an obstruction just past the entrance of the vagina. I put in a speculum and took a peek inside. I'd never seen anything like this before. The hymen was a wall of tough skin more than a quarter of an inch thick with just a pinhole opening in the center that allowed some of her menstrual blood to seep out. No matter how much her young stud tried, there was no way his penis was going to bring that wall down. I must confess I admired his perseverance as he battered away at this immovable obstruction. I explained the problem and offered the solution. She readily accepted.

She was admitted to hospital and given an anesthetic of intravenous pentathal. I made a series of radial cuts and removed a good amount of skin, leaving just enough tissue so that when her husband next penetrated her, he would have the feeling of some resistance. By so doing he would feel victorious and she would feel equally pleased in being able to fully receive him. Both egos needed to be gratified. When the tissues healed, everything proceeded as expected. I rather enjoyed the role of facilitator in a situation that had such a rapid, happy ending.

Infidelity was always painful for our women patients to discuss; consequently, it was often disguised by symptoms such as fatigue or tension. In these cases the somatic complaint could not be explained by anything of an organic nature, and my training was to probe for what was really gnawing at the patient's insides. The woman's initial presentation of body symptoms was her way of seeking help while simultaneously hiding the problem through repression of conflict. Unconsciously she hoped to be rescued and have the problem solved by the doctor.

Mrs. H., a polite woman in her mid-fifties, complained of severe abdominal pain that had no organic base. I had the impression that in spite of her outer pleasantness she was unhappy. After she understood that I could not identify any physical reason for her misery, I said, "The symptoms you are having could all be produced by something that is distressing you. So let's just talk." I asked her to return to the office a second time and then things began to unfold. Her husband was a very successful farmer, a leader in the community and an elder in their church. He also headed a number of community organizations, one of which was the hospital board. A proud and arrogant man, he seemed to thrive on his self-importance. His wife had discovered that he was having an affair with a young divorcee in town. It just happened that I also knew that the divorcee was carrying on with two other men and that she had recently abruptly terminated an early pregnancy. I believe she must have gone to some local abortionist because I did not have any indication that it had been done by my boss. In fact, I seriously doubt that Frank did any abortions during my tenure with him.

After a few meetings with Mrs. H., I asked her husband to come in. Men rarely refused my request to come for a talk, even though they would never initiate the consultation. Mr. H. was cooperative and seemed concerned, almost as if he expected me to tell him that his wife had cancer of the stomach. Even though he was old enough to be my father and had an aura of aloofness, I nonetheless told him my findings. "Your wife is in good health, but all her physical symptoms were due to the stress of living with the knowledge that you are having an affair with Mrs. X." He was shocked at first and then his demeanor changed to that of a man filled with shame and guilt. He was actually relieved that all was in the open and wanted to cooperate in resolving his marital difficulty.

Mrs. H. admitted rather shamefully that her libido had been decreasing and that she had not been sensitive to her husband's sexual needs. He said that he was worried that he was no longer appealing, so when this young woman flirted with him, he allowed himself to be seduced. It was an ego trip for him and made him feel like a man again. After three meetings with his wife and me, he voluntarily gave up the extramarital relationship and reconciled with the woman he really loved. Her depression lifted and her belly pains disappeared.

That little "operation" had none of the glamour of surgery, but it had much to do with saving two lives. No one in the community even knew that anything had happened, and although I could talk about surgery cases or the management of illnesses with colleagues, there was no way that I could mention to anyone that one of our town's leading citizens had gone astray. But it was satisfying to see this good couple get back on track.

A brief postscript about the "other" woman. She was attractive, divorced, and sensual. One afternoon I had to go to her place of work. I walked in and waited. Suddenly there were loud noises, moaning, sighing and shouting, "Yes! Yes! Yes!" A few moments later a rather shy, timid married clerk from the local general store walked out. "Hi Doctor Ben," he said cheerily. "How are you doing?" I suspect he thought I was waiting my turn. Soon after he departed, our lady appeared and in a business-like manner asked if she could help me. I had to stop myself from saying, "Am I next in line?"

One evening when I dropped by the hospital to finish up some chores, knowing that Frank was delivering a baby, I stuck my head into the delivery room to say hello. I found Frank in obvious distress. The woman he was attending to was a healthy young woman whose three previous babies Frank had delivered without difficulty. But this fourth child had been born precipitously, exploding out of the birth canal before anyone could react. The patient was still in the lithotomy position with both legs in the stirrups. The sheets were soaked with blood. The placenta was just coming out. More blood and mess!

The suddenness of the event had taken everyone by surprise, especially my boss. He was gray and seemed totally drained. The nurse on duty seemed bewildered. Standing behind Frank, I could see clearly the damage that had resulted from the sudden eruption of the baby, catapulted by one powerful contraction of the uterus. The baby's head had acted like a battering ram, and the soft tissues of the woman's bottom, her vagina, rectum, and perineum were caught off guard. The vaginal wall was torn through its entire length, the tear extending through the posterior wall of the vagina into the rectum and through the anal sphincter. I could see that the upper wall was sagging, as the bladder must have been dragged down as well. The damage was indeed extensive.

Realizing at that moment that my boss just could not take any more, I said, "Frank, you look tired. Would you allow me to repair the damage?" He seemed immediately relieved. For once his strong and positive attitude was gone. At the time it did not occur to me that there was any more to his emotional and physical state than that, although in retrospect, this was clear evidence that his capacity to cope with drastic situations was diminishing. I was reminded of the time when he reacted in much the same way when his patient died after being crushed by a tractor some months earlier. This sort of stress event just added to the wear and tear of 25 years of pressure during which time he had little relief. Each event took a little more out of him. I think his capacity to respond was beginning to run on empty.

"Please go ahead, Ben," Frank said quietly.

"Get some rest downstairs, Frank. I'll stop in and see you after the job is done." He went down to the nurses' quarters, had a drink and fell into a deep sleep. I let him sleep for a few extra hours.

I'd assisted on a few of these cases during my rotation in obstetrics, and I had a lot of confidence in my knowledge of the area from constantly reviewing anatomy and physiology. After scrubbing up and reassuring the patient, I explained the situation to her and told her that her little boy was just fine. In later years, I often wondered what sort of young man he'd turned out to be. I imagined him playing hockey and football, running over and through anything that got in his way.

The damage was so extensive that I decided to take my time and just follow the simple fundamental rules of tissue repair. After tying off the bleeders and getting the patient comfortable I started, sewing muscle to muscle, mucosa to mucosa and skin to skin, taking the most time to sew up the anal sphincter and the extended tear into the rectum. I did not want to leave her with an opening between these structures because, if I did, stool and flatus would find their way into the vagina and create a very upsetting and embarrassing situation for this young woman.

I recalled a time while horseback riding, where I had noticed that the mare in front of me was passing gas through her vagina with each step as she walked along. I knew this was due to the same sort of birth trauma that Frank's patient had suffered. Sewing the anal sphincter a little too tight would result in her hitting high 'C' notes every time she passed gas and having bowel movements would be most difficult. Sewing the sphincter too loosely could result in some incontinence; losing control of her stool.

When it got to sewing up the tears in the vagina, I used lots of stainless steel wires, digging them into the deeper muscle tissues in order to avoid a prolapse of the upper and lower walls in later years. That's when, with aging, wear and tear, the weakened walls give way and the bladder and rectum begin to herniate or prolapse through the vaginal orifice. While I was doing my stitching I thought of a passage in the beginning portion of the morning prayers of the Old Testament that states, "I pray God keep my openings open and my closings closed." I guess in those old days, hernias, fistulas, and prolapsed organs were commonplace. They don't kill people but they sure can make them miserable.

It took me nearly two hours to finish up. Everything seemed neat and tidy. However, the stainless steel wires along the entire length of the vagina had about 1/4 to 1/2 inch of wire protruding into the vaginal cavity, and I wondered if they would cause her any discomfort as she moved about. I knew that all discharges from the bladder, bowel movements and urinating would be painful for a time. I instructed her in detail how she might best care for herself during the next six weeks and advised her to avoid intercourse until after the wires were removed. I could not conceive for a moment what it would be like for her husband to attempt penetrating that vagina with its mess of sharp spiked wires. It would shred the skin right off the man's penis. Freud wrote about the Dentate Vagina (the toothed vagina) and the fears that it instilled in men's minds, but he didn't write of men's fantasies about the "Barbed Wire Vagina" because that situation just did not exist in his day.

Six weeks later our patient came in for a checkup and to have the wire removed. But when I told her that it would now be safe to have sex, she calmly stated that they had been having intercourse for the past five weeks and that everything was comfortable for both parties. I was absolutely amazed. It boggled my mind that he could insert his penis into a minefield of sharp strands of wire without apprehension or injury. I never did get to ask the husband how he did it.

Frank thanked me for taking over and for the good job I had done. He said that he was especially upset because this woman was like a daughter to him, and that was the reason for his overreaction. I believed him but felt that there was somehow more to the story.

Shortly after this incident, Frank and Marjorie went away again for a few weeks, leaving me with the practice. The weather was good and everything was running smoothly when I was suddenly swamped with a run of emergencies and other serious problems. My mind has jumbled the order of events, but I think it all started with a nice elderly lady going into left ventricular heart failure, which meant her lungs were filling with fluid. She was on the verge of dying, drowning in her own body fluids. Within the next seventy-two hours, a diabetic patient was admitted to the hospital in a coma; one patient had acute appendicitis necessitating immediate surgery; several farmers were admitted with bone fractures; two children came in with acute ear infections, and three women went into labor, fortunately giving birth to three healthy babies. And on and on it went.

Besides being on my own with these emergencies, I also had to get through regular office hours and hospital rounds. The constant demands for my attention drove me to eat on the run and gulp down enormous quantities of coffee, so that I was performing on pure adrenaline. Tasks such as repairing fractures, removing an appendix or delivering a baby were easy in comparison with the management of my cardiac and diabetic patients who demanded constant attention and sound clinical judgment. Their vital signs, urine and blood required regular monitoring, and their medication had to be tailored to their individual needs at each moment. I became obsessed with the idea that I could not let anyone die on my watch. I must do everything humanly possible to get people well.

The more mechanical work was done rapidly and with a minimum of stress or cerebral demand; nonetheless, it was work that contributed to my mounting fatigue. I remember going to the toilet frequently to void but I do not recall taking the time for a bowel movement. I washed frequently, but had no time to shave.

From my days as an intern I knew how it felt to work around the clock dealing with a constant flow of critical situations, but that was nothing compared to the stress of going without rest for three days and nights. I became aware of erratic behavior. I was beginning to have visual and auditory hallucinations. I found myself talking and responding to people who were not there. I became a zombie, carrying on with my work while my brain was shutting down, and I realized that my reality and dream states were becoming one.

I had just enough sense left at the end of seventy-two hours to tell the nurses at the hospital to cover for me. "Call me only in a life-or-death situation," I said, but recalling vividly how, when I was an intern, I had slept through the complaints of the patient with the too-tight cast, I was determined I would not make that mistake again, no matter how exhausted I was from sleep deprivation. When I lay down, I collapsed into a dead sleep, totally exhausted both physically and mentally. Fortunately for the patients and myself, things settled down. When I woke, my lady in congestive heart failure and the patient in diabetic coma were out of the woods. They would live.

Those three days gave me another view of the stress faced by the solo country doctor. Where was Frank when I really needed him? "My God!" I thought. "How in hell did he manage to cope with demands like this over a quarter of a century?" My respect for the man rose to even greater heights, and I was happy that this time it was I who had been faced with such exhausting demands.

I understood then that everyone has a breaking point; I was no different from any other human being that reaches his or her limit. Doctors, soldiers, explorers, and laborers all have their limitations that ultimately bring on biological rebellion in the form of brain shutdown. My breakdown ended after eight hours of solid sleep. That was the longest I have gone without rest or sleep, before or since.

A few days after my marathon hours of duty, just as I was writing up my notes after the last office patient had left, the nurse on duty at the hospital called to tell me that an injured logger needed immediate attention. I ran over to the hospital and saw a man in his late thirties in good physical shape, but with puncture wounds on his face. He was quite alert and able to tell me what happened. "I was working alone running a log through my sawmill when the blade suddenly ran into a hidden spike," he told me. Apparently the teeth that were severed from the big circular saw when it hit the spike had reacted like bullets, peppering his body from head to toe. He looked much like a battle casualty sprayed by machine gun fire.

Luckily, his eyes and most of his head had been spared. And because the heavy clothing he was wearing had provided some protection from the force of the projectiles, none of them had penetrated the chest or abdominal cavity. I spent the better part of the evening digging the teeth out of his body. I got them all. The logger felt lucky to come through the mishap with minimal harm, but he sure was angry with the person who left a spike in the tree trunk, and he returned to his one-man logging camp with the lingering fear that this could happen again.

The next morning the first patient I saw in the office was Mrs. A, a fifty-year-old woman who lived in a small community about 25 miles from Eckville. A married woman with grown children, she had no history of prior illness, pain, discomfort or disturbance of bodily function. She looked healthy and well nourished, her only complaint being the recent onset of a profound malaise. "I just feel so tired these past few days!" she told me.

I took a careful history, checked her thoroughly, including a vaginal and rectal examination, and carried out blood and urine tests. Everything was within normal limits. I had not the slightest inkling what could be causing her symptoms so I suggested that she return in a week for a follow-up examination. I wanted to see if anything different would present itself or if the picture of fatigue would change. She agreed.

The very next day a member of the family called to tell me that she was dead and that the funeral would be held the following morning. I was stunned! Although the family was not at all interested in knowing the cause of death, I was determined to discover the reason for it. I wondered about suicide, poisoning, even the unlikely possibility of foul play. When the family refused to allow an autopsy, I called their local mortician, explained my concern, and told him that I planned to come to his place late that evening to examine the body and do an autopsy in total secrecy. The man understood and agreed to cooperate. Being a mortician was an extra job he did to subsidize his earnings as a clerk in a small store.

In preparation, I refreshed my memory on how the British had performed autopsies in secret in the past when autopsies were illegal, using a technique that made discovery highly unlikely. The procedure as described in my textbook on the history of medicine was so clear and precise that I knew I could duplicate it. I packed a few scalpels and a two-foot-long knife of the type used by butchers to cut and trim beef or fishermen to fillet salmon. I added a pair of scissors, forceps, some suture material with a fine silk thread, and a few specimen bottles just in case there was tissue that needed to be sent away for pathological study and interpretation. I was ready, but I was beginning to feel much like the doctors in nineteenth century England who robbed fresh graves in the middle of the night in order to examine the bodies of the recently deceased.

It was around 10 p.m. and pitch black as I neared the mortician's home. I switched off the headlights so as not to arouse curious neighbors, then parked in the alley behind the small wooden building that served as the morgue. The corpse was lying on a makeshift slab in the center of the room with a white sheet draped over her naked body. I uncovered her and saw no evidence of anything different from what I had observed the day before in my office. I then made a neat transverse incision through her pubis just a little above the pubic bone so that I could hide any evidence of a cut. It was highly unlikely that anyone would check out that area after she was neatly groomed for her funeral. All I needed was enough room to insert one hand through the cut. As I probed the contents of the abdomen I then used a small sharp scalpel to dissect the gut tract away from its attachments so that the entire stomach, small and large bowel could be removed intact. I followed this up by removing her liver and spleen.

The next step would be more difficult. My task was to remove the contents of her chest cavity (thorax) using essentially the same technique but with the long fillet knife. This would mean removing such organs as the lungs and heart together with the contents of the mediastinum, the esophagus, trachea and the large vessel that leads to and away from the heart and lungs, but everything that I did from this point on would be blind. Reaching up with the knife, I visualized the organs just as I remembered them from the anatomy lab in my first year of medical school. The knife was now guided by my memories of past dissections. Everything came neatly away, and I had in front of me the complete and total contents of the two major cavities of the human body.

To my total astonishment I saw that her organs were riddled with cancers of all sizes, each tumor firm and individual. The entire picture had the look of a classic massive end-stage malignancy with extensive metastases. I could not tell the exact origin of the cancer but my hunch was that it started in the bowel and spread through her body by way of the lymphatic system. I suspected that the immediate cause of her sudden demise was the extensive invasion of the cancer within the mediastinum, the area between the heart and lungs, as compression there in the right spot could cause sudden death.

I was satisfied. The mortician was amazed and grateful for being part of the investigation. I then replaced each organ into its proper cavity and sewed up the pubic incision with sutures that were totally hidden beneath her skin. The only evidence of a cut was a thin bloodless line hidden under her pubic hairs.

It was past midnight when I got into my car and returned to Eckville. I felt a little guilt tinged with remorse for doing something so personal without the family's permission, but I could justify my action with the same reasons that today make it legally mandatory to investigate deaths of patients in whom a diagnosis was not established or in situations where the deceased had not been under the care of a physician.

As I drove, I remembered that when I was a teenager one of my mother's closest friends had gone to the Mayo Clinic for a routine examination, a common practice for people of the west in those days. She had received a clean bill of health, returned home feeling reassured, only to die within weeks of extensive undetected abdominal cancer. Things like that happen. In this case, my one consolation was that even had my patient been diagnosed at the time of her office visit, she had been already beyond all help. The end would have been the same.

On a day much like the one I saw Mrs. A., the quiet and peace of the office was suddenly disrupted as all hell broke loose. A strapping farmer in his mid-forties was brought to the office in a state of excitement that bordered on acute agitation, announcing to all present that he was the Messiah. His eyes were wide and blazed with excitement. His speech pattern was so pressured that he just talked on and on without a stop. He had to get the message out to all that he was here to save mankind.

His wife told me that he had not slept for three days and nights. Psychotic and totally manic, he had no awareness of his surroundings and refused to stop for food or drink. I already knew that if I worked without sleep for that period of time, I would start to hallucinate and eventually collapse with exhaustion, but this man showed not the slightest evidence of fatigue. Quite the opposite, he seemed more elated and more energized as he pursued his messianic mission of saving the world. His mania was as malignant as any I'd ever seen in the past.

Knowing that if I could not slow him down within the next few hours he would die of exhaustion, I said, "I want to thank you very much for coming to my office to offer to heal the ill. It would honor me if you would come to the hospital where you could heal the multitude that are in dire need of your powers." He obliged immediately, spun around and charged out of the door with his wife and I running to keep up to him as he led the way to the hospital.

When we got there, I maneuvered him into a private room and injected him with a potent intravenous sedative. Just as soon as he slowed down, we undressed him, put him to bed, applied arm restraints and hooked him up to an intravenous drip in order to hydrate and nourish him. I could also use the line to pump pentathal, a rapid-acting anesthetic, directly into his blood stream. It took about three days of feeding, hydrating and the administration of sedatives before I could chance shipping him to Ponoka Mental Hospital, about 60 miles away. A week later the hospital superintendent called to tell me that they had been unable to slow him down, and that in spite of all they had to offer, he had died of exhaustion.

I requested an autopsy and offered to drive down to perform it as they had no pathologist available; from my past experience at Ponoka, I knew that the postmortem was something the staff did not care to do. They were happy to accept my offer. I was particularly interested in the farmer's brain, so I carefully sawed through the bone to remove the top of his skull and examine his brain as it lay within the cranial cavity; I then removed the brain to examine it further. Everything seemed normal on gross examination except for what seemed to be a small scar on the front part of the brain (the left fronto-parietal lobe). Hoping to discover that the man's illness was all due to some demonstrable organic brain pathology, I shipped this specimen and other sections of the brain to the pathology lab in Edmonton for microscopic examination. Their findings offered no clue as to the cause of the man's illness. We had no understanding of brain chemistry at that time.

When I talked with the deceased's wife, I discovered nothing that suggested a family history of mood disturbances, nor had he exhibited any signs in his normal life of being ultra-religious. In retrospect, I'd say that it had all been due to some subtle imbalance in the brain neurochemicals that regulate mood; today with a pill like Lithium his prognosis for becoming a functioning citizen again would be excellent.

WITHOUT QUESTION, OBSTETRICS WAS THE SOURCE OF MY greatest delight and greatest apprehension during my tenure in general practice. Nature is wonderful! In most situations, a nice healthy woman gets pregnant, carries for nine months and delivers a healthy baby, all without a hitch. In fact, ninety percent of the time a woman could squat alone in a field to give birth to her child, but when there is a problem, the lives of both mother and infant can be endangered. That is why it is always best to have a trained person present.

With most deliveries I used a epidermal block. The technique is to inject a local anesthetic into the lower end of the spine inducing numbness to the woman's saddle (lap) area. She can still move her limbs, be awake and participate with the process, all the while being free of pain in the area of the birth canal, the perineum and the anal area. Most importantly, she is able to witness and enjoy the arrival of her baby. This greatest of natural miracles is missed when the mother is under a general anesthetic. She and the baby miss out on an early important bonding experience.

The drama in the birthing room is always contagious. During the last stage of labor the mother is doing most of the hard work. Moans, groans, screaming, crying, cursing, and even orgiastic ecstasy are expressed. All inhibitions are gone. There is no shame. Husband, doctor and nurse are all coaching at the same time.

Suddenly and dramatically the scene changes when the baby arrives. The hollering and cursing are replaced by the sounds of pure unadulterated joy. Mother and father cry and laugh and "ooh" and "aah" as they go through the family bonding just as humans have been doing since the beginning of time. The infant, who was able to hear sounds while in utero, is quick to recognize the mother's voice and seems to attach to her in a way that is different than towards anyone else. Everyone is happy and relieved, but it is around that time that the mother might apologetically say, "Oh my goodness, I didn't say anything terrible, did I?"

While the parents are bonding and crying and laughing, I am able to proceed with rather routine surgical repairs such as suturing an epesiotomy without the patient's awareness. The nurse cleaned up the baby while I aspirated mucous from its mouth and trachea to avoid plugging of its airways. After first identifying and announcing, "It's a girl or a boy," I ran a quick but careful check to make sure that all the parts of the body were where they were supposed to be, as well as listening to the newborn's heart and lungs. We put drops in the eyes, swaddled the baby in a soft sheet and returned the infant to the mother for further bonding. By this time the mother was cleaned up and the sheets, covered with a mix of blood, urine, amniotic fluid and feces, removed. We helped the mother onto a gurney and wheeled her to her room. The baby, neatly swaddled and comfy in the newborn crib, was wheeled to the small nursery across the hall from the mother's room and the nurses' station.

Just as soon as everyone was settled, the baby was returned to its Mom. This part was always the most loving and exquisite time for me to observe. This first bonding of mother and infant is very touching and so vitally important to set the stage for what will follow for the rest of their lives. Not only is it organically necessary for the symbiotic pair, but it sets the stage for the basic ingredients of loving and trusting. The mother's instinct is to hold the baby on her bosom, usually on her left side next to her heart, as she talks softly in a tone so characteristically universal between parent and infant, all the while tenderly patting and stroking her baby. Vocal tenderness and communication through holding, patting, and stroking from the very first minutes serve as the prototype for getting and giving love.

After nine months, it's the beginning of mother and child really getting acquainted with each other. The baby responds by trying to focus on the source of this familiar tone. With great effort the newborn turns its head, searching, as if wanting to nuzzle and burrow into the mother. The physical closeness not only brings comfort and security but also brings the baby to the breast for all the benefits derived from suckling. From this time and for about the next nine months this special bond between mother and child continues. It is the one time in life when symbiosis is a healthy biological necessity for both. It's the same throughout the mammalian kingdom. Dogs, cats, monkeys, horses, pigs, otters, all do the same thing. The genetic pool continues to operate in a species-specific way, to be repeated again by the newborn, just as development of the baby repeats the origin and development of our species.

I must confess without shame that I envy the woman who can carry and give birth to a baby. I do feel cheated at being a minor player in this, the greatest of life's miracles.

I delivered many babies during my time in country practice. Fortunately, I neither maimed nor lost a mother or newborn, even though there were times when things could have gone bad. The most common obstetrical problems occurred when the baby was not in the proper position such as a breach delivery (butt first), face or a transverse (side) presentation. We would manipulate the breech baby and manage to flip it into the proper birthing position; that is, head first with face down as if the baby were taking a quick peek at the mother's bum. It was a lot like maneuvering a doll covered by a quilt.

Frank was very skilled at turning babies. I would watch how simple he made it seem when he would manipulate the unborn baby by applying pressure on the mother's belly. His judgment and timing were perfect. He never seemed hurried nor did he take any shortcuts. His strong hands worked together with delicacy and precision. When he had me have a go at it, I found it quite awkward pushing on the baby's top and bottom while simultaneously turning the baby in the right direction.

Sometimes the delivery would be touch and go when there was a question of the birth canal being too small for the baby to get through. As we did not have ultrasound and all of today's wonderful technology, we depended completely on measuring the inside and outside of the pelvis by physical examination only. The technique was to measure the inlet or top of the bony pelvis by sweeping the examining hand from one side of the inlet to the other. This provided a crude but effective guide as to its diameter. The inlet is important because it is a solid bony structure that will not give. In contrast, the vagina is elastic so that it can stretch beyond any-thing I ever imagined as a kid. It can also be cut or torn and will heal rapidly.

If it was a clear case of disproportion between the birth canal and the size of the baby, then we did an elective cesarean section. However, if there was some borderline narrowing of the pelvis, it would mean a longer labor and usually the application of forceps to help the baby along. Those cases always frightened me. Would I damage the baby's head by pulling too hard or injure its neck or break a limb? Babies are so tiny that one tends to forget they are like elastic bands that can bend, stretch, mold and endure the immense power of the contracting uterus.

Both Frank and I were in the office enjoying one of our rare slack times, when a farmer called in a panic. His wife, seven months pregnant, had suddenly gushed bright-red blood from the vagina. We grabbed Frank's "kettle of fish," a homemade ten-inch by three-foot-long copper box with lid, that he kept stocked with emergency surgical instruments. Frank told the farmer to start boiling water, keep his wife calm and in bed, with the bottom end of the bed elevated until we got there. We were out of the office within minutes. Frank drove the big Chrysler and we got to the farmer's house in record time.

A hasty examination showed that she was bleeding from a condition where the afterbirth is attached too low in the womb so that it covered a portion of the opening to the cervical outlet, a partial placenta previa—a potentially serious complication of pregnancy. We had all the tools and other paraphernalia to do a Cesarian section on the kitchen table, but as the bleeding was showing signs of slowing down, we decided to risk the ride back to town to be close to the hospital operating room.

Just as soon as her bleeding stopped, we carried her to the back seat of the Chrysler and laid her down with her butt elevated by pillows. Frank drove slowly, and we got back without incident. After three days of total bed rest and no more bleeding, she was sent home on bed rest, with only bathroom privileges for the duration of her pregnancy. Both patient and husband were told that at the first sign of cramps or bleeding we were to be called immediately, no matter what time of day or night. When she approached her due date, I made it a point to stand by just in case com-plications developed that would require another set of hands, but Frank delivered her daughter and the placenta without further complications.

Once again my boss demonstrated excellent judgment. I knew that even if he were alone he could have done a C-section on the kitchen table, if it had been absolutely necessary. When I asked if he had ever had to do something like this on his own, he gave me his big boyish grin. "Yes, I have, Ben. A number of times," he said.

It wasn't long after I had saved a little girl's pet from dying in July 1950 that her mother, Martha, had come into the office in a state of undisguised agitation. She was sure that she was pregnant, and when I confirmed it, she was in even greater turmoil about carrying through with the pregnancy. I had her get dressed and met with her in Frank's office so that we could talk. She recalled vividly the extremely difficult time that she'd had eleven years earlier when her first child was born. From her story it appeared that there had been a tear of the vagina that extended into the rectum and the anal sphincter, leaving her badly damaged and very sore for months. For her, recalling the trauma was very much like reliving a recent nightmare. She was convinced that another delivery would only lead to a repetition of the experience, and this was the reason for her apprehension. However, at the end of her story she admitted that had things been different she would have wanted another child.

It so happened that Doctor Reed's book on natural childbirth had been published in 1950, just before I entered general practice, and I had been waiting impatiently to try it out on some willing obstetrical patient. Here was my chance, and I went into great detail about this new approach, and the process of educating both the patient and her husband, and the special attention that I would give her throughout the pregnancy and delivery. My enthusiasm, support, reassurance, and the promise of a different approach must have worked because her position softened and she agreed to work along with me. I was elated. Martha was to be my first maternity case whose child would be delivered without caudal, general, or spinal anesthetic. She would not even be given whiffs of gas to take her out of her misery. Everything was going to be natural!

Her pregnancy went along beautifully. Each month she came in for a regular prenatal checkup and each time we talked about the labor and the delivery and about how I wanted her to breathe, relax, push, and cooperate to participate in the birthing process. Martha was soon my model obstetrical patient, enthusiastic and upbeat. She was going to help me reach a new level in managing maternity patients.

So in February when Martha started to have regular contractions, I had her go directly to the hospital. It was late in the afternoon. I'd finished up my office work so I was free to attend to her just as I had promised seven months earlier. Her husband and I were there to give her comfort and to promote maximal relaxation to conserve her strength for the ordeal ahead. When the hour got late, I sent him home to do his farm chores, assuring him that I would stay right there with his wife. Martha knew I was tired and encouraged me to rest, telling me that it made her feel safe to know that I was with her. When she was not contracting, I would close my eyes and lay my head on the bed to grab a quick catnap.

When she was just about fully dilated, I called her husband to come to the hospital. I then wheeled Martha into the delivery room so that she could be prepared. In those days women were given an enema, shaved, catheterized and washed up before plugging an IV into the arm, a safety measure to establish a quick route into her circulation should the need arise. While this was going on, I began the process of scrubbing up and getting gowned and gloved. When her husband arrived, everyone was relaxed, chatting and joking, having fun and ready for the new arrival. Martha was especially enjoying the whole process and voiced her delight at being able to participate in the delivery of her baby.

When she began to bear down, I could see that I'd have to do a double epesiotomy in order to avoid any chance of a tear. This meant my taking a pair of surgical scissors and making cuts on either side of the labia majora. I told Martha what I had to do and said, "Please let me inject the area with some local anesthetic so as to numb it. You can still participate fully in the delivery but there is no need to endure this kind of pain!" She responded by saying, "Don't worry about me, Ben. Just go ahead and cut. No injections! I'm doing just fine!" I went along with her wishes and made my cuts. She didn't let out a whimper or even flinch. If her husband had any concerns, he was doing a good job of keeping them in check. So far so good!

As soon as the baby's head presented, I once again offered Martha a little pain relief before I applied the forceps. Once again she refused. So I applied forceps in order to carefully guide the head through the birth canal, thus minimizing the risk of a precipitous delivery and subsequent damage to the soft tissues of the vagina, bladder and rectum. The baby slithered out, let out a howl and was placed immediately on Martha's abdomen for her to see and hold even before I cut the cord. She was a healthy, robust little girl with all fingers and toes intact. I cut the cord, put in the argyrol eye drops, cleaned her up, had her swaddled and then turned her over to the ecstatic parents. The afterbirth came out without any problem. Her husband had been supportive throughout while Martha was completely euphoric. I quietly reveled in the glory of successfully applying the principles of natural childbirth.

When it came time to sew her up, I pleaded with her to let me inject the cut areas so that I could do it without causing pain. "There's no more need for natural childbirth, Martha." Once again she politely refused. "Ben, go ahead and sew me up. I'm doing just fine." So I sewed her up, and when I was finished, the baby was taken to the nursery, and I rolled Martha onto a gurney and wheeled her back to her room. All the while she kept talking without stop which even under normal circumstances Martha tended to do. It was not until I rolled her onto the bed that it all became clear. A bottle of scotch fell from under her pillow onto the floor. Then it all flashed before me, and I burst into howls of laughter.

Apparently while I had been napping, Martha was nipping. She told me that even though we had worked so hard to get her in shape for the delivery, she just wasn't going to take any chances. The scotch was her insurance. She felt no pain because she was mildly looped. So much for natural childbirth!

Not all births were as happy as that one. Early one morning, a woman walked into the hospital, announced that she was pregnant and ready to deliver. From her casual attitude, one would have thought she was just browsing in a bookstore or that what was going on had nothing to do with her. I'd seen her around town and knew that she made her living as a prostitute, but she had never once consulted either Frank or me. She was probably about forty and built like a tank; obese but square and solid. I thought that her customers must have had unusual needs or else she had something really special to offer that was difficult for me to fathom.

I could not detect any of the usual external signs of pregnancy, but after the nurse on duty got her signed in and prepared her for the delivery, I quickly checked her over and determined that she was indeed in labor. Her cervix was fully dilated. Her contractions were strong and coming more frequently. In taking a quick history, I learned that she was single and the mother of two daughters by unknown and different fathers; she didn't know who the father of this baby was either. This did not seem to trouble her, or if it did, I could not detect any signs. I decided to stay close to the hospital that day because I knew that when she began to bear down it would all go very fast.

The delivery was a piece of cake. The baby just popped out like a cork from a champagne bottle. There was no need for an epesiotomy or even an anesthetic. She didn't cry out or utter a sound. It was eerie to witness. She showed none of the usual euphoria of a new mother, and in fact, seemed absolutely indifferent to the baby.

As we waited for the placenta (afterbirth) to be delivered, I felt deeply saddened by her apathy and absence of maternal instinct. I missed the delivery high I normally experienced, and I felt a terrible sadness for this woman who made her living by selling sex while being sexless and joyless herself. She would live her life removed and isolated, without understanding the meaning of joy, passion or love. Lord knows what would happen to her three daughters by the time they grew up.

Normally the uterus would quickly rid itself of the placenta and then contract tightly down so that the rich and abundant supply of open blood vessels would be clamped off, but as time passed, this woman's uterus remained flaccid in spite of external massage that should normally stimulate this massive muscle into activity. Then instead of the placenta being delivered, arterial bleeding began. I knew she would quickly bleed to death without immediate intervention.

I instructed the attending nurse to ready some pitocin, a drug that induces powerful uterine contractions. I then removed my gloves and went to the sink and scrubbed both arms almost as high as my armpits because I would have to go into the uterus and manually dissect the afterbirth from its attachment to the powerful inner muscular wall. Gloves would cover only my hands but I put them on anyway, probably out of habit, then told the woman what I must do. After saying that she understood, she lay in stony silence. I then inserted my entire arm well above my elbow through the vagina and into the cavity of her flaccid uterus. By letting my hand blindly follow the inner wall of the uterus, I eventually felt the boggy, spongy-like texture of the placenta, but as I began to rapidly dissect it away from its muscle attachments, the bleeding became profuse. I instructed the nurse to add the pitocin into the IV tubing so that it would instantly reach the womb by way of the blood stream.

Within seconds the massive and powerful muscle of the uterus clamped down. My arm was trapped in a hundred tourniquets. As it continued to squeeze tighter and tighter, my arm became progressively numb. I knew that within seconds all feeling in the fingers of my dissecting hand would be lost. With all the will I could muster, I swept my totally numb hand over what I thought was the last of the attachment and pulled my paralyzed, useless arm out of her body. To my relief the afterbirth followed quickly behind. All bleeding stopped. It was over. She would be okay as long as she did not develop an infection. Whatever small chunks of placental tissue still remained would slough out over the course of the next few weeks.

Within three days she left the hospital with her baby. She never returned for a follow-up visit, she never said thanks or good-bye. She didn't even pay us the $50 charge for all the services we provided. Somehow, I really didn't mind. The whole event meant nothing to her, but it did to me. I was left with the rather unscientific thought that the absence of her life force and the lack of response of her womb were in some way connected.

Later that same evening, having finished rounds, I was going down the stairs on my way home for some sleep, when the front door was pushed open by a man carrying a woman. In her arms was a newborn infant. It was apparent that the delivery had taken place moments before their arrival because the infant was covered with blood and mucous and the cord was still attached. They were taken immediately to the delivery room so that I could attend to the newborn. I went through the routine of clamping the cord, checking the baby out, and putting drops in its eyes. I handed the baby to the nurse and then turned my attention to the mother. To my surprise, there was another baby inside. The parents were not just amazed, they were ecstatic!

There was enough time to get the patient cleaned up and properly prepared for the next delivery, and as we waited until Mother Nature was ready to do her thing, there was time to talk. It seems the couple farmed in a rather remote area about 30 miles from town. She was in her mid-40s, and even though she had understood that she was pregnant, she had never consulted a doctor. I thought that this could have been for several reasons—they had little money and it was a long and difficult trip over dirt roads. But I was wrong! She was actually reacting to the death of her one and only infant daughter during the time that her country, Ukraine, was under Nazi occupation.

She still grieved for her dead child, and even though she desperately wanted another baby, she was afraid that it would only be a replacement for her dead baby girl. She had rationalized her feelings by telling herself that it wouldn't be fair to the new child. As the years went on, she never conceived in spite of the fact that they did not practice birth control. When she discovered that she really was pregnant she just carried on letting nature take its course. Her seeming indifference was her way of protecting herself from another major disappointment.

Our talk was interrupted by the sudden return of vigorous contractions. Within moments she delivered a second healthy baby. Now she had fraternal twins—a boy and a girl. She felt that the tragic loss of her only daughter was profoundly assuaged and as if by divine intervention everything was made right. The birth of twins was a testimony to the emergence of life from the ashes of war in spite of the invader's intent to destroy all. This was a new beginning and the continuation of the family genetic pool.

It seemed that emergencies always happened late at night when Frank was away. Perhaps there was some higher power that was testing me in ways that I just could not imagine, or maybe I'm inclined to remember these events because I faced the unusual alone. One evening, having delivered a baby and done an emergency appendectomy, I got my patients settled down, took a shower and was well into bringing the records up to date when Agnes, the night nurse, rushed into the room where I was doing charts. "Quick! There's an emergency!" I dropped what I was doing and ran to a young woman who was lying motionless on a stretcher. She was about nineteen years old. In contrast to her dark hair and dark eyes, her lovely face was deathly pale and her skin cold and clammy. The nurse reported that her blood pressure was very low and her pulse rapid and thready. She was hovering close to unconsciousness, but she managed to tell me that she was pregnant and had tried to abort the fetus by sticking a wire hanger into the uterus. She was single and terrified to confide the fact that she was pregnant either to her parents or the young man who impregnated her. Whoever had brought her to the hospital had not stayed around, so I was unable to get any more information.

All my feelings of fatigue disappeared. I became emotionally detached, my mind absolutely clear and focused. Strangely enough, I felt no fear even though the girl was rapidly bleeding to death in front of my eyes. My thoughts were only on what needed to be done to save her life. While I examined the patient, I instructed the nurse to get the operating room set up for an emergency laparotomy. As the girl's belly was grossly distended and hard as a board, I figured that she'd perforated her uterus and possibly some bowel as well. I also knew that the internal bleeding was arterial in origin because of the rapid onset of (hemorrhagic) shock. Her abdomen was acutely tender due to the irritation of the nerve-sensitive (peritoneal) lining of her abdominal cavity.

By now Agnes was busier than an one-armed paperhanger and running to follow my orders for plasma, morphine, ether and getting the instrument tray set up. She was fast, efficient and cool. Since we did not have whole blood, I hooked up an intravenous and got some blood plasma dripping into her circulation. I gave her a little morphine through the same tubing in the hope that the combination of the fluid, oxygen and analgesic might help keep her from slipping into irreversible shock and then death. I knew I had to open her up as quickly as possible. I couldn't wait for her to be stabilized because that would not happen until her bleeding was stopped. She was too vulnerable to withstand a general ether anesthetic, and there was just no way that I could administer it and open her up at the same time. This left me no option but to inject the skin and the underlying tissues with the local anesthetic Novocain.

I fed her just enough IV morphine to keep her from feeling pain but not enough to depress her vital signs any more than necessary. Agnes set the instrument tray handy so that I could pick up whatever I needed without hesitancy, then she went about monitoring the girl's pulse, respiration and blood pressure. With one swift sweep of the scalpel I made an incision from her belly button down to the top of her pubis through the linea alba (the white line) which lies in the exact center of the abdomen between the two large belly muscles. It was much like gutting a fish. I wanted plenty of room to work and not be hampered by a small incision. I'd worry about cosmetics later.

Within a few seconds I had the abdominal cavity completely exposed. I could see a middle-sized artery still pumping as she continued to lose blood. I quickly clamped the bleeder and left the clamp in place. I couldn't waste time tying it off. A cursory examination of the area told me that the bowel had not been punctured. I then shifted my attention to the belly cavity that was filled to the brim with fresh arterial blood.

I was faced with a dilemma. *What the hell do I do now?* Then it came to me! My mind flashed back to my bedtime reading on the history of medicine. I recalled that long before whole blood transfusions were invented, surgeons had scooped up their patient's blood and run it back into the circulatory system as a heroic life-saving procedure. *That was it! That is what I would do!*

Agnes found me a large sterile glass funnel that I stuffed with sterile gauze. I then hooked it up to some sterile tubing and at the far end of the tube attached a large needle that I inserted into one of the large veins of the abdomen. I think it was the iliac vein, a huge vessel that I couldn't miss. While Agnes held the funnel in place, I scooped the belly blood into the funnel. The many layers of gauze snagged the large clots, necessitating many gauze changes. In the meantime Agnes continued to give me readings of our patient's vital signs, one hand holding up the funnel, the other checking pulse, blood pressure and breathing.

Within minutes after starting the autotransfusion, our patient began to look better. Her skin lost its ghostly color and stopped feeling cold and clammy. Her pulse got stronger and her blood pressure began to rise from its dangerous low. The first crisis was over. She was out of immediate danger of dying, and as she came out of shock, she began to stir on the operating table. As that danger abated, I then silently prayed that no small clots had slipped through my crude filter as they could do immense damage if they lodged in her lungs or brain.

Now I had time to get things tidied up. Agnes gave the patient a few whiffs of ether that rapidly induced sleep. We eased up on the morphine but continued with the IV fluids and the oxygen. I finished returning the bulk of her "free" blood back into her circulation, then cleaned up her abdominal cavity as best as I could with some swabbing and suction, rather like cleaning debris from a kitchen sink. I tied off the bleeders and made sure that I didn't leave any medical garbage—such as gauze, swabs and clamps—in the belly and happily proceeded to sew her up. I inserted a temporary drain just in case of unnecessary fluid accumulation as a result of all the debris and tissue trauma. Before we moved the fortunate young lady off the table, I loaded her with intravenous penicillin as a precaution against infection. We put her into the room that was in full view of the nurses' station so that she could be closely monitored.

It was over! It felt as if hours had passed, but in fact, it had been just under ten minutes between the incision and the beginning of the auto-transfusion. Time had been moving in slow motion while Agnes and I raced to save the patient's life. I thought a lot about how neat our teamwork was. Agnes had done everything I needed her to do with a minimum of coaching. It was just the two of us, in contrast to what it would have been in the city with a team of surgeons and a support group of skilled nurses, aides and lab staff. Certainly that would have been a much more comfortable way to handle such a crisis, and I had been part of such teams, but what I experienced with one nurse was something I would not trade for anything.

Our young lady recovered without any complications and was discharged after a week in hospital. I called her folks in and we had a nice chat about what happened. They were loving and supportive and so happy to have their daughter back safe and sound. I think she eventually married the lad who got her pregnant. I saw her a few times in town and she seemed very well and looked as if what happened was all in the distant past. She never asked about the details of the surgery. I don't think she had any idea how close she had been to death.

As for me, I wondered if I would have had the presence of mind to do an autotransfusion had I not read that particular section of the history book. I suppose I'll never know the answer to that question, and I can live with the not knowing. Still, I like to think, "You would have figured out something!"

I've always been a believer in the right of a woman to choose to carry or not carry her fetus to term; however, I will do everything within my power to help the woman consider all the issues and alternatives to save the life of her unborn child. Never have I done an abortion for the sake of "family convenience."

Much like my mother back in rural Bruderhiem, who would warn women to avoid the local abortionist, Frank and I preferred to educate women in the use of birth control. But I went one step further than he did, for when it was time to instruct the woman in birth control, I made sure that the husband was part of that discussion. At that time we did not have the pill, so my first choice was either a diaphragm or using both a diaphragm and condom together, with some spermacidal jelly.

I did not favor post-coital douching, withdrawal, or timing based on the cycle of ovulation because the odds of getting pregnant were much greater. All patients got the same instruction, no matter what their religious beliefs. I did have a few devout Roman Catholics who refused contraceptives, so I spent more time with them detailing the ovulatory cycle and cautioning the man on withdrawal prior to ejaculation.

Every once in a while a couple or an individual would request surgical sterilization. Most of these people had their families and felt certain that they did not want any more babies nor did they want to risk other forms of birth control. Usually it was the woman who volunteered to be sterilized, in spite of the fact that the procedure for the man is so much simpler. It seems that the women felt that making such a request of their husbands might injure their pride or reduce their virility, so I would take the initiative and suggest that he be part of the decision-making. In almost all instances where the husband was brought in on the discussion, he volunteered to have his spermatic cords tied off rather than subject his wife to an abdominal operation.

I can only recall one or two cases where the wife had the operation because of her fixed belief that sterilization in the male was the same as castration. I am sure that the psychological problems leading to this conviction had deep and distorted roots. Much later I learned from a research project that I did on the wards of Temple University Hospital that poor, ghetto black women believed that the uterus was the origin for sexual drive. In their minds, frigidity and hysterectomy went together.

My beliefs about birth control and abortion were sorely tested when, on another occasion that Frank was away, one of his patients came to me in the latter part of the first trimester of her pregnancy. Her medical record indicated that with each of her three previous pregnancies she had signs and symptoms of toxemia that became progressively worse each time. On examination I found her blood pressure to be alarmingly high, her face was puffy, and she showed evidence of kidney failure. I realized that her heart was failing, as evidenced by the accumulation of fluid in her legs and in her lungs, and I felt that she would die before she reached the ninth month if she chose to have the baby.

The only alternative that I could see was to have the pregnancy terminated. In a conference with the patient and her husband I reviewed her past and present medical history. It was with considerable personal discomfort that I said, "There is a possibility that you will not survive or you might have a stroke or some other medical catastrophe if you carry on with this pregnancy." I was almost certain that this news would be met with a great deal of pain and discomfort.

I was wrong. There was little discussion. They both seemed relieved and requested terminating the pregnancy as soon as possible. They did not want to take the chance of invalidism or death, especially since they had three healthy young children. Her husband volunteered to be sterilized. In a most compassionate voice he said, "I don't want my wife to suffer any more than is necessary." She added one more significant comment that gave me some relief when she said, "Doctor Frank warned me of the danger were I ever to get pregnant again. This was a terrible accident."

The choice, though medically sound, had a terrible effect on me personally. I knew it had to be done, but I had great difficulty in reconciling the equation that I take one life to save another. I admitted her to the hospital and prepared her as best I could medically. A few days later, I anesthetized her with great caution, dilated the cervix and with a curette (metal scraper) removed the fetus and its attachments from her womb.

Even though the debates go on and on about abortion, I still believe—based on psychology and not on religious law—that there is a price to pay for taking a life. I know from my later work as a psychiatrist that women in particular endow the unborn fetus with a gender, birth date and age. If the pregnancy is terminated for whatever reason, their unconscious continues to count on as if the fetus had gone to term and lived. They say such things as, "My second pregnancy that I lost after two months would be eighteen years old next month," or "I dreamed of my little girl that I aborted. She would be six years old today." The memory is locked in the reservoir of the unconscious and is expressed in one way or another.

In this particular life-or-death situation, the seriously ill mother did not verbalize any remorse or guilt. For the time being she was just happy to be alive and to be around to raise her children. She did well after the abortion. Her blood pressure dropped, her kidney function slowly returned to normal and her heart muscle strengthened, thus ending its failure.

I did not do as well. To this day I think about the life I sacrificed. Right decision or not helps little to take away the feeling that I took a life. What I did was something that all my schooling did not or could not prepare me for. My whole being, from the time I was a young lad, was to preserve life. No matter how I reason and justify my actions the pain remains. I often think that if I am so tormented by such an action it is little wonder that the mother never forgets.

It was during that same winter that a terrible blizzard descended on Eckville with sudden fury, the worst that I can ever recall in all my years of living in northwest Canada. Within hours the temperature dropped to 60 degrees below zero, with constant wind, sometimes gusting up to 75 mph. In those days we didn't use nor need chill factors—we just knew it was damned cold! But I calculated the chill factor to have been around minus 200. The snow fell continuously. It wasn't ordinary snow, but ice crystals that felt like needles as they pelted down. It was so cold that if any part of the body were exposed, it would freeze almost immediately. Fingers, feet, and face were especially vulnerable, and I just didn't dare even write my name in the snow while urinating for fear that precious organ would freeze as well.

Breathing was difficult. Were it not for a protective woolen scarf wrapped around my face and mouth to filter the freezing air, any exertion could have resulted in lung frostbite and gangrene. The vapor from breathing condensed and froze on the scarf, making me feel that I was wrapped in a collar of frost and icicles. My watery eyes dripped tears that instantly froze on my face. The cartilage in my knee joints became so cold and stiff that bending my knees was like bending rusty hinges. I swear that I could feel the outline of my stiffened ligaments and cartilage so much that they actually hurt.

Farmers worked with haste to get as much of their livestock under cover as possible so that they would not freeze or starve to death out on the open range. As the day wore on, the snow began to drift, threatening to keep people house-bound, and we sent urgent calls to all women in the last trimester of pregnancy to get into town. Most were picked up and brought in by farmers who had ingeniously rigged their vehicles with snow skids; other women came in by horse-drawn sleds and cutters. In all, ten women came into town to stay in the hospital or to be with friends. We felt safer having them close at hand, even though not a single woman went into labor during that blizzard emergency.

Within twenty-four hours all traffic stopped. The snow drifting off the flat plains piled up everywhere. Roads and their markers disappeared, and by the end of the storm the drifts had risen high above the hydro and telephone poles, packing the icy snow so tightly that the drifts had the physical properties of huge blocks of ice. I remembered as a child building igloos in this kind of frozen crusted snow. We would carve out blocks of it and build a little one-room snow house where the inside would be much warmer than the outside. In this blizzard, however, a person would have frozen before cutting half the blocks required.

Fortunately, since few trees on the prairies were big enough to threaten the lines by falling on them, the telephone lines remained intact, so it was agreed that Frank would answer calls to the office while I took care of our hospital patients. Even though it was only a short hundred yards to the hospital, I had to be very careful to bundle up well for that brief walk outside. It was like stepping into a frozen hell. The road was a solid slick of ice, and as the frozen flakes hit it, they whirled off to join the growing drifts. At the hospital I found everything quiet and calm even though everyone felt concern for those caught or isolated in the storm. There was nothing to do except hope and pray that all would be okay.

By the end of the second day calls began to come in from people in the outlying districts. Most were suffering from simple flu symptoms or upper respiratory infections such as colds and scratchy throats, but under these blizzard conditions, their symptoms had become exaggerated as fear and panic set in. Frank's job was to separate what was real from what was exaggerated, so much of his time on the telephone was spent calming people down and giving them realistic advice. He certainly did not want anyone setting out to bring in a sick person and take the chance of being trapped along the way and freezing to death. However, one call came in that could not be dealt with over the phone. Simple reassurance or home remedies would not help this child, who was suffering from a raging fever, chest pains, cough, weakness and shortness of breath—all symptoms of an acute pneumonia.

He needed to be treated immediately, but there was no way that we could risk his being brought in because the family lived in an isolated area about seven miles due north of town. Frank told the mother to sponge the boy with cold water, give him plenty of fluids, some aspirin and wait until I got there. Then he put together an emergency supply of medication, called Larry Knudson to get a jeep and some volunteers and pick me up at the office. While I traveled, he would continue to command the phones and take care of those in town. I could tell that he was worried about me, but all he said was, "Be careful. Take care of yourself, Ben." I knew that were it not for my being there, he would have made the journey himself.

Larry said that the grease was frozen in most of the cars in town, but fortunately his jeep had been inside his shop when the blizzard struck and it was ready for travel. He and three other able-bodied men equipped with shovels and courage would do what they could to get me as far as possible. We were on our way in minutes, but it was stop, shovel, push, and slowly move forward again. After less than a mile of this I grew impatient and decided that I'd make better time on my own. So while they turned back, I plowed my way on foot the few hundred yards through the hard-packed snow to the nearest farmhouse. The crust on the snow was so thick that it could support a man on snowshoes, but I had no snowshoes and I broke through, sinking down to my hips, making walking even that short distance exhausting. I'd never met the farmhouse's occupants before, but they were good folks, and the wife gave me a hot drink while her husband went to the barn to bridle a horse. He didn't say a word about how or when he would get his horse back. He was only interested in getting help to a neighbour. I guess he knew I wasn't going to run off with it anyway.

It's strange the way my memory works at times; I have a clearer memory of that horse than of the people who gave me shelter. The horse was white and had a thick shaggy winter coat of fur. He looked hardy and seemed calm and ready to challenge the elements. I started out to ride in the saddle but quickly decided to ride bareback, lying flat on his back to protect myself from the wind and to give at least part of me some warmth. My emergency bag was tied with rope onto my back. We made good progress as I let the horse pick his way around the deeper snow-drifts until, after another five miles, that too became impossible, and he began sinking up to his belly through the crust. Abandoning this great horse as I had the jeep earlier, I patted his head, thanked him, then slapped his rump and told him to head home.

By now my back was freezing cold in contrast to the front of me where my clothes were damp from the heat of the horse. That changed quickly as they froze solid within seconds after I dismounted. I was encased in ice. Once again I plowed my way to the nearest farmhouse. I knew I was getting near my destination but could not go further in my frozen clothes. The people in the next farmhouse had been alerted that I was headed out to their neighbor's place, and they greeted me warmly, amazed that I had made it that far.

My clothes were now frozen on the outside and quite damp inside from the physical effort of slugging through the crusted snow, so they gave me a complete change of clothes and fitted me out with a pair of snowshoes to complete the journey. After I was fed, I thanked them and again headed out into the cold. Travel was much easier as I glided over the crust. I had no trouble with fences or small trees because drifts covered them completely.

Within a short time I arrived at my destination, examined the

House call, 1951, at 61° below Zero, Eckville, Alberta

child and confirmed my diagnosis. The boy had pneumonia. I gave him a whopping dose of penicillin by injection, left the family with some oral medication and told them to bring him in when it was safe to travel again. I stayed for an hour, observing the boy and talking to and reassuring his parents. Then I bid them farewell and started back to home base on my borrowed snowshoes. Even though this was my first real experience with this sort of travel, I soon got into a good rhythm as I cut through the fields, traveling in a straight line back to town. Frank's relief at my return was obvious.

After a total of three days the blizzard ended, and little by little things started to return to normal. Snowplows began clearing roads, and where drifts were high and ice-packed, crews used dynamite to clear the way for the plows. A week later the child was brought to the office for a checkup; the crisis was over and he was recovering rapidly. I still remember the child's face, but not those of his parents. Another week went by and the first farmer returned my clothes all nicely folded and clean and I handed over his, also clean and neat. The hardy gentle white horse had experienced no difficulty finding his way home, returning there in good condition. I thanked God that the blizzard had only lasted three days and that no one died, although I did hear later that more livestock froze to death than was initially estimated.

When I look back on that experience, I wonder if I would have had the courage or strength to do it again. It could be that growing up in the northwest and being exposed to the raw elements all my youthful life gave me a sense of confidence, so that facing this challenge seemed like no big deal at the time. If I could tramp around the open fields that surrounded Bruderheim as a little boy, I could certainly handle something like this blizzard as a grown up! After all, I was twenty-five years old, in excellent shape, and looked upon with respect by the community. I think now that I wanted so much to live up to their high expectations of me that I simply did the job at hand and to hell with the risks. However, I did do all I could to prepare for the dangers that I knew existed out there, in spite of my confidence that I could do anything I set my mind to. I understood the risks and did take appropriate caution to avoid stupid blunders that might cost a life—mine or someone else's.

One bitterly cold mid-winter day I was called to the hospital for an emergency. A native man had brought in his 14-year-old boy with a blood-soaked towel wrapped around the boy's left hand. The father told me that his son had been helping rope horses, and the lad had inadvertently put an extra wrap of rope around his left hand. Suddenly, the horse spooked and took off, dragging the boy with him. Unfortunately, the rope was locked on itself and could not release when the horse ran away. Quite the opposite; it got tighter. By the time the horse was stopped and the rope was removed, the damage to the boy's hand was extensive.

I asked the father to leave us alone while I examined the boy's hand because I knew it would be a frightening sight. The bloody towel was removed to expose an unholy mess of severed tendons, bare bone and dangling pieces of skin. The bulk of the skin on all four fingers was pulled off. Luckily the rope did not trap the thumb; it was also fortunate that he didn't have all his fingers just yanked out of their joints. I gave the boy morphine for pain, penicillin for infection and a tetanus injection because of the possibility of fecal contamination. The rope had to be dirty and contaminated and the field he was dragged across was open range.

We cleaned him up in a separate room so as not to contaminate the operating room. When I was satisfied, I carried the boy to the operating room table. While changing into surgical greens and scrubbing up, I cogitated on how to approach the job of reconstructing the hand and thought back to times I scrubbed on cases involving tendon repairs of the hand at the university hospital. Dr. Ted Hitchen had done most of the hand surgery, assisted by a resident and an intern; I had only been privileged to hold a clamp or cut a suture. However, I had absorbed as much as I could. Now I would have to rely on what I could recall.

The scrub nurse set up the operating room with all the dressings and operating tools, after which she became nurse and first assistant. The other nurse kept the anesthetic going after I'd induced the lad. She also kept a sharp eye on his vital signs.

The wound still had lots of dirty pieces of hemp rope and other foreign debris deeply imbedded in all parts of the exposed tissues. Cleaning it up properly was my first priority. The nurse and I worked together picking out the solid debris, frequently flushing the wound with sterile water. When I was satisfied that it was clean, we removed all surrounding dirty drapes and swabs, changed our gowns and gloves, painted the skin, then draped the entire arm and trunk with sterile drapes, leaving only the mangled hand exposed. Now I was ready to start the reconstruction of the torn parts.

I tied off all the bleeding vessels so that my operating field was clear and dry, then began with the tendons, grateful for the long needle-nosed forceps that the blacksmith had crafted for me. Their narrow points allowed me to have an unobstructed view of the area being worked on. I used very fine black silk sutures attached to thin curved needles as I went about hooking the torn tendon ends to each other. I recall using a special stitch that would hold the severed ends so that they would remain connected and hold firmly together. I was concerned that if I attached the wrong tendons together the kid would have a lot of problems with hand function, but carefully going from one tendon to another I gradually had them all linked up. I did not even attempt to deal with the small nerves that traveled up the sides of the fingers because I was at a loss as to how to sew thin fragile nerve fibers together. They seemed intact and if they were not, there was little that I could do to repair them.

It took hours of tedious work to tie up the tendons and draw together what skin was left. I was very careful to sew the skin so that the suture lines would be located where they avoided contraction that might further interfere with normal hand function. It was most fortunate that the bulk of the skin was hanging on and was thus useable. Skin is a truly remarkable organ. It can be stretched, patched and moved around, and it will still grow. I inserted some drains in the wound to allow for serum, blood and whatever other fluid might accumulate to drain because fluid accumulation due to improper drainage serves as a breeding place for harmful bacteria. The resultant infection can result in a nightmare of complications.

The last step was to dress the wounded hand in a pressure dressing that ended up looking like a boxer's glove. It was just snug enough to give constant pressure without impairing circulation. The barometer would be his fingertips which I left exposed so that we could observe the color of the nail-bed. Pink is good. Blue or purple is bad.

It took about 5 hours to finish the repair. The time zipped by because it was such absorbing work, much like putting a puzzle together, with mounting excitement as the pieces fell into place. My operating time would not break any records, but it was about as fast as I could work at something that I'd never done before. And I consoled myself that if I'd messed up and hooked the wrong tendons together, he could always go to the city and have it fixed by a hand surgeon.

As was the custom, I had a mattress placed beside the boy's bed for his father so that when the patient woke up, his dad would be there to comfort and reassure him. When the boy was comfortably settled in bed, I went home and collapsed into a deep sleep.

It was around 3 am when the nurse on duty called to report the following scenario. "I was at my station, which allowed me to see into the patient's room. As the anesthetic wore off, the boy began to wake up. In his state of (post operative) confusion he sat up, seemed alarmed by the strange environment, leapt out of bed and landed on top of his sleeping father, who in turn cried out in alarm. The confused boy was so terrified that he ran for the hospital exit in his bare feet with hospital gown open at the back, exposing his bare ass as he ran outside. That was the last I saw of him."

"What about the father?" I asked.

"He went after him without his shoes or his coat," she said. It was well below minus 30 degrees that night, but that was the last we saw of either the patient or his father.

One nice spring day, about two months later, Dr. Alex Greenway of Rocky Mountain House, 60 miles west of us, stopped in to pay us a social call as was his habit whenever he was in the neighborhood. In the course of chatting he asked, "Do you happen to recall repairing the hand of a young Indian boy?"

"Of course. Do you know what happened to him?" I responded.

The doctor told me that about six weeks after the operation, the father and son came to his office to have the original dressing removed. It was still intact and relatively clean inside. When it was removed, it exposed a clean and well-healed hand with sutures still in place. The boy had good use of all his fingers. There was no evidence of impaired movement or any contraction due to scarring.

I felt great relief. This was the most time-consuming operation that I'd ever performed, and the shortest time that I'd ever spent with a patient after surgery. It still puzzles me how those two got back to wherever they lived without freezing to death.

The next winter event I was about to face was nothing like the episodes just described. It was far more dangerous.

Every winter it was traditional for the doctor to play goalie at one of the local hockey games, and that winter Frank suggested that I take his place. Every kid in Alberta started skating and played hockey at about the age of four. The sport went on from November to the spring thaw, with the best of them going on to play professional hockey. Small farm towns like Eckville were the breeding grounds for our best players. To stand exposed to this bunch of wild young Canadian hockey players was a truly frightening experience, especially since all I had for equipment was a pair of ill-fitting ice skates, wool gloves and a goalie stick. My strategy when these lads got the puck and headed my way was to simply turn the net around and hide behind it. There was no way I was going to risk getting my teeth knocked out by one of those wildly aggressive Canucks. I couldn't wait for the game to end so that I could get warm and get the hell out of there. This was not my idea of fun. I much preferred the delicate pleasures that appealed to my other emotional needs.

Every once in a while I'd head out on a Saturday night to do some barn dancing. The dances were held in real barns on real farms, and the bands consisted of locals who played the fiddle and accordion, good musicians who ground out a lively beat of classical country folk music. The crowd was made up chiefly of young singles and marrieds with a sprinkling of older folks, all from the farms in the area. They drank endless amounts of beer and stomped around with total abandon to the wild country music. The steps were all new to me except for an occasional waltz. There were no fox trots, twirls or dips. It was just "grab your girl and swing her around," charge down the barn floor with hips banging and feet stomping, closer to a game of mixed sex rugby than any of the dancing that I had experienced before.

The frolicking would go on until the wee hours of the morning. From time to time the young studs would leave to drink more beer and to empty their bladders against a tree. Women would also leave the barn to satisfy their thirst or the passion of the moment, then return for more dancing. As for me, after a few hours of dancing I felt as if I'd had a tough workout on the football field, but the wild abandon was great fun and a welcome relief from the intensity, seriousness and caution of practice.

One winter evening, I was invited to the home of some Finnish farmers for a sauna and food, after which we were to go off barn dancing. Patients of mine, these folks were gracious, warm people who lived about ten miles out of town. The sauna was in a little wooden shack in back of the farmhouse. Before entering this male-only spa, we all had a few drinks of good homemade moonshine whiskey. So far so good. This was living. We shed our clothes in a small room attached to the sauna. Then we entered what I soon came to realize was not a steam bath such as I had enjoyed at the YMCA, but a torture chamber for the naïve and the unprepared.

The room was small with an upper bench for the hardy and the insane. I sat on the lower bench because I was sober enough to know that heat rises. We faced a pot-bellied stove surrounded by white-hot stones. A bucket of ice cold water, a dipper, and some wooden switches completed the inventory. As soon as we were all settled, one of the guys took up the dipper, filled it with water and chucked it onto the white-hot stones. Then it happened. A white cloud of steam rose from the bricks and hit my naked body. It felt like someone had just turned a blowtorch onto my white and delicate skin.

The more the water was poured, the hotter the room got, until I felt like a boiled lobster. It was so hot that I found it painful to breathe, and if I did take a breath, I felt as if my lungs were being seared. I couldn't understand why the others seemed relaxed and able to carry on a good conversation. Whenever anyone felt the need to cool down, ice cold water was dipped from the bucket and poured on top of his head, causing momentary cool-down and possible avoidance of heat prostration.

Sometimes an overzealous nut would expedite the cool-down by dumping the full bucket. However, most of my insane hardy hosts ignored the cold water treatment and went outside to roll in the snow instead, the temperature being a mere 20 below zero. I guess they had something against water. I declined the kind invitation to join them in a snow bath, so my hosts, recognizing my need to cool down, were happy to oblige with frequent dousing. Like any sane doctor, I was sure that my heart would stop as I went from the extremes of the hot blast of steam to being drenched with ice cold water.

Finally it was over. It was time to get dressed for supper. I felt weak and faint and prayed that I wouldn't pass out. That would be most embarrassing, especially as I'd never fainted. Back at the farmhouse, the women had prepared a huge feast that would normally have delighted me. It was a typical farmers' Saturday night dinner: steak, potatoes and all the trimmings with lots of homemade bread, pickles, greens, butter and milk, and all topped off with wonderful freshly baked apple pies with home-made ice cream and tea to wash it all down. I stuffed myself with food and drank large amounts of tasty well water. Eating was an activity in which I excelled. We had a few more shots of booze, piled into one car and headed out to the dance. By then it was about 10 PM. The night was young but I felt old and ready for bed.

I was stuffed, buzzed, drained and weak. The bumpy road did not help my queasy stomach, and they had to stop the car two or three times so that I could heave out my guts and be separated from all that good food. I felt like hell. The hardy Finns seemed amused. They clapped me on the back, gave me words of encouragement, and seemed to enjoy seeing the young doctor in such a state of vulnerability. I spent the rest of the evening leaning against the barn wall near the exit, so that I could regain my strength as I gulped in the nice crisp cold air while musing over my evening of pain and pleasure. That was the first and last of Finnish saunas for me.

Meanwhile, my life had taken a new turn. I had become attracted to a new nurse at the hospital from the first moment we met, although for a long time our relationship was strictly professional. She had come to work for a few months while her two children visited their grandparents in Edmonton. Tall and slender with a lovely figure, she was soft spoken and reserved in manner, a little afraid to speak her mind in contrast to the other females on staff. This was not a woman that I would tease or joke with—it just didn't seem appropriate—but she was an excellent nurse who was able to anticipate her patients' needs.

Our friendship began one winter day when it was about 40 degrees below zero, and she approached Frank Coppock to tell him that the ice machine was malfunctioning. "What would you like me to do about the ice pack that you ordered for Mrs. X?" she asked.

Frank put an arm around her shoulder, led her to a window and said quietly, "If you open that window and piss through it, by the time you run out there, you would have your ice cubes!" He seemed amused by his teasing response to what he considered to be a rather naïve question.

The nurse, whom I'll call Betty, was visibly upset. She went pale, then flushed as she turned and, without a word, walked away. I could see that she was terribly hurt and guessed that this sort of thing must have happened to her on other occasions. She seemed very fragile. I felt annoyed with my boss for his lack of sensitivity but said nothing. Later I went to Betty and apologized for his behavior and said that he really meant no harm.

"It's just the way he relates. He's that way with his family and with both sexes. It really wasn't anything personal." It was then she explained that she was healing from a recent divorce. Her parents were baby-sitting her children in order to give her time to heal. Betty did not volunteer any of the details nor did I ask, but from that time on our relationship subtly changed. She became attentive to me whenever I was in the hospital. I felt that she liked me and felt comfortable with me. And I admired her.

One night when Betty was on duty, I was called in to deliver a baby. It was almost daybreak by the time I finished so I figured that there was no point in going back to bed. In the tiny doctor's lounge, I stripped off my bloody OR greens and stepped into the shower. The water was hot and felt good as it beat down on my tired body, and I topped it off with a brief burst of ice cold water. When I stepped out to towel myself off, I looked up and saw Betty leaning against the wall, gazing at me with a look that needed no words. I forgot my towel as we moved toward each other.

I was soaking wet and not the least bit embarrassed as we embraced. Betty's passion was fierce as she clung to me. I forgot the advice that Dr. Fulton Gillespie had given us back in medical school about not becoming romantically involved with co-workers. I was gone! Not a word was spoken as we gave full expression to our passion. When it was over, she quietly composed herself, straightened her uniform and left as if embarrassed by her sudden impulsive display of uninhibited passion. I just collapsed on the sofa and slept soundly for two hours. The memory of her standing in the room as I stepped out of the shower and the ensuing lovemaking seemed like a terrific dream. It was as if one of many favorite fantasies had become real. I wanted more.

I knew that she would be concerned about how I would respond to her after our brief intimate encounter, so the next time we had an opportunity to talk with some degree of privacy, I asked her how she felt about what had happened. I wanted to know if she would like to be with me away from the hospital. She seemed relieved to be asked and said that she would love it. When the next opportunity to have a few days off came up, I asked if she could join me on a trip to Ray's isolated log cabin in the foothills. She readily accepted. I suggested I would come for her at four in the morning so no one would see us leave.

"It will be pitch black then, and I won't even use my headlights."

Once again I would live out another favorite fantasy; only this time I was the aggressor. Betty and I would be completely alone for 48 hours to indulge ourselves as we chose.

The weather was cold, dry and crisp, and the snow crackled under the tires as I drove to the hospital to pick her up. The town folks slept peacefully as we drove away. I had a lovely girl at my side, a snow shovel, chains in the trunk, some blankets, lots of good food and a remote hideaway to go to. Everything was perfect.

I knew that the logging trail would be easy to negotiate because there had been no fresh snow and all the creeks would be frozen solid. The only time I stopped the car was when deer stood on the trail staring at the headlights. Their eyes seemed huge when they looked at us from just a few feet in front of the car. The dawn light with its muted pastel colors greeted us as we arrived at the cabin. The beauty of it made me feel like crying and singing at the same time.

Betty put the food away as I gathered more wood and got a roaring fire going in the huge open stone fireplace. The bed was of simple construction, an elevated wood frame supporting a wooden platform that was topped with the thin, tough mattress. During the day the bed frame served as a place to sit, adding to the comfort of the cabin when there were more than two people. I'd brought a sheet to throw over the mattress's rough ticking and thick woolen blankets to keep us warm at night.

In this perfect little nest there was simply nothing to do except spend time in bed sleeping and making love. Betty found it quite amusing to see me walking around the cabin in my long johns. I guess the flap in the back was a sort of funny-looking to see whenever I'd get out of bed to throw a few more logs on the fire; but there was no way I'd wander around nude, exposing my body in that ice cold cabin when the fire died down.

It's the way I had slept with my brother on an open back porch through many Edmonton winters, but it sure was much cozier sleeping with Betty than it was with my brother Norman! When our passions were temporarily satiated, we'd bundle up and go for long hikes in the woods, following one of the numerous animal trails that led from the forest to the water's edge. There was little danger of getting lost because I always kept the borders of the lakes in my mind's eye.

When it was time to go back to civilization, we timed our return so that the townsfolk would be asleep. As I approached the hospital, I turned off my headlights. There was little left to say when we parted. We kissed goodnight and off she went quietly to her own room. Our adventure had been carried off without a hitch. I got to bed and slept peacefully after our perfect weekend. It had been so good to share those primitive surroundings and total isolation with a wonderful woman.

The next morning when I did some town chores that brought me to the hardware store and the drugstore, I was shocked out of my socks when people coyly greeted me with, "Well, Doctor Ben, how was your trip to the cabin?" or "Have fun at the cabin, Doc?" To this day I have no idea how the word got out. How did they know?

I recalled passing a local young man on the highway as we headed west. There was a possibility that he could have recognized my two-tone brand new Pontiac with the canoe rack on top. Of course, everyone in town always knew where I was every time I left the office, but they never would smile coyly at me and ask if I had a "good time." When I told Betty about the town gossip, she'd heard nothing, so I decided that even if they knew I'd been to the cabin with a woman, they hadn't been able to identify her.

Soon it was time for Betty to get back to her children, and I hated to see her leave. She thanked me for caring and for the good times we had together. She must have taken a page out of my mother's book because she'd made her intentions towards me clear before we entered into our intimate relationship. That eased my sadness at seeing her leave. She was a lovely person and in spite of our good times together she still seemed sad and alone. I never heard from her again.

GROWN-UPS ARE NOT MUCH DIFFERENT THAN CHILDREN, for in spite of age difference, they both feel concern, apprehension or anxiety about their health. This is illustrated in medical practice by the fact that simple reassurance and some basic teaching will do for adults exactly what it does for children. I think it was Sigmund Freud who said, "Scratch a grown up and you will find a child!" Knowing this, I would always try to involve them in my findings as best I could. If a person had a hernia I'd say, "Now, Jim or Jane, just place your hand here, lift your head and cough. You should feel a sudden bulging take place. That is because there is a weakness in the tissues at that spot. I don't want the defect to enlarge as it will in time, so the best thing to do is repair it with a simple operation as soon as possible."

A close second to the joy of delivering a baby into this world was the time I spent with children both in the office and the hospital. I really enjoy being with children, finding it is easy to identify with them and to be grown up at the same time. It is much like having two personalities with the capacity to swing easily from one to another, and so my ability to establish rapport with children of all ages came naturally.

When small children need to be examined, they cling to mother for comfort, apprehensive of the stranger and his strange environment, while at the same time reacting to her reassurances. Transference of the child's trust from mother to stranger can take place rapidly if the parent and doctor participate willingly with each other in a friendly, positive manner, such as the mother and doctor playing pass the percussion hammer or tongue depressor to each other. The child observes and is quick to perceive that this is a non-threatening interaction. Soon the transaction includes mother's passing the hammer back and forth to the child, and eventually the doctor is included in this trust-developing behavior. Just as soon as this happens, the physical examination can take place in comfort for all. All of this just takes a few moments while the mother is relating her observations and concerns.

Curious children love to play with the doctor's "toys"—the stethoscope, tuning fork, percussion hammer, tongue depressor and whatever else is around. They like to try the stethoscope and hear the rumblings in their abdomens and the beat of their hearts. It is also interesting to note how quickly the mother relaxes when this takes place. This bond between mother and child is amazing; in fact, if you tickle a child, the mother is usually the first to laugh.

I remember once when Frank was busy with his regular patients that he asked me to take care of a timid 8-year-old girl whose mother had brought her in to have a tooth pulled. When I took her to our back room to examine her teeth, she cringed with fear, openly terrified of what I might do to her. Deciding to go slowly, I gave her a lollipop and had her sit on the dental chair while we chatted about school, her playmates and her doll. I told her that there was no need to rush the business of taking out her tooth. I'd rely on her judgment to tell me when she was ready. So over the next few weeks, she would come to see me after school, sit in the chair, eat a candy and talk, her comfort level improving as her trust in me grew.

Then one day when she arrived after school, her speech was a little slurred and her clumsy movements suggested that she was intoxicated. As we began going through our regular ritual, she told me that she had been drinking vanilla extract because she had seen her mother do that frequently in the past. Frank and I already knew that the mother was a chronic drinker, but now I learned that she was drunk most of the time. The youngster then announced that she was ready to have her tooth pulled, which I did without a hitch. She seemed to feel absolutely no pain, probably because she was still a little numb from the vanilla extract. Having made such a comfortable attachment to me, she often returned to the office after school for a lollipop and a chat.

In the meantime, we had the mother come in to talk about her addiction. I told her of her daughter's confession about the vanilla extract, and with a little persuasion she agreed to go away for drying out and rehabilitation. She spent two months there and I know that she remained completely sober throughout the remainder of my time in Eckville.

Nowadays it is well-known that the children of alcoholics are prime candidates for succumbing to addiction at some time in the future, but I knew even then that the little girl would be lucky to avoid later complications.

One day when Frank was away I was making rounds at the hospital when a curly-haired little girl, who had just passed her third birthday, was brought in by her parents. The child's face was wrapped in a blood-soaked towel. A neighbor's dog had viciously mauled her face, and she was in terror as she desperately clutched onto her mother.

We went immediately to the operating room, and while the parents held and comforted the child, I gently removed the towel to check out the damage. From my cursory examination I could see that the dog's mouth had been large enough to do extensive damage to her entire face. Its teeth had gone through both eyelids, her cheeks, ears, nose and chin. The scary part was the eyes, and I took plenty of time to assess the damage. Most of the other bite marks seemed like deep puncture wounds with some tearing of skin, but as the dog's jaws had clamped down, its teeth had caught both eyelids, tearing the skin off the lids, resulting in total exposure of the cartilage beneath. This cartilage is the tough tissue lying under the skin of the lid that helps the lid open and shut. Now this cartilage and the skin that covered it hung down like a pair of curtains without any support from the upper area of attachment, leaving the surface of the eyeball vulnerable to drying up. Fortunately, the dog's teeth had not penetrated her eyeballs.

I told the parents exactly what my concerns were and what I intended to do. "I'll do the best I can in patching up the lids so as to protect the eyes. The other wounds seem straightforward. Then we'll ship her out to the city for a checkup and further reconstruction, if needed." They seemed relieved and asked me to proceed. Once they were persuaded to leave the operating room, the nurse and I got on with the repair work.

I quickly anaesthetized the child and cleaned up her face as the nurse kept a Ringer's solution constantly dripping on the exposed eyeballs.

Ringer's is very much like a body solution and resembles serum in its salt constituents. My primary concern was to get her eyes covered as quickly as possible. If the outer surface of the cornea broke down and ulcerated from lack of moisture, it could be very, very painful for the child and could even lead to blindness.

My biggest problem was that I'd never witnessed such a repair. During internship I had never scrubbed up with an ophthalmologist. Now I figured I had no choice but to say, "To hell with it, just do the best you can and get those eyes covered!" If I were lucky the lids might even work afterwards. In spite of being faced with a procedure I'd never seen before, the repair presented an interesting challenge, although it turned out to be easier and faster than repairing the torn finger tendons of the native boy injured by the horse.

I used the smallest curved needle we had in stock with a very fine thread to stitch the parts together. It is now vague in my mind, but I seem to visualize fine muscle fibers in the skin of the eyelid. With both cartilages back in place and covered with skin, the nurse—my cosmetic consultant—and I agreed that the lids looked equal and symmetrical. After applying some antibiotic eye ointment, I shut the lids and bandaged them closed with just enough pressure to keep the lids from swelling too much.

In the meantime, the nurse gave the child a tetanus shot and a large dose of antibiotics. The rest of the repair was simple. I cleaned and thoroughly irrigated all the facial bite marks. The ones on both cheeks went completely through the flesh and into the mouth. Tooth bites also went through the nostrils and the bite marks on the ears penetrated through to the other side. This, however, made the cleaning easier and presented less chance of infection, as there were no pockets where debris could lodge. I cut away loose, ragged or badly injured skin, creating clean, sharp edges that would heal faster with less chance of ugly scarring. When it was all done, the child's face looked like a battlefield, with scars sewed together with hundreds of black thread sutures, but it was clean, closed and all repaired. I carried her to a crib and had her mother sleep in the same room so that the child could get all the comfort a loving mother can provide.

I decided to keep the child in hospital for a week at least to be certain that the eyes would be okay and that the wounds would not become infected. For the first few days I kept her reasonably sedated in order to diminish agitation and to relieve her pain. A pressure dressing covered all of her face except for her mouth and nostrils. She was fed by spoon and could suck fluids from a straw.

Both parents were willing to take turns sleeping in her room and tend to her needs as much as possible throughout her hospital stay. This was great for the little girl and easier on the nurses.

I changed her bandages frequently, before each change holding her on my lap and talking to her, telling her stories and praising her for being so cooperative and being such a "big girl." It never ceases to amaze me how responsive children can be when they know that something is seriously wrong and that they have to lie quietly and not tear at the bandages. Like any injured animal, they passively submit to the caregiver.

Within a few days I removed all the dressings and allowed her to roam the corridors of the hospital. She could see and open and close her eyelids, even though they still had stitches. Best of all, though swollen and bruised, the lids completely covered her eyeballs. She was soon so used to our routines that she would get up on my lap, give me a big hug, tell me that she loved me, and then and only then I tended to her wounds. The ritual worked well for the two of us. When I made rounds, she would tag along behind me like a little puppy. She won everyone's hearts and seemed to infuse the patients with a sense of joy and enthusiasm as she went about visiting.

She showed no signs of post-traumatic stress, and she was without any evidence of anxiety or sleep disturbance. It was as if the dog attack had been totally repressed. When I was satisfied that all was well, I had her grateful parents take her to Edmonton to see Dr. Hitchen, who in turn called to tell me that all was well and no further cosmetic surgery would be necessary. He suggested that he see her in follow-up to be certain that the lids and facial scars continued to heal well. I felt euphoric.

Less than a month after this little girl was rushed to hospital, another little girl was brought in by her horrified father. A young farmer, he had been using a liquid poison to kill rats around the farm while his two-year-old child played nearby. Without thinking, he had set the Coca-Cola bottle containing the poison down on a bench and inadvertently turned his back on the little girl.

The bottle was within her reach and she simply reached up and took a swig from it, thinking that it would be that nice-tasting, bubbly drink. The horrified father scooped up his little girl and, in less than an hour after that terrible mistake, they came through the front door of the hospital looking for help.

As soon as the man said, "She drank rat poison," I instituted a poison treatment protocol even though I did not know what I was doing or what to expect. All I knew was that the poison was caustic and probably contained arsenic or phosphorous. I induced vomiting; then I pushed a tube down into the toddler's stomach to wash its contents with water, hoping to suck out as much poison as possible and at the same time dilute the caustic toxic substance. The child was encouraged to drink lots of fluids and was given whatever she needed to relieve symptoms. The book on poisons did not give me any comfort because it offered so little that one could do in these circumstances. Now it was a case of wait and see.

She was placed in a crib in a private room that was in clear view of the nurse's station. Her parents were in constant attendance, sitting with her in twelve-hour shifts to help keep her feeling secure and comfortable. Their coverage was of immense help because we did not have the constant nursing help she needed. But within twenty-four hours the child began to evidence some difficulty in breathing. Her lungs were clear, however, and I saw no evidence of surface irritation when I checked out her throat. I figured that the poison must have irritated the structures beyond the back of her throat, causing irritation and swelling to the trachea and bronchial tubes.

My concern was mounting, so I called for guidance from Dr. Carlton Whiteside, chief of thoracic surgery at the University Hospital. He heard my story and suggested that I do a tracheotomy to provide an airway. "Call me any time for further guidance or assistance," he said, then added, "If you need me, I'll fly out."

This was my first tracheotomy on so small a child. The procedure is simple but I was struck by how narrow in diameter the trachea of a two-year-old really is. I found the opening clear so I inserted a tiny metal tube and tied it into place. Her breathing was immediately relieved, which suggested to me that the obstruction was above the area of the tracheotomy. I put her on oxygen and steam to help with breathing and to give her extra comfort. I looked in frequently as did the nurses. I knew that there were more complications to come, but I didn't know how or where the poison would strike. In the meantime her urine and blood picture remained within normal limits.

On the third day her condition suddenly changed for the worse in spite of all that we were doing. Her breathing became more labored and she seemed to be turning a little blue, a disastrous sign. I called Dr. Whiteside, who said that he would get a private plane and be at the girl's bedside within two hours.

My relief was short-lived. By the time I returned to her room, the child was no longer alert and seemed to be getting progressively drowsier and less responsive to her surroundings. She was deteriorating rapidly. Our fears and anxieties mounted as we watched her struggle desperately with each breath. Her cyanosis worsened. She was slipping into a deep stupor, becoming listless and limp. She was suffocating, choking to death.

I knew that she would die before Dr. Whiteside arrived. But if she was choking, then perhaps there was something I could do. It was a silly thought, but I couldn't just stand by and watch her die. In desperation I took out a long pair of curved forceps and began to blindly probe the trachea below the tracheotomy opening. The child could not feel anything; she was now comatose and near death. As my probe slipped slowly down, I felt it butt against a soft obstruction. I pushed on just a little further, then clamped the forceps on whatever it was and proceeded to slowly pull back.

To my utter amazement, I pulled out a solid mucous plug. A tiny pinhole through its center had been providing the only passage for air to get in and out of her lungs. It would have been a matter of seconds before it shut down completely, and within minutes she would have died.

The plug was thick, sticky and relatively solid. It held its shape, as if it were carved out of play dough, in the form of an upside down "Y." The single straight line was a perfect cast of the trachea and the two arms of the "Y" were complete molds of the two major bronchi where the trachea splits to deliver air to and from the lungs. Later, when I examined the opening within the mucous plug I discovered it was even narrower than my first estimation, so small, in fact, that it would not even admit a tiny insulin needle. She had been about 99.9% obstructed.

As soon as the "Y" cast was removed, she sucked in air in great gasping gulps. Within seconds a blue child who was suffocating became an alive, breathing, pink child. She soon became alert and responsive to her mother and father and her surroundings. Everyone in the hospital, patients and staff, cheered, laughed, and cried in relief and celebration.

Twenty minutes later my old professor of chest surgery walked in. He heard the story, examined the child, looked at the cast and said, "My services are no longer needed." Though noted for his brevity, he also added, "She's just fine. Congratulations." He left after spending about five minutes in our little hospital.

Apparently, when the caustic solution had gotten into the trachea and the two major bronchi, it caused the lining of these pulmonary tubes to excrete excessive amounts of mucous and to slough material from their linings. As the sloughing process continued, the mucous, having nowhere to go, formed a thick tenacious plug that slowly choked off the airflow.

I think this is about as close as I ever got to saving a life by doing something that was just a pure wild guess. What a fortunate child, and what good luck for me! This was a miracle.

I ended the summer of 1950 by holding a clinic in the resort town of Sylvan Lake, about fifteen miles east of Eckville. The town was jumping with family vacationers, and most of my work was taking care of people with earaches, sore throats and some cuts that needed stitching. The office was slow so I spent most of my time standing at the store front just watching the people go by and soaking up some sun.

Suddenly a squall came up with wind, black clouds, thunder and lightning, and within moments after the squall hit, I got a telephone call. "Get out here fast, Doc! A kid's been hit by lightning!" I'd had no experience dealing with lightning casualties. The closest I'd ever been to such an event was when I was a kid, having fun in a swimming hole on a neighbouring farm, when a similar storm came up. We grabbed our clothes and ran for the woods. Suddenly, lightning hit a tree next to where I stood. At the same time I felt the hair on my body stand straight up. Now all this flashed through my mind as I grabbed my "doctor bag," jumped into my Pontiac and raced out to the lake.

A motor boat was waiting to take me to the raft on which the victim, a boy about twelve, lay just as he had fallen. He was not breathing, and there was only a faint thready heartbeat. His skin seemed to be cooked in a strange pattern. I started giving him CPR, but it was useless. It was a desperate attempt on my part because I knew from the start that he was a goner. At no time did he breathe on his own, and in spite of everything that I tried, he never responded. The boy was dead.

As I worked, witnesses explained what had happened. They said they were diving off the raft when the storm came up. The young lad had gone out onto the diving board to have one last dive, when a bolt of lightning struck him and flung him back onto the raft. Nobody touched him. Others on shore heard their screams for a doctor and within moments someone had called me.

I lifted the boy off the raft, placed him in the boat that had delivered us from shore, and took his body to Red Deer where I did the autopsy in the hospital morgue. My external examination revealed a fascinating pattern on his skin. There were grayish white lines all over the body as if an artist had drawn a picture of the nerves in the skin—the superficial cutaneous nerves—outlining them in a beautiful lacy pattern like ice crystals fanning out on a windowpane in winter. And when I examined the larger nerves that emerged from the spinal cord, I found that they were all cooked to mush. In fact, the jolt of electricity from the lightning bolt had cooked his entire nervous system. There was not a remote chance that this poor kid could have survived such a direct hit. His death was instantaneous.

I often remember the kids who have died and find myself counting the years. That young lad would be in his early 60s if he was alive today. All was for naught, just because he wanted one more dive.

One day when Frank was away in Edmonton, Marjorie asked me to see one of his patients who had come in for her annual check up. With her was a curly-headed blonde child who looked like a pale fragile China doll. Her skin was bloodless. She clung to her mother's hand as if she needed the extra emotional support. Something was not right! I asked the mother if she would mind if I took a closer look at the child. She seemed a little surprised but readily agreed. I was certain she was in denial because it was obvious that her child was very ill.

What I quickly discovered made me feel ill inside. The lymph nodes in her neck, arms and groin were numerous, firm and discrete. This was what I had dreaded during my internship rotation in pediatrics. I wanted to run away, to cry, and to scream but there could be none of that.

A drop of blood under the microscope confirmed that she was the victim of an acute fulminating leukemia. The white blood cells were very immature, suggesting that it was a very malignant cancer of the blood that carried with it a terrible prognosis.

It seemed needless to prolong the investigation. When I went to talk to the mother, she knew immediately that something was terribly wrong by the grim look on my face. I could not hide my overwhelming distress. I did the best I could to explain my findings and to suggest that this was something that we were just not equipped to handle. I tried to be gentle, but even the simple presentation of some of the basic facts seemed cruel. The young mother listened to my words quietly in a profound state of shock. Her sadness was beyond shedding any tears. All the while the fragile little girl clung to her mother as if she herself understood that something was terribly wrong.

I made arrangements for the child to be seen by a pediatric oncologist at the University Hospital for further evaluation and whatever treatment they could offer. The child remained in the hospital as they vainly attempted to alter the course of the disease, but there was not a thing that they could do that would provide any hope. She died within two months. I believe that current cancer therapies could have prolonged her life for years.

The memory of that pale child holding onto her mother's hand is still vividly etched in my mind. I see her before my eyes, so helpless, so pale and with such a short time to live. How terrible for the mother and child to be torn apart forever at such a vulnerable time in both lives!

I had known in medical school that I could never be a pediatrician, and this fact was confirmed again that day. I love little children, but I cannot bear the agony of working with them if they are hopelessly ill. They are the one group of patients with whom I have great difficulty in being clinically objective without being overwhelmed by my emotional feelings.

I found myself remembering the first time I had attended a funeral service. I had been about ten when Morris Haifetz, a good friend of both Norman and I, died after of some medical illness had kept him bedridden for weeks. He was a nice kid who lived a few blocks away from us, a very active, energetic, tough, blond, curly-haired lad. We often played together. How could he have died?

I recall sitting near the front row during the memorial service held at our Hebrew school and feeling surprised and embarrassed when I found myself quietly laughing during the eulogy. Yet I knew then that I was just on the verge of crying when this inappropriate response emerged. I vividly recall struggling to control both emotions. Up until then I seldom was brought to tears by physical or emotional pain. Tough guys don't cry. Tough kids shouldn't die.

When I was about seventeen, I dated a bright, attractive girl who had recently moved to the city. I took Rachel out six or seven times over the course of about six months and found her to be very good company. I kissed her goodnight, but that's about as far as our physical relationship went. Then one day I called her for a date and she declined. "I'd like to go out but I'm not feeling well," she said. "Why don't you come over and visit?" I accepted and was let into her home and escorted to her bedroom. Something was not right. She was quite pale and seemed rather frail. I was shocked because only a few weeks before she had seemed perfectly healthy. After a few moments of polite chatter, I asked, "What seems to be wrong with you, Rachel?" She turned to me with tears in her eyes. "Oh Ben," she said, "I suddenly found myself feeling very weak. We went to see a doctor and he sent me to a specialist. He says I have a cancerous melanoma that has spread through my body and there's nothing that they can do for me."

I held her and we both cried. I felt helpless and sad. After that, I visited her almost every day. Sometimes we would talk and sometimes she just slept. Then one day they took her to the hospital, and she died within twenty-four hours. I grieved for months. I could not get over the death of someone who had been so full of life just six months earlier.

During medical school and internship we were given little instruction on how to work through this final step of life with our patients. In a big hospital, the dying person was usually isolated and only visited briefly by the medical staff. I got the feeling that the needs of the dying were just too time-consuming or that caregivers were either uncomfortable or threatened by what was happening or what the patient actually needed. Nursing aides were left to do most of the bed care and once a day a minister, priest or rabbi would come around and pay a brief visit or recite a prayer and then be gone. None of this measured up to my expectations of how a dying person should be cared for.

But what should be done for the dying patient? I asked myself. This was obviously something I would have to work through myself since none of my teachers of medicine could or would instruct me. Then gradually the constant exposure that I had to the sick and dying while I was in medical school and interning brought me face to face with my own feelings of mortality together with an understanding and acceptance of the fact that death was an inevitable part of life. I learned to see it as the last stage of life and that those who were dying needed as much, if not more, attention and compassion than those who were simply ill. As I sat with the dying, what I came to feel was a mutual emotional experience, a mix of love and sadness and the intimacy brought on by talk that is focused entirely on the last thoughts that these patients had. For me this communion was the last thing I could do for people in my care.

In country practice, just as I had the opportunity to help people live, I had plenty of opportunities to help people die. I did all that I could to be there for the dying, to help them get through this last journey, making every effort to have them surrounded by loved ones, offering the opportunity for talking, reminiscing, laughing and crying together, to get the last wishes out, and to say their good-byes. I could not bear the pain of watching someone die alone, without dignity or the opportunity of being comforted by loved ones. I know I don't have the courage to make this journey without someone to help me.

During the spring of 1950 two people, a man and a woman, lay dying of cancer at opposite ends of the corridor in our small community hospital. The time and the place were the only things common to them.

I recall walking into the dying woman's room and meeting her for the first time. Her room was dark and stuffy with the unpleasant odor that greets one in so many homes for the chronically ill, the odor of decay and death. Thin and frail, she lay facing the wall of the room in the foetal position. I knew that she was in her mid-forties and that she was dying of breast cancer that had spread to just about every bone in her body. Whenever she moved, she screamed in pain.

Each sudden movement meant the breaking of another fragile, nerve-sensitive bone, thin as egg shell, each one evoking terrible pain as it fractured. Morphine gave her little relief. She only wanted the blinds pulled and the door closed. She turned away from visitors and was so negative that people, including her family, did not stop to chat with her or give her emotional support. Staff did only what was required of them. She refused to accept the fact that she was dying. Her fierce denial was reinforced by her continuing belligerence and relentless anger.

When I talked with her, she made it perfectly clear that she wanted to live and would not tolerate any other discussion. She was abrupt and bitter, uttering only a few angry and insulting words. I did not politely excuse myself to get away from her as others on the staff had done. I sat down next to her and tried patiently and futilety to engage her in conversation. She responded by tightly closing her eyes and turning her head away from me. Frank had the same experience with her. He just shook his head as if to say, "It's just hopeless, Ben." In spite of this, I did continue to try, hoping that at the end she might reach a point of acceptance and die with some degree of quiet resolution. To no avail. Her actions so alienated friends and family that she was finally left to die alone. Her last screaming words were, "I want to live!"

At the opposite end of the hospital corridor was a sixty-four-year-old farmer whom Frank had admitted to hospital with inoperable stomach cancer. When I had first seen him in the office I was struck by how thin and frail he looked, but even though his clothes hung on him, he had a demeanor of serenity. He was a handsome man with a full head of hair, bushy eyebrows and warm dark eyes. In spite of his excessive weight loss and his pallor, he carried himself with dignity.

I recall how sensible he was as we discussed his condition and his options. His constant pain and inability to swallow food brought him to acceptance of the fact that he was dying and he said, "Frank, I'm ready to go to the hospital." We understood that he was prepared to have help for this last step of his life. He asked only that we keep him comfortable so that he could continue to visit with his family and maintain some dignity. He elected to take morphine instead of nourishment through his intravenous feeding tube, knowing that without food, death would come sooner. I saw time running out as if I was watching an ancient hourglass, once filled with sand, now nearly empty.

Whenever I stopped in to say hello, if he was not asleep, he would greet me with a smile and a pleasant comment. This man understood and accepted and made it seem easy and natural. Someone in his family was always in attendance, including his young grandchildren. They talked, tended to his needs and helped make things go well until the end when he finally closed his eyes and stopped breathing. He died peacefully, without fear, and with the sight and touch of loved ones at his bedside.

It seemed so foreign and strange to me that two people dying in our little hospital at the same time illustrated the two extremes when facing the end of life. Their dying said more about who they were and how they viewed life than could be learned by going into past life histories.

The older I get the more I have been able to accept the fact that death is inevitable. So I see each day as a gift and make the most of it. I believe that it is my responsibility to live life to its fullest through work, play, community and family. Then when it comes time to let go and pass onto the next and last phase of life, it will come as no great shock. The only sadness should be the last farewell to your loved ones.

I remember it wasn't long after the premature death of my mentor, the excellent internist Dr. Edward Weiss, that his wife Babs developed terminal cancer of the liver. She chose to remain home to die and she asked me to help her through this difficult time. At the time my son Geoffrey was about four years old. He would come in and say "hi" to Babs who loved to see his bright cheery little face. After a little chat she would say, "Geoff, Anna has baked some chocolate chip cookies for you," and he would run into the kitchen and have milk and cookies while Babs and I visited.

Not long after she died, my son asked, "Dad, are we going to visit Babs?"

"No, son," I told him. "Babs has died."

"Where is she?" he asked. I explained that after a person dies they are buried in the ground. "So Dad, let's just go dig her up so I can get some cookies!"

He did not have the slightest inkling of what death was. Eight years passed and one morning while I was shaving in the bathroom, Geoffrey, who was sitting on the radiator chatting as he did most mornings, said casually, "You know, Dad, it's okay if you die now." It was a wonder I didn't cut myself as I turned suddenly to face him.

Without having to say anything myself, I knew that he wanted to explain what he meant. "I just wanted you to know that if you died, I would be able to take care of myself," he added. That was immensely reassuring to me. It is something most parents want from their children before death strikes.

In the beginning young people think that death is something that happens to older people like grandparents. Later they realize that it happens to parents and eventually to oneself. Once this is understood and accepted, it allows the individual to get on with the business of living.

My parents both died suddenly without suffering any invalidism, so there was no opportunity for saying a last "good-bye" or having to be in constant attendance for a slow death. I had mixed feelings about this. On the one hand, I wanted to be with them for every precious moment and on the other hand, I was grateful that they were spared needless lingering and suffering. I knew in advance how and approximately when each of my parents would die, but this was information that I kept to myself.

Towards the end of my internship, Dad offered to take me on a trip to California to give us time together and visit family there. In Los Angeles he had me make him an appointment for a checkup with Dr. Elliot Cordes, an old friend from Edmonton, who had become a renowned and respected cardiologist as well as cardiologist for Hollywood's stars. Elliot was very pleased to hear from me, saying, "Please bring your dad in this Sunday morning so I can take all the time I need to check him out. I'll look forward to seeing Bill." After the examination, he called me into his X-ray room to look at the pictures of Dad's heart. I was shocked. The wall of his left ventricle, the major pumping chamber of the heart, had an aneurysm the size of a golf ball with an outer wall as thin as a piece of paper. I knew that this is what he would die of. Elliot said the only thing that he could offer was to drastically cut down his thyroid function and in so doing dramatically slow down all bodily functions. The alternative was to do nothing. This was long before the days of open-heart surgery. I made a rapid decision. Knowing Dad as I did, I realized that stopping his thyroid function would be worse than death. I asked Elliot to say nothing. He had a nice chat with dad and said in effect, "Bill, you look good. Just carry on doing what you've been doing."

I did not tell anyone about this grim finding. I watched Dad go about his life and held my breath every time he leapt over our back fence or when he lifted a 100-pound sack of flour. Five years later my folks were at a party where dad proudly read out letters from his kids. Afterwards they went home and a few moments after he went to bed, his aneurysm ruptured and he died within a minute. The year was 1956. He was just 67 years old.

Mother's story was a little different. It was around 1959 when Mother came to visit us in Philadelphia, and asked if she could have a check up. I asked my mentor, Dr. Ed Weiss, if he would do this for me. Mother was admitted and examined by him and Dr. Hugo Roesler, a cardiologist. After the check up Dr. Roesler told me that mother had severe aortic stenosis that was a complication of childhood rheumatic fever. There was no treatment for this condition. Mother was only told that she had a heart condition and that she could do as she pleased but to avoid excessive cold or physical exertion.

Though Father was now gone, mother was not alone. From the time he died, she had rented a room to a graduate nurse from either the General or Misericordia hospitals. She also had the companionship of Howard and his family who lived next door. Meanwhile she continued her busy life, going out to her clubs and to visit her friends, but she insisted on walking the two long blocks to catch a streetcar. She refused to take cabs because of the expense involved and she refused money from me to pay for this sort of transportation. The big problem was that when the weather got cold she would have to stop and rest along the way because of angina pectoris. I had to find a solution, so I spoke to my cousin Mickey, who owned the Dollar Cleaners in Edmonton, and we came up with a plan.

He would tell my mother that he got free taxicab tickets in exchange for promoting a certain cab company. Since both he and his wife had cars, would Aunt Rose help him out by taking the tickets off his hands? "Of course," she said. "If this will help you out, Mickey, then I will do it."

From then until she died, Mother used an unlimited number of tickets to go wherever she needed to go and also treated all her girl friends to rides around the city—thanks to Mickey! Each month I got a humorous note from my cousin together with a bill for the money I owed him. Mother died never knowing the real story.

As the years went by the aortic ring leading to my Mother's heart continued to shrink, resulting in the progressive decrease of vital oxygenated blood to her body. Gradually her body began to waste away. Then one day in 1963 she got up from watching television to check on the chicken soup that was stewing on the kitchen stove. The nurse boarding at our house was sitting at the kitchen table. Later she told me that Mother came into the kitchen, lifted the lid of the pot and said, "My, that smells good!" then collapsed to the floor and was dead before the nurse got to her. "She did not suffer for a second," said the nurse. Mother was 74 years of age.

I keep my parents close to me and think of them every day of my life, keeping them up-to-date by sharing with them my thoughts and experiences. And I still draw from their wisdom and love. Thus their continuity is ensured. If the same thing happens to my offspring when my end comes, with continuity from one generation to the next, then I will be satisfied.

About ten years after I left Eckville I organized a symposium on aging in Philadelphia where I was then living. During the introduction to the conference I read a brief letter that had been found in the personal effects of a woman who had died a few months earlier in an old folks' home in Jerusalem.

It started out with the words "Look at me. Look at me. What do you see? A little old lady unable to move. Look at me. I am a little baby held by my mother...." and I continued reading her beautiful description of her life, herself as a child, young girl, young woman in love, wife, mother, widow, and then as an aging person. It was a most sensitive version of Shakespeare's "All The World's A Stage."

I had a cold and was a little nasal as I read the piece to the audience. When they heard me sniffling, they all started to cry. It was a little comical because my sniffling was from the cold, but they perceived me as crying. I had the letter duplicated immediately and distributed to everyone because of the instant request for copies.

THERE HAS TO BE A GOOD REASON WHY I HAVE SPENT almost a third of my life in small towns. During my formative years, the village of Bruderheim offered me a safe place to roam, explore and express myself in ways that could not have been duplicated elsewhere. In those days there was no need for car-pooling, travel or special classes in order for a child to engage in play and school. Life in a small town was conducive to the development of resourcefulness in order to offset boredom or the need for excessive direction.

With the help of my folks and the people in and around town I was able to develop in a secure setting. I never got lost, acquired lots of friends, and was free to spend time with folks of all ages ranging from teenagers to octogenarians. There was so much to be gained by exposure to what amounted to an extended family of good and some not so good people. I learned to take care of myself.

When I went to Eckville to work for the most important and most respected man in town, I found life there to be much the same as I remembered from my childhood. The social structure of both villages— though over a 100 miles apart—was much the same. The community was a family. Within a few days I knew the town and all the people who lived there. Actually people knew me before I knew them. They accepted me and welcomed me into their homes, so different from the city where a neighbor told me, "Don't be upset if you don't get to meet your neighbors. It can take years!"

In Eckville, I never suffered from boredom or lack of things to do. Often I might have a few moments to wander around town and just chat with folks that I would meet. There was no pattern to my strolling, no special order to where I stopped just to say, "Hi." I loved the warmth and respect in people's voices when they called out, "Good morning, Doctor Ben."

I'd stop in at the drug store and chat with Tom Forhan, the lean and lanky pharmacist who looked more like a baseball player. We chatted about sports, local medical problems or about new drugs that had appeared on the market. Then I would stop in at Knudsen's garage and take a peek at what he was working on. I liked the smell of the oil and grease and was always curious about any contraption he might be creating. Larry was a man of many talents. Not only was he a good mayor for the town but he did a excellent job administering ether when Frank was short-handed. If time permitted, I'd stroll down to the creamery and help Jack Neil dump milk into the large vats or steam down the stainless steel equipment. No germs would grow in his shop. Jack was a gentle, soft-spoken person, and our talks tended to be more philosophical in nature than those with Tom Forhan. Then we'd go next door to his house and have a coffee with the missus. But my favorite stop was the blacksmith shop.

The tools were the same as the ones I knew as a kid, and the sounds of hammer striking metal and the smell of charcoal fire mixed with the aroma of horses and farm equipment brought the past right back to me. There were others, but the person I spent the most time with was Ray Sestrap. He was my closest friend in town. Ray made a living as a farmer but his first love was fishing. Whenever I called he was ready to set aside his chores and go fishing on the stream that ran through his farm. In return, I was always ready to help feed his hogs and chickens.

There were so many remarkable people in that town. One morning just before Frank set off for a consultation at the Parsons Clinic in Red Deer, he told me that a patient coming in for a routine examination was a retired farmer who had been a travelling magistrate in the old days. As a lover of western stories and of cowboys, I was excited about the prospect of talking with one of the last of this wonderful breed of frontiersmen who upheld the law during Alberta's pioneering days, just like the sheriffs in Hollywood movies.

A little later that day, when Ida informed me that he had arrived, I went to the front door and there, sitting straight and tall in his saddle, was my sheriff. I went out, introduced myself, shook hands and then, because he was unable to walk, carried him into the office for his examination. After I attended to this 93-year-old man's medical needs, we chatted and he told he had been born in 1857 and became a magistrate in the late 1870s when Alberta was still part of the Northwest Territories.

The area had been wild and primitive then and he had practically lived on horseback as he tended to the business of punishing lawbreakers. He said that even though he was unable to walk now, he still felt completely comfortable sitting in a saddle and getting around on a horse. I wanted to keep him talking, telling me stories of the old days, but desisted because he was so frail.

I carried him back to his horse, lifted him onto his saddle and bade him farewell. He waved as he rode off, sitting straight in his saddle and looking very dignified. *The town was safe now*, I thought. *Law and order was restored. The job was done. The old sheriff got on his horse and rode out of town, never to be seen or heard of again.*

And I never did see him again.

But during my time in Eckville, it was the members of the Royal Canadian Mounted Police who did the bulk of the work of maintaining law and order in the rural communities of Alberta. An elite group of men, dressed in their strikingly handsome uniforms—bright red coats and blue riding pants, with a broad yellow stripe down each side—they looked just like Nelson Eddy in the old movies.

Although there was little need for policing locally, every once in a while I'd see a RCMP officer making his rounds of the small towns west of Red Deer. No one locked doors. Children roamed the town and countryside as if it were a big back yard. Fear of child kidnapping, sexual abuse, or a child getting lost just did not occur to the folks in our community. For the entire time that I was in country practice there was not a single reported crime.

However, on two occasions an officer of the RCMP consulted me. A few years older than I, he was a nice, polite young man who seemed thoughtful and intelligent. The first time he stopped in the office, he introduced himself and asked politely if he could have a few minutes of my time to discuss a complaint that had been filed with him. I felt somewhat flattered and was quick to reassure him that I would be happy to hear him out. I made it clear that anything we talked about would remain confidential and off the record.

He presented the story in a simple, clear-cut manner. Apparently, a local farmer had observed his bachelor neighbor having intercourse with a sheep. It wasn't that the sheep in question belonged to the farmer; rather, it was being witness to this sexual act that had upset him so much that he had felt compelled to report the incident to the police. The officer had investigated the story and found that it was true. For twenty years the bachelor had lived alone on his farm in a remote area of the foothills due west of our town and during that time had never bothered anybody, nor had he ever broken the law. He admitted to the officer that he did have intercourse with his sheep.

Although jokes are often made about one's favorite sheep, it was the first time that I had been actually consulted about a real farmer/sheep episode. The officer wanted some feedback about this rather unusual, embarrassing and delicate situation. He was uncertain what to do. In response I began talking without any particular direction, drawing from a mix of what little I had learned in psychiatry about sexual perversion and the anecdotes I'd heard about such acts when I was a child in Bruderheim. Now, as I look back on my reactions, I find it strange that I was reacting as a grown professional and as a child simultaneously; my collective wisdom was a blend of childhood rumor and naïve scientific information collected during my internship.

I said that to the best of my knowledge this sexual perversion was not uncommon among single men living in isolation for long periods of time. In addition, I did not know of a single case of such a man violating any woman or child. It seemed to me that the bachelor favored a sheep as his outlet for his frustrated sexual needs, and that no one other than the voyeur was upset. I certainly would have difficulty thinking that this act might be construed as animal abuse. On the contrary, I could imagine that it might actually give the sheep some temporary pleasure.

On the other hand, perhaps seeing the event had stirred up something in the witness that threatened some unacceptable unconscious sexual impulse of his own. So it would seem reasonable to this upset viewer that punitive action against the sexual perpetrator would serve to help suppress the dangerous unconscious impulses in himself and thus keep him safe from carrying out a similar act. After revealing my unedited thinking, I summarized by saying, "What's the big deal? There was no harm done to the sheep. Who knows? They may both have enjoyed the act."

Taking everything into consideration, it seemed that the best thing to do was to do nothing. There followed a very interesting philosophical discussion between the officer and myself about sex with animals and about other forms of sexual perversion, all of which was a bit of a change from the routine of office practice. I do know that the officer spoke to the complainant and in essence told him that everything had been taken care of.

A few months later, the same constable stopped in to chat about another dilemma. This time I was in the midst of a busy day, so I asked him to drop back after he'd finished with his other police duties. Apparently, an amorous young logger had gotten off work early, rushed home to surprise and please his wife, but caught her having intercourse with his good friend and neighbor in the logger's own marital bed. His unexpected early arrival was indeed a surprise to all.

The neighbor grabbed his clothes and fled in panic, only to be pursued and caught by the furious husband. The guilty man was wrestled to the ground and punched out. Not satisfied that justice had been done, the logger then pulled out his hunting knife and cut off the man's balls, castrating him on the spot. As I did not get to see or examine the 'castrated' man, I really had no way of knowing whether he indeed had his testicles cut out of the scrotal sac.

I do not recall exactly how it was that the RCMP had been notified, but fortunately our young officer was the one assigned to the case. When he went to investigate, the first one he talked to was the unfortunate "good friend." The castrated victim shamefully admitted his guilt and was extremely remorseful for having betrayed a good friend. He asked that no action be taken and that his friend should not be charged with a crime.

The betrayed husband could well have killed his old friend, but he showed restraint, limiting his violence to taking the revenge of 'an eye for an eye.' He now felt that all should be forgiven and forgotten and that they should all get back to life as it was before this shameful episode. I found it especially interesting that the unfaithful wife did not volunteer any opinion, for it seemed that she was kept out of all discussion relative to the events that took place. Her crime was adultery.

The constable was torn about his responsibilities, for each of the three had committed a crime and as a result all were guilty. To me it seemed that some primitive law had satisfied both men. After considerable discussion, we felt that if they were satisfied and willing to go about the business of getting their lives together, so be it and the best of luck to them. My only advice was that they be asked to get some counseling and that the officer keep tabs on all parties to make sure that things would not deteriorate again. He needed to be sure that there would be no more acting out of violence or sexual misconduct. Six months later the officer stopped by to report that all was well when he last contacted those involved. Much to my surprise the friendships had been rekindled and all was peaceful and quiet.

I felt that the constable understood these people and their environment in much the same way as a cultural anthropologist or sociologist would view them. In the first case, what could possibly have been gained by dragging the sheep-loving bachelor into open court and charging him with sexual perversion or of charging his outraged neighbor with his unnatural interest in his neighbor's sexual preference? In the second, who should be charged with what? I still can imagine the damage that would have been done by dragging such a group into court. It would have ruined three young lives and been a source of community gossip for months. I may be biased, but I believe that it all worked out for the best.

In the late summer of 1951, Premier Ernest Manning of Alberta and a small entourage made plans to drive west to check out a route for a proposed section of the Trans-Canada Highway, and as soon as word got out about their proposed trip, I got a call from a few of my friends in town asking me to join them in an adventure. Ray Sestrap was especially persuasive. Manning's plan was to head west past Eckville towards Rocky Mountain House, at which point they would follow a trail paralleling the North Saskatchewan River, past the town of Nordegg, to link up with the Banff-Jasper highway in the heart of the Rocky Mountains. Our plan was to follow them. Quickly we gathered a group of eight locals, including Ray, his two brothers, and his teen-age nephew Ken. We lined up an old farm truck and piled it high with sleeping bags, plenty of food, a few cooking utensils and headed west after the politicians.

We were all experienced mountain campers, so it really made no difference to us where we went. All we wanted was to have a little fun and to share in the adventure. This was not to be as difficult as Alexander MacKenzie's expedition, but like him, we would be on an expedition to explore something new. Less subtle differences were that we understood the language, and had a truck, fresh food, a doctor to take care of emergencies, and the premier of Alberta to lead us.

All in all there were about fifteen men on the trip. Three of the politicians' vehicles—one of them a jeep—and our truck made up the caravan. That was about as intimate as we got with the politicians. They simply had nothing to do with us. We followed the highway to somewhere between Rocky Mountain House and Nordegg where we branched south, heading straight for the North Saskatchewan River. It was beautiful country, rugged and untouched by civilization.

Our first overnight camp was next to a fast-flowing glacial stream that we planned to ford well before daybreak. It was important to be on the other side before the sun was high enough to warm the snow on the glacier that fed the stream, because within a short time this shallow, fast-moving water would become a raging, freezing, torrential river. We knew that any vehicle that did not cross in time risked being swept away, endangering the lives of those aboard. Naturally, as we were tag-alongs and had a truck, we would be the last to cross. I couldn't imagine that the head and leader of the province would take such a chance.

We made camp. Within minutes our experienced group of campers had a roaring fire going to keep out the evening chill and to serve as a place to cook thick juicy steaks with onions and potatoes, with fresh apple pie for desert. We had beer and coffee to wash everything down. The premier's party stood around eating sandwiches and canned food, looking wistfully at our fire and feast but determined to keep to themselves throughout the journey. In the morning, we had the fire going again for our bacon, eggs and coffee before we readied ourselves to cross the river.

It was not yet daybreak when we broke camp. The first car crossed gingerly. When it reached the other side safely, the remaining cars in the Premier's party crossed the stream one by one. By the time it was our truck's turn, the water was already rising rapidly and the current picking up velocity. Time was running out. We were in mid-stream with the water

Ben before swimming to shore with the line that the Premiers party would use to winch them out with.

four feet deep and halfway over the engine and still rising, when the truck's engine died. The eight of us were stuck in the middle of this torrential water.

It was decision time. A line had to be secured to the truck's undercarriage and then taken across to the opposite side so that we could be winched out. I volunteered as I was the strongest swimmer and best fit to enter the ice-cold stream. I knew that I could take it for a few moments before succumbing to hypothermia.

I stripped down to my shorts and sneakers, and with a safety line tied to my waist and the free end of another line in my hand I entered the water. The current was so fast and powerful that it was all I could do to hang onto the truck to keep from being washed away. Wedging my feet against the rocky bottom, I crawled under the truck to secure the hitch. By then my body was numb, and I had no sensation in either my hands or feet. When I was sure that the hitch was set, I worked my way across the remaining sixty feet of the river and up the bank into helping hands on the other side. The Premier's men secured the rope to the winch of a jeep that was in their entourage and pulled the truck to safety. Another fifteen minutes and the eight of us would all have been washed away. An hour later that lazy glacial stream of the night before was a frothing torrent of freezing water.

The guys got a roaring fire going again to help thaw me out, covered

Almost to shore; if they had waited even a minute longer, the car, Ben and his friends would all have been swept away.

me with blankets, and fed me hot coffee. My teeth chattered and my body trembled uncontrollably from the cold. When I took off my soaked sneakers, my right big toe was blue and red and about twice its normal size. Apparently I had broken it while I was jamming my foot against the rocks in the freezing water. The numbness in my limbs and the opium-like endorphins I was producing had prevented me from feeling any pain. I made a crude splint and taped the toe to keep it from moving about. But that's the way it usually happens—the doctor is the only casualty on expeditions like this.

In the wake of the Premier, our party followed Indian and animal trails through a dense forest of evergreens into a valley filled with lush deciduous growth and long stretches of white aspen. The valley floor was covered with wild grasses that had never been cut. Herds of wild horses grazed and romped, oblivious to our presence. The air had a balmy quality to it that reminded me of the warm Chinook winds that sometimes blow over southern Alberta in winter, lifting the prairie snow within moments. It was a place of such breathtaking beauty that I thought that this is what Shangri-La must have looked like. I felt as if I was hundreds or even thousands of years back in time.

Further on, we met an Indian tribe moving camp just as they had done when this land was theirs alone. Some were walking, some were on horseback dragging their gear and provisions on travois, a clever contraption consisting of two poles, each tied at one end to either side of the horse, with a sling between them to carry supplies. It was a brief glimpse into a tranquil past that I have never seen since, but the memory is as fresh and vivid in my mind today as it was when we left the valley. It could have been a dream it seemed so brief and so fleeting.

I prayed that the proposed route for the Trans-Canada Highway would not go this way. I wanted this little piece of serene, isolated, pristine wilderness to remain untouched, left to itself forever. My prayers were answered; the highway was eventually routed well to the north.

Led by the premier's vehicles, our convoy began climbing after we reached the North Saskatchewan River, traveling along its right side towards its source on what might have been an animal trail. Though partially covered with grass, it was dry and dusty. As the steep slope fell sharply towards the river more than a thousand feet below, our truck began listing strongly to the left, and we stopped to assess the risk. Several of our more apprehensive members decided that I should drive the truck. Since they were all good drivers, I thought that they had lost their wits, but they insisted that "Doctors don't get nervous. They always remain cool in the presence of danger." No one gave a thought to my broken right toe. However, I figured that I would rather be behind the wheel than sitting in the back of a tilting truck, so I accepted the job.

We continued our climb in a line that followed the river and the con-

Warm and dry again, Ben and everyone make camp along the banks of the North Saskatchewan River.

tour of the hill until suddenly we came to a sheer drop of about 2000 feet to the river on our left. Our truck wheels were just a few feet from the cliff's edge and potential disaster. The Saskatchewan River looked very small from so far up. Ahead I spotted a sharp turn in the river's direction, and at the far end of the turn was a gigantic whirlpool, swirling in a monstrous vortex like some black hole in the universe. It looked dark and menacing as if it wanted to draw us in, and I stopped the truck so we could climb out and have a better look at it.

When we got back into the truck, the four men in the back leaned over to the right to keep the weight on the far side; the other three were on their knees praying, their eyes closed. I got back into the driver's seat, shifted into low gear and proceeded cautiously forward, holding my breath all the time, but we passed through this hazard with no problem other than the sheer terror of it. When I examined my own state of mind, I saw myself as having had an out-of-body experience. I had no fear, I was cool and alert, and I did not shake or perspire as would be expected, and aside from being thrilled with the frightening beauty below, my only thought was how I would escape from the truck should it begin to slide towards the cliff.

When we eventually arrived at the highway again, I felt a little let down to be back in civilization. I wanted to explore the mountains and forests further and eventually end up at the Pacific Ocean, the way Alexander MacKenzie had done. Except for that first river crossing, the Premier and his entourage remained distant and aloof throughout the journey; and they certainly did not look as if they had any feelings about the primitive beauty that surrounded us.

Thirty-five years later, I finally finished my journey to the Pacific, and when I bought my home in lovely Pender Harbour, BC, I found it to be much the same as Bruderheim and Eckville. This small community had built its own hospital and later a medical clinic, a golf course, a cultural centre for music art and literature, a swimming pool and now the citizen volunteers are remodeling and landscaping the town. The incentive and enthusiasm inspired by gifted people like Don Fraser and Martin Nicholes and others have generated a wave of excitement among young and old in the community. People filled with pride and pleasure are participating in this creative adventure. This is what small town living is all about!

WHILE THE PROCESS OF LEARNING ON THE JOB HAD BEEN going on, I had become increasingly aware of my deficiencies in two special areas of medicine: psychiatry and surgery. And by the summer of 1951 it had become perfectly clear to me that I needed to be better equipped in these areas to meet the needs of country practice.

There is an old joke among doctors that a psychiatrist is a person who wanted to be a surgeon but couldn't stand the sight of blood. I've often thought that this joke must have been invented by a surgeon, and that's why he had it a little wrong. It should be that a surgeon is a person who can't stand dealing with the inner person he is operating on. In reality there may be some truth in both versions.

What is definitely true, however, is that these two seemingly diverse fields actually have some interesting similarities. Both involve probing and cutting. One discipline is bloodless and the other bloody. In one you can see and feel what it is you are cutting while in the other the probing, cutting and removal of debris is done with the abstract and the symbolic, much more difficult to visualize. Both require skill and patience.

An abscess, whether physical or emotional, hidden in the body or mind, needs recognition and treatment. The surgeon anaesthetizes the area, cuts through the tissues and drains out the pus. The psychiatrist helps the patient identify the hidden emotional abscess, then as he cuts through the patient's protective psychological defenses, the problems pour out in a verbal and emotional catharsis, thus draining the emotional abscess. In both, healing takes place from within as the physical or emotional wound is freed of its toxins. With surgery there is a mess of blood and pus to clean up. In psychiatry the mess is in the form of tears, runny noses, and various emotional discharges such as laughter, crying and screaming. If I was to seek more training, which of these two should I choose?

I had already discovered that surgery was usually dramatic in its presentation and often immediate in getting results. Things were either fixed or messed up, with few in-betweens. I did not feel the least bit muddled in surgery, unless it was some procedure that I'd never seen or even imagined before, but I knew that I needed more training to deal better with the unexpected. I also knew that I was lucky to have gotten away with so few complications as a result of my inexperience. Surgery had provided me with instant gratification, a rush of power and the most in drama.

On the other hand, psychiatry is a much more complex process that involves interaction between doctor and patient—a two-sided process where the patient does most of the work. But for me, dealing with emotional conflicts had been like plodding half blind through a muddy maze. Results had been difficult to achieve and to measure with little in the way of drama. At best, I could only get a little below the surface and when I did, my ability to work through conflicts was amateurish. I had read some of Sigmund Freud's *Interpretation of Dreams* which I found interesting, but I must confess that I understood little of what he wrote, nor did I find it helpful in my daily work. My mother could have done a better job.

The patients and the community still talked about the case of the little girl who was mauled by the dog, and I confess that I enjoyed the praise and the awe in which others held me. I could talk about repairing her eyelids and know my listeners were impressed. But I could not tell anyone how Mrs. X had reacted to her husband's infidelity and how she had felt responsible for it. Certainly I couldn't brag, "You know, it was tough going but I saved the marriage of the president of the hospital board by getting him to give up sex with the very pretty, popular, and promiscuous Miss Y." My reward in that case was only in knowing that the job was well done, but I couldn't be sure the results would last. There was no praise to be had there.

I also realized I was stuck between two powerful emotions: vanity versus the satisfaction of doing a good job. I needed both. I was ashamed to admit that my vanity was related to my life-long need to show off and win praise from others. As a teenager I had become aware of my need for praise from my parents. Part of the reason I became a physician was to make them proud. Not only would I be the first in our extended family to ever go to university, I would also become a doctor. Now I had found that surgery could satisfy my need for praise, but something inside me said that this was a little excessive and immature. I knew that the satisfaction in doing a good job for Mr. and Mrs. X should be enough.

Another significant conflict was related to the issue of love and marriage. I was torn between the impulse to get married and settle in and yet I knew that I was just not ready to settle down at this time. The last time I had developed a romantic attachment had been in the final months of my stay in Eckville.

Anna was a lovely young woman who had returned from the city, newly graduated from university, to spend the summer with her parents, a prominent farm family who lived outside Eckville, before taking up her first teaching position. I had liked her immediately. She was fair-haired and tall with a nicely proportioned slim figure. Bright and quick-witted, she was subtly sensual and challenging. It was soon apparent that she had her sights on me and that I was to be her playmate companion for the duration of her visit home. In retrospect, I think she was in command and that I was merely a willing and cooperative subject.

We started to see each other, keeping a low profile. We both knew that tongues would wag if we were perceived as a couple, so most of our time together was carried out with considerable discretion. When I went to Edmonton, she would come with me and visit with her own friends there while I visited with mine. Our talks and times together were filled with fun, intimate talks and passionate making out. She would accompany me when I made house calls in the countryside, and after I attended the needs of the sick, we would attend to our own needs.

One night I told her that when I was a teenager, my mother suggested that if I went out with a girl more than six times I should declare my intentions. I did not want to lead her on since I could not allow myself to be serious yet. I had years of training ahead of me before I was ready to settle down to marriage. Anna's response was, "When I was a teenager, Dad's advice was keep your legs crossed when you go out with boys." We laughed and shared more about how differently our parents had discussed such personal issues as sex and marriage.

In growing up, I had felt totally comfortable discussing matters of intimacy with my mother. There was no embarrassment or shame. Mother was very sensible and wise. Dad, in contrast, though an openly affectionate and loving man, rarely expressed his thoughts and feelings on such matters. Anna's talks with her parents had been more like lectures on the dangers of sex and intimacy with boys. Open, shared discussions were infrequent. For her, it was mostly about the dos and don'ts.

Then one evening while I was in bed in my room below the office, reading up on medical matters, my door opened and Anna entered. Her unspoken intent was clear and my response was one of complete acceptance and submission. I tossed my books aside and watched her in total fascination and admiration. She simply took off her clothes and got into bed with me. We made love in silence. We had done all our talking; now it was simply a matter of satisfying each other's needs and in expressing the pent-up desires of our weeks together.

Knowing and trusting each other as we did paved the way for a wonderful few months of intimacy and romance. The only pain was in knowing that we would soon be going our separate ways, pursuing paths yet unexplored. Although I was falling in love with her, I knew that I was not ready to get married; I had no savings and my next priority was to complete my professional training. However, the most important reason for my hesitancy was that Anna was not Jewish, and from early in life it had been made clear by both of my parents that my brothers and sisters and I were expected to marry persons of our own faith. The reality was that there simply were no Jewish girls within miles of Eckville.

Our days together went by quickly. I felt wonderful, for I had both a woman and the work that I loved. When it came time to separate, we never did say "Good-bye." For years after she left the province to teach high school, we wrote to each other. When she told me that she had met a man whom she loved and planned to marry, I was very happy for her. Four years later Anna developed a malignant disease from which she did not recover. She was just 30 years old.

When I think of the girls I have loved, beginning with Velma in Bruderheim and the others as the years went on, I still love them all and still see them in my mind as they were then. Velma is 5 years old with her beautiful blue eyes and light blond hair. Anita is 9, Esther 12, Clara 16,

Queena 19, and Anna 20. I feel a great sense of comfort to know that my love for those and others has remained with me through the decades and that the memories remain fixed in my mind as if it were only yesterday. Those and other loving relationships comfort and nurture me as the years slip by. When I add them to the inventory of others—friends and family whom I continue to love—I feel rich and blessed.

Meanwhile, I talked my career problems over with my friend Dr. Sid Spaner who suggested that I write to Temple University Health Science Center in Philadelphia and the University of Pennsylvania for permission to spend a year studying in each place. Temple was noted for pioneering psychosomatic medicine and Penn for its training in surgery. To my surprise, both institutions expressed interest in having me and urged me by letter to apply in person. I think they were impressed that a western Canadian country doctor wanted more specialized training.

Months before I decided to journey east, I told my boss of my intent and was happy to have his blessings. "I'm not at all surprised, Ben," he said. "It's the right thing to do." Frank knew and understood that I was not content with what I felt to be my serious limitations. But he added, "It's not likely that you'll ever return, Ben. Once you get involved with one or the other of these specialties you will stay with it." I didn't tell him he was wrong but I was pretty sure I would be coming back to country practice.

"I know of a good man to replace me, Frank. His name is Bryan Sproule and he's just finishing his internship at the University Hospital," I said. Frank took my word for his competence and promptly hired Bryan.

A week before I left Eckville, Frank and I were reminiscing about the wonderful times and the great learning experiences I had gained during my tenure with him. I told him that he was the best teacher I'd had in all of my exposure to medicine. He had shown me that country practice provided a unique opportunity to treat the total patient and had made it possible for me to face situations that I might never have come across in a lifetime of city practice. I wanted him to know how much I appreciated his trust in me as evidenced by his letting me go it alone so often, right from the very first day of my arrival in his town.

The conversation shifted to the work I had done, and jokingly I said that I'd done just about everything except brain surgery and the repair a ruptured viscus, an internal organ of the abdomen. About four days after this conversation, Frank woke me with a phone call around two in the morning. "Well, you got your wish, Ben! I've got a ruptured viscus for you, so get your ass out of bed and get over here! You'll do the case. I'll assist you." I rushed to the hospital and went directly to examine a man who was in tremendous pain. Frank, who had already started an intravenous and given the patient a narcotic to relieve his intense suffering, greeted me with his boyish grin, pleased that he could give me the gift of repairing a ruptured viscus. "This will have to do, Ben. Sorry I won't be able to come up with a brain surgery case!"

The patient was a slim 50-year-old, who lay on his back, not moving a muscle as he complained about the tremendous pain in his abdomen. He had a long history of stomach ulcers. The previous night he had eaten a hearty meal and gone to bed, only to be wakened shortly after midnight by a sudden, catastrophic, unbearable and unrelenting pain in his abdomen. His belly wall was as rigid as a board and had classical rebound tenderness. This was evoked by gently pressing down on the abdominal wall, then suddenly lifting my hand to let the belly wall bounce back; the result for the patient was an immediate sharp stabbing pain. I knew this was indicative of an acute irritation of the tough, nerve-sensitive lining of the abdominal cavity—the peritoneum. He had ruptured an old ulcer of the stomach or duodenum.

Less than ten minutes after my arrival at the hospital, we had rushed him into the operating room and Frank was administering the anesthetic, first knocking the patient out with chloroform, then switching to the much safer ether. He was a whiz at giving anesthesia. Few people ever mastered the use of the volatile and dangerous drug, chloroform, as did my boss.

That done, he sat back with a big grin on his florid face and said, "Well, Ben, here's your wish. Fix it up!"

I made an incision down the center of the patient's belly wall from his breastbone to his belly button. I was beginning to like opening people up; it was like opening a gift package and looking for the surprise inside. In this case the surprise was to see the belly filled with tomato rice soup. It looked as if it had just come out of a can of Campbell's best, although the presentation was not too appetizing. It was also apparent that the man had eaten a good amount of it for his evening meal.

A hole about the size of a 5-cent piece had been blown out of his stomach, and all the stomach's contents—including the recently eaten food and the digestive juices—had immediately poured out. Hydrochloric acid, which is the number one ingredient of the stomach, especially after a meal, is very strong and corrosive. When it hits the sensitive nerve endings of the peritoneum, it causes intense, unrelenting pain, something like pouring vinegar or a corrosive-cleaning agent over an open wound on your lip, only fifty times worse.

I scooped and sponged and sucked out all the food from the inside of his abdominal cavity. After that was done, I tackled the job of patching the hole, and the patient was back in his bed within the hour. The pain subsided and he never complained because the memory of what it had been like before the surgery helped with his perspective and morale. He knew that he was on the mend and would soon be home with his family.

That night I returned to my room confused about whether I should go or stay. Maybe I could get enough training by staying on with Frank, I thought. But in the end I recognized that he could not advance my training in psychiatry and there was also a limit to what more he could teach me in the area of surgery. While I'm certain that he was capable of doing any operation, he would never voluntarily do complicated elective surgery.

When I arrived in Philadelphia, I called both medical institutions to set up interviews. My first appointment was with the distinguished Dr. O. Spurgeon English, chairman of the department of psychiatry at Temple University Medical Health Science Center. He greeted me warmly and invited me into his office. I handed him my medical diploma, the only thing I brought with me. He glanced at it, and then we chatted for an hour, with him asking me such simple questions as, "Tell me about your family," and "What was it like living in a small town up in the northwest." Then he wanted to know about my hobbies and interests outside medicine, and he asked, "What made you want to leave country practice to study surgery and psychiatry?" I assumed these questions were preliminary to his asking about my knowledge of psychiatry, so I was a little shocked when he said, "I would be happy to have you join our program."

Afterwards, I called the head of surgery at the University of Pennsylvania and told him I would be starting my year of psychiatry the next day. I thanked him for wanting to see me and said I would call him again in a year's time to make arrangements for my year of surgical training.

Dr. English had explained that there would be no salary and no perks other than free meals for the time I would be in postgraduate training, so I quickly found a night job working in a private mental hospital taking emergency calls and examining newly admitted patients. The pay was room and board and $200 a month. Not bad! I knew one thing for sure— I would not go hungry.

After working at Temple for about a month and meeting the small number of bright, friendly residents there, I knew that I not only wanted to do good psychotherapy but also wanted to do some teaching and research. I had no idea where this would take me, but I did know that this would begin to satisfy some of my mixed learning goals and my insatiable curiosity.

In looking about for a research project, the first person I sought out was Doctor Edward Weiss, professor of internal medicine and senior author of the authoritative textbook, *Psychosomatic Medicine.* He told me that there was nothing specifically organized for this specialty, but he suggested that my best course of action would be to get

Ben as a resident at the Temple University Health Centre; Department of Psychiatry.

as much training in psychiatry as was available and to also train in internal medicine. At the same time he suggested that I focus as much of my time as possible on hospital patients who were suffering from organic illnesses which appeared to have a psychological component. Heeding his advice, I then began to take all the consults that came to our department of psychiatry. I also attended Dr. Weiss's weekly psychosomatic conferences.

The only other psychiatrist who had a keen interest in this field was Doctor H. Keith Fischer, a brilliant and innovative man, who had also worked with Dr. Weiss. I approached him during the first month of my residency and said that I'd like to do some research in the field of psychosomatic medicine and would appreciate any ideas and help he could offer. A short time later he arranged a project on how and why placebos work, and I was given a grant of two thousand dollars from the Sandoz pharmaceutical company to carry out my first research project.

It was an interesting project that led us to discover that the transference and interpersonal relationship with the doctor was primarily responsible for the effect the pill had on the patient. Since it was a double blind study with pills looking all the same, the treating doctor did not know which pill was an anti-anxiety agent or the placebo sugar pill. I was amazed to learn that some who took the placebo medication became violently ill with symptoms such as throwing up, severe headaches, dizziness and so on. I was more amazed to find that about an equal number had a miraculous recovery of conditions such as migraine headaches, stomach ulcers etc. These patients reported that they now "never went anywhere without the (placebo) pill." We also concluded that placebo response whether good or bad is a normal phenomenon with most people, which is why one of my teachers suggested that "When a new drug hits the market, use it while it works!"

By the time the results of this study were presented at a medical meeting and then published in 1956, I was launched into this new field of medicine and knew I would not be returning to general practice. I had also developed close personal and professional relationships with both Doctors Weiss and Fischer that lasted for as long as they lived, a most productive and rewarding experience for me.

Within my first month I had also discovered that all the other residents were undergoing personal psychoanalysis in order to recognize and understand inner conflicts that they might be totally unaware of, conflicts that could interfere with their treatment of patients. I learned that every transaction between patient and therapist involves transference of feelings from one to the other.

For example, if the therapist needed praise from his parents, he might look to his patients to fulfill that need. On the other hand, a patient may want to give in to his need to be cared for and treated like a child or, feeling angry, he might act out his feelings against the doctor. By undergoing personal psychoanalysis, the doctor could be guided in such a way as to avoid perpetuating both his patients' and his own neurotic or immature needs.

It became clear that if I expected to be a good psychiatrist, I should follow the lead of the other residents. The recommended training psychoanalysts were all very well qualified, so I decided to select one whose life style was well balanced and reflected some of my own values. I assumed that such a person was not likely to do me much harm. To my surprise and delight I found the entire experience to be one of the best investments of my life, a wonderful opportunity to focus entirely on myself and to learn all that I could about the workings of my own mind and my life. It was here that I learned more about my reasons for leaving country practice.

It took me the better part of a year to train myself to sit hour after hour listening to patients talk about their problems. I just did not understand what the hell was going on. I had left country practice feeling up and ready to challenge anything, and here I felt terribly inadequate and sometimes just plain ignorant. The other residents seemed to know so much and could quote from books and the literature, while I did not really understand anything that I read.

The language of psychiatry was as foreign to me as Latin had been in high school. I would leave the hospital each day feeling exhausted and drained, but it was in no way similar to the exhaustion I had experienced in Eckville. It was more like the way I had felt in my first year of pre-medical school—pure brain fatigue. I found the only thing I could do was take my notes and what I observed in my patients to anyone who would listen to me—senior residents, social workers and a few of the psychologists.

Mostly they were patient with me and supportive.

But I couldn't wait to leave the hospital in the evening and drive to Eugenia mental hospital to examine new admissions and write up a history of my findings because this was a lot more like what I was used to doing. I got myself a collie dog to be my friend, and I would sneak away from the hospital and take a subway to Center City to sit in the bleachers listening to the Philadelphia orchestra. This was an escape I continued for the duration of my first three years of training.

I returned home for a visit during that first year of psychiatric training. Mother and I were chatting about dreams when she said, "You know, I have been having a nightmare that has been recurring for years and years. I don't understand why it won't go away." In her dream she was alone on the top of her family's old apartment building in Odessa, looking down on the square below. "There was a funeral. The people standing around the grave were my family. They were crying. The coffin was for a little baby. I felt very sad and had a terrible feeling of guilt." When I suggested that this nightmare might be related to her infant brother's death and that she still felt the same responsibility for the event that she had when a child in Odessa, she seemed very interested.

"Ma, I think that is what drove you to be such a good and concerned caretaker," I told her. "And it may even be why, when we were ill, you would be at our bedside day and night. You couldn't allow the death of a child to happen again." Mother was thoughtful.

"That makes sense," she said. "It does seem to fit." She never had the nightmare again. She was the first person to respond so well to my dream interpretation.

While all this was going on, one of the social workers with whom I often consulted on patient welfare, a maternal woman named Carol Schultz, began to invite me to her home for dinner. Carol and her husband always had guests who were bright and stimulating, but it took me most of a year before I realized that there was always a single woman invited to the meal, a different one each time, and it finally dawned on me that Carol was doing a little match-making.

Unwilling to be manipulated, I decided to have just one more dinner there and then end it. At that last dinner it so happened that the only daughter of one of their good friends was visiting, and I found myself feeling immediately attracted to her. She was Jewish, and I even liked her name—Lorna. My courtship of Lorna lasted a year and a half; then having accumulated a bank account of a whole two thousand dollars, I married her. Carol Schultz was thrilled that she had been finally successful.

However, before that happened, I nearly got thrown out of residency. About six months after I came to Temple, I was invited by Dr. English for a chat about my training thus far, and I was delighted to have the opportunity to tell him how much I was enjoying the program. Dr. English had just published a book entitled *Fathers are Parents Too*, and the subject of his book came up in the course of our conversation. I told him that I had read it and enjoyed it, but there was one thing about it that troubled me. He was curious and asked me to go on. "In your book, you champion the value of fathers," I said, "but how do you find time to be at home with your wife and four children? You seem to be here working all the time." His response was to tell me that our meeting was over.

The next day I was called into the office of Dr. Vic Hansen, head of resident training. "What did you say that got the Boss so angry?" he asked. "He wants you thrown out of the residency program!" I told him what had happened, he interceded on my behalf, and the boss cooled down. It was a number of years later that Dr. English admitted to me that all he knew how to do was work. Play was something he had to work at; it never came spontaneously to him. I felt sorry for the man for he continued to work until he was past his 90th birthday.

I still kept in touch with the Coppocks after I left Eckville. Marjory and I wrote to each other on a regular basis, with Frank adding a few lines onto the end of her letters. I learned that Bryan Sproule had left after a year to do post-graduate work, but Frank had been joined by Dr. Gordon Gibson and everything was going well. Then just about fifteen months after I left, Marjory called to inform me that Frank had suffered a massive heart attack and died.

I was stunned by the news. I cried and grieved for this man whom I loved, but even as I grieved, I knew that there had been a certain inevitability to his end. I had seen quite clearly the toll that twenty-five years of hard work, total dedication, and the extreme demands of the practice had taken on him. I had recognized his incipient, progressive exhaustion, and twice I had seen him crumble when the stresses had mounted too high. I knew that he had needed to rest, get away, have a drink to relax, and yet that was not enough.

He could not stop what he was doing. He was not pacing himself. Exhausted as he was at times, he could not quit. It was as though he believed that his drive and strength would get him through whatever hardships he faced. After all, he was just in his mid-50s, in excellent health and rarely missed a day's work because of illness.

However, the concern on Marjorie's face had been evident when she looked at him. She worried that he drank too much, but I had told her, "Marjorie, I know he likes to drink but I've not seen him drunk nor have I seen it interfere with his ability to function. I think it helps him wind down and relax." Other than relieving him of some of his practice burden, there was little I could do to help. In looking back, I really think he should have taken a leave of absence and spent a year recovering from decades of accumulated wear and tear. The man was burning out, and I was too naïve and ignorant to do more to rescue this giant. But he was old enough to be my father, and I doubt he would have taken my advice if I had spoken up.

At the same time I saw similar character traits in myself: pride of accomplishment, fearlessness, dedication, love of hard work and the inspiration of a challenge. Although I was working very hard and holding up just fine, I was thirty years younger, filled with zeal and inspired by the novelty of the work. But this man had been tougher than I, and the more I emulated him the more I began to realize that if I returned to country practice and worked at his pace for thirty years I would not survive either. I could run a mile in a little over six minutes, but I knew that I could never run a marathon at that pace.

It was another forty-four years before I learned the next part of Frank Coppock's story. It was 1997 and I was attending a medical school reunion in Chilliwack, BC. Two classmates, Dave Klassen and George Gibson, and I were playing golf when they invited a man playing alone to join our threesome. "Hey, Gordon," Dave said, "do you know Ben Dlin?"

The stranger exclaimed, "Bennie Dlin? You're Bennie Dlin?" He explained that he was the Gordon Gibson who had joined Frank Coppock in Eckville after Bryan Sproule left. What a wonderful and fortuitous surprise! I knew this man could fill me in on the last part of Frank's life.

Gordon told me about the events that had begun in early November

1953 which had led up to Frank's death. "It was my weekend off, and as I was driving out of town with my wife, I noticed Frank standing just adjacent to the office building beating at a brush fire with a broom. I stopped the car and offered to help, but he waved me on. He had everything under control."

The following Monday Frank took patient X-rays to be read by Dr. Bill Parsons in Red Deer, and while there, he told Bill that he'd been having chest pains for the past two days. An electrocardiogram showed that Frank had a serious myocardial infarction, and he was immediately admitted to the hospital. After three weeks, he was allowed to return home but was told to take it easy for another four weeks. Then one day a few weeks after returning home, he went to the hospital to administer an anesthetic, something he could do with little effort. The next day he stopped by the hospital again to see how the patient was doing, and while there he collapsed with sudden and severe chest pains. "I was called immediately," Gordon told me.

When Gordon arrived, Frank said, "Gordon, this is it. Get Marjorie and the girls." While they waited for the family, Gordon gave him morphine to ease the pain. Frank insisted on Gordon staying for his last instructions. His final act was to complete the sale of his practice, thus securing the economic well-being of his loved ones. Then after saying goodbye, he died.

"He was given a Masonic funeral and buried in Red Deer," Gordon said. "The funeral procession was more than two miles long."

Two years after my meeting with Gordon Gibson, when I was at work on this story of my time in Eckville, I made contact with Donna, Frank and Marjorie Coppock's younger daughter. During one of our conversations I mentioned how back then I had felt concern that her Dad had missed some obvious signs of coronary disease in some of his patients. This error in his judgement just did not fit with his medical astuteness. "Did your dad expect he would live to a ripe old age like his parents and his Uncle John?" I asked her.

Donna didn't know the answer to my question. "Dad never talked about heart disease in the family," she told me, "nor of his concern about dying prematurely." She decided to research her family's medical history, and what she learned finally drew back the curtain on Frank Coppock's life.

Frank's father, a pipe-smoker and social drinker, died at age 85, but he'd had many cardiac episodes over the years. Of his four children, only Bessie, the second child, escaped heart troubles; although a smoker, she died in 1983 at the age of 84. The third child, Jack, a heavy smoker and drinker, died of a heart attack at age 47. For three years prior to his death, he had been under the care of his local doctor in Saskatchewan, although Frank had arranged for him to see a cardiologist at the University Hospital in Edmonton. The fourth child, Margaret, also suffered a heart attack; she was only 51 when she died in 1958.

But it was what Donna learned about her father that came as the greatest shock. The heart attack that he had in November 1953 and the one that killed him at age 57 a month later were not his first. That one had occurred in the winter of 1952 while he was taking part in a curling bonspiel in Lethbridge. He had been admitted to the Red Deer hospital, but it had been mild enough that he had been released within a few days. He told his wife she was to tell no one, not even their daughters. Apparently, he had been concerned about his family's economic future; he needed more time to save money for a trust account which would manage the assets for Marjorie after he was gone. He was afraid she would give most of it to her church if left to manage it herself.

The data Donna assembled not only shows a strong history of coronary disease in her father's family but also reveals that with each generation it strikes earlier. Of Jack's seven children, four of the boys have had surgery for coronary disease. Margaret's only son had a heart attack while in his 20s. Although Frank and Marjorie's elder daughter suffered from early onset multiple sclerosis and eventually died of stomach cancer at the age of 58, Donna herself, a cigarette smoker, told me she had been "afraid of dying in my 50s, but nothing happened until I was 64 when I suffered a mild heart attack."

What is also clear is that Frank was fully aware of the family heart problem but kept it quiet and was even secretive about it. But the fact that really stunned me was that his brother Jack's death had occurred on November 1, 1949, and I came to work for him just six months later. He never at any time mentioned his brother's death to me, and his bravado as he rode the bucking bronco at the rodeo and his escapades on his motorcycle were both indications of his denial of the disease. The family's history of heart problems also explains at long last why Marjorie was so concerned and protective of him, getting him away from the practice as much as she could. I understand now how during those fourteen months that I was with him, he was being torn between providing for the future of his family and tending to the welfare of his patients, even knowing inside that his heart would eventually kill him if he kept up the pace. And I believe that in telling me that I would not return to country practice, he was also encouraging me to escape his fate.

Death at fifty-seven was a tragic premature ending to the life of such a good man, so outstanding in his profession and community. He was a hell of a good boss and one hell of a doctor. He was my hero.

Frank Coppock, M.D., 1953

TO BECOME A PSYCHOANALYST, IT WAS NECESSARY TO HAVE completed the first year of residency before applying to the Philadelphia Psychoanalytic Institute. After that, we had to be interviewed and approved by three of the senior faculty. Each candidate had to enter into a personal psychoanalysis conducted by a training analyst, attend classes, and be supervised in his psychoanalysis of four patients. The focus of training was on learning how to get into the deeper recesses of the mind. As the years rolled on, I found that my ability to get good data from patients improved rapidly, and my understanding of the dynamics of emotional illness began to take shape. Reading, seminars, classes, and clinics were all helpful. I discovered, however, that individual case supervision was the best way for me to learn. Not only did this format expand my thinking about the patient, but it opened my eyes to my own feelings about the patient, often exposing feelings that I had not previously recognized or acknowledged. I also noticed that each of my supervisors had their own style of working, so I was able to pick and choose useful clinical tidbits from each of them

Around the third year of training I recall being involved in a Thick Chart study. Dr. Ed Weiss, as both internist and pathologist, came up with the idea of studying every patient in the medical clinic whose chart weighed over one pound. Our team of four physicians, all trained in both psychiatry and internal medicine, did a thorough examination of each patient and his or her chart. These were people who had been shunted from one clinic to another, taking medicine and having tests and undergoing surgery. The files showed us that they had been seen by a long parade of young doctors of various specialties who had been genuinely anxious to remove these patients' symptoms, but they had little if any recognition of why the patients kept returning. To our amazement we discovered that most of them had been coming back to the clinics year after year because they were lonely and wanted not only the attention of the doctors but also the companionship of other patients in the clinic. Over time they still had their original symptoms, and though minus an organ or two, they had the pleasure of adding yet another drug to the piles that filled their medicine chests. The charts got thicker but the patients were the same. This would not have happened if each had been assigned one primary physician responsible for his or her care, a process that would have taken a little more time initially but in the long run would have saved time, money and suffering.

Aside from organizing our data, our group of psychiatrists and internists would meet once a week for an open discussion of each and every project we worked on. These sessions were so productive that they continued for over 20 years after Dr. Weiss died, with leadership divided between Dr. Fischer and myself.

In 1956, I completed my training in psychiatry, psychoanalysis and internal medicine, then returned to Canada with my wife Lorna and our daughter Melissa. I set up a practice in Vancouver and joined the faculty of psychiatry at the University of British Columbia, the first qualified psychoanalyst west of Toronto and east of Japan. Shortly after my arrival, I was asked by UBC to organize a program called "Family Medicine" for first year medical students. At the heart of the program was the assignment of each student to a family in the community that he or she would follow for the entire four years of medical school. Each student was also assigned a practising doctor to act as his or her preceptor. It was only the second program of its kind in North America; the first had been the brainchild of Dean Patterson in Cincinnati, Ohio. I had recommended a similar program to my dean, John Scott, at the University of Alberta six years earlier, but he had not acted on the idea. I was delighted to be doing something at last to raise the practice of family medicine to a level of recognition and respect in the work of academic medicine.

My decision to return to the United Stated two years later was made for personal reasons: I'd promised my wife that if after two years in

Vancouver she was unhappy, we would return to the USA. Initially I felt certain that she would love the area as I did, but that did not happen. A deal is a deal, so we returned to Philadelphia. As soon as I returned, I rejoined my colleagues Dr. Weiss and Dr. Fischer to pick up where I had left off in our research.

Dr. Weiss had organized a long term project on cardiovascular research, beginning in the early 1950s. This was a study of all acute heart attack patients admitted to our hospital. Each patient was seen immediately by one of four doctors who did an intensive analysis of all physical, emotional and social factors, seeing each patient for an average of nine hours over the course of their stay in hospital. Early on we rediscovered what had been known for a long time—that both chronic and acute stress played dominat roles in the onset of heart attacks. However, one of the more surprising discoveries was that close to 20% of these people had the attack on specific anniversaries. This Anniversary Reaction (AR) had been described a few years prior to our observations, but only as it was related to the sudden onset of schizophrenia. Subsequently we found that the AR was present in a wide spectrum of physical and mental illnesses. The most common AR was when the patient reached the age at which a parent died, and the younger the patient was at the time of this traumatic experience the greater the likelihood of an AR taking place.

We speculated that two mechanisms were at work simultaneously in this reaction: the impact of painful memories usually hidden from the conscious mind and the role of conditioned reflex as described by Pavlov and Gantt. Sometime later it was demonstrated that the immune system in animals could be conditioned to respond to noxious stimuli that caused severe vomiting. The animals were then given a lengthy period of freedom from the drug. Later when they were given a placebo that was similar in taste and colour, it resulted in the death of the animal. The immune system remembered and reacted! These data excited us as well as Dr. Horsely Gantt who had worked with Pavlov and at the time of WW1 he had come to John Hopkins University and introduced the west to Pavlovian medicine. Dr. Gantt became especially interested in our cardiac work and AR in particular, and he invited Dr. Fischer and I to his place for a day. He told us that in Pavlov's experiments the first organ to respond to an electric shock had been the dog's heart. So when he came to the USA he had focused on this study. He told us about one of his dogs whose heart had raced rapidly after one shock was administered. After six years in which the animal was kept in a kennel, he brought the back into the same lab, and its heart began to race just as it had the day it was shocked. Gantt said, "I think the human and the dog are reacting through similar psycho-physiologic memory mechanisms."

Shortly after Dr. Weiss died in 1960, Dr. Fischer and I set up a study of patients admitted for open-heart surgery. We knew that in the early days of this remarkable procedure a large percentage of patients became psychotic and it was not uncommon for them to commit suicide. Our study was a simple one. We examined patients both physiologically and psychologically prior to surgery. We found that fear, anxiety, sadness and depression were common and to be expected, given the nature of what they would face, since death and invalidism were common following the surgery in those days. We noted, however, that the incidence of death, postoperative complications and psychosis was highest among the patients who exhibited apathy prior to the operation, regardless of the severity of the heart defect. Apathy was the emotional indicator of feeling helplessness and hopelessness—a mind ready to give up. Once we were aware of this condition, our surgeons sought help for the patient prior to surgery and with good results.

Medical students and residents participated in the heart surgery research. I recall that we did a little experiment using our younger colleagues as guinea pigs. We were interested in the phenomenon of the simultaneous presence of human sensory overload that we felt had much to do with post-operative psychosis or other weird behavior. At that time all post-operative cardiac patients had to endure an unbelievable amount of physical and emotional stress. Confused by the pain killers and sedation, they were not able to move or speak because they were intubated, had an indwelling catheter to collect urine, both arms had intravenous running and their heads and torsos were encased in plastic tents that piped in steam and oxygen. They could neither speak nor hear voices above the hissing of steam and oxygen. They were overloaded with stimuli and cut off from the outside world.

Our young, fit medical researchers were asked to act as patients, duplicating these conditions, though without the drugs or the surgery or the intubations. The rest was the same. After only one hour they became very uncomfortable, and after a few hours they felt their senses leaving them. They were disoriented and their hold on reality was rapidly slipping away.

Because so much of our work was conducted in the Intensive Care Units, I suggested that we do a simple around-the-clock monitoring of all transactions that took place between the staff and the patients who occupied two specific beds of the unit for the duration of their stay. The number and nature of all interruptions by nurses, aides, doctors and others were noted at the same time as a continuous record was kept of the sleep and rest the patient had. Since each young researcher and most of the staff worked an 8-hour shift, they came in well rested and ready to do their job, but their interruptions caused a lack of proper rest for the patients. They reacted with basically two types of behavior. One was to lie passively without complaint and just go along with the team. The other type of patient would complain, make demands and want to be more informed as to what they were being given or why things were being done to them. The staff preferred the docile patients, but these patients' time in the unit was significantly longer than the assertive ones who did better because they participated in their own recovery.

Perhaps the most interesting study I did was on patients who had suffered from cardiac arrest; of these a special few had been given up for dead. When the heart stops, the resuscitators have just four minutes to get the blood circulating to the brain. The longer the brain is deprived of blood the greater the likelihood of permanent damage. Since hearing is the last of the senses to go, even if the patient is unable to respond in any way, most can hear what is going on. I recall one survivor who heard the doctors say, "He is gone." The patient's brain was saying, "Don't give up, doctors! I'm still alive!" In most cases there was no fear, only a peaceful state with a life review or thoughts of loved ones, all going in slow motion as the seconds ticked by. A good percentage of these survivors of arrest had religious experiences of seeing heaven or even God. After my paper was published, the media got hold of it and wanted to know about the religious experiences that were reported. "Tell us about God," was the central question. They were not very pleased when I stated that these people had, in fact, not been dead and that what they had were comforting, out-of body hallucinations.

In the early days of pacemakers the power box that kept the pace-maker going was a large battery in a sort of small suitcase. The big box was the patients' lifeline, and it was not long before this vitally important battery became an extension of his body image. However, the short life of the battery resulted in serious sleep loss because anxiety of it stopping was almost constant. Fortunately, that picture changed with the rapid development of pacemakers that will beat for decades, and are only the size of a cigarette lighter.

When I was asked in 1974 to give a paper to the Pennsylvania Ostomy Society on sexual problems, I found that the only thing of significance in the literature at that time was that the operation on males resulted in impotence due to severing nerves in the pelvis. This information was in all the surgery textbooks, and male patients were always informed prior to the surgery of this complication. This operation, a rather common one which involves the removal of a chunk of bowel because of cancer or inflammation (ileitis or colitis), results in closure of the anus and the creation of an opening of the bowel on the belly of the patient. The bowel contents are thereafter collected in a bag that envelopes this opening. With the help of the American Ostomy Association and Dr. A. Pearlman I was able to survey 400 patients, and the bottom line answer to the sexual question was resolved: most of the men who had been sexually active prior to surgery had experienced a return of their ability to have erections. The reason for the reported impotence had mostly to do with the fact that researchers had not waited long enough before drawing their conclusions. The patients they studied had been exhausted from the pre-existing illness and surgery and did not even think of sex until they were healthy and robust again. The myth of permanent impotence was established as not true.

In the mid-'70s I participated in a research project dealing with the two phases of gastric secretion: the results led to the successful medical treatment of peptic ulcer disease. The Mayo Clinic had gotten its start when the renowned Mayo brothers developed the vagotomy operation to cure stomach and duodenal ulcers. The only problem with their procedure was that it only took care of the first phase of gastric secretion which lasts approximately two hours; it was decades before the second phase which lasts about four hours was discovered. One of the first teams which worked on studies of these two phases in humans was the Shay Institute, which specialized in diseases of the gastrointestinal tract. Since it was part of the Temple Medical system and I had worked with them over the years, the leader of the Shay group, Dr. David Sun, asked me to help them by doing some experiments of the relationship between the emotions and gastric secretion.

Dr. Sun had by this time worked out a technique to block pathways controlling gastric secretion using pharmacological agents. Ulcer patients admitted to the study would sit in a lab for six hours relaxed and reading while their gastric juices were being sucked out by a nasal-tube. The contents were analyzed as the experiment progressed. My job was to conduct a benign, non-threatening interview just gathering general information while the ulcer patient was being monitored in the lab. My first patient was a quiet, slender, middle-aged man who was pleasant and cooperative throughout the one-hour visit. He told me about his work, his long suffering from ulcers, and his family's origin. Unbeknownst to me or the patient, during our interview his juices during the second (pituitary-adrenal) phase had shot sky high. Dr. Sun and I decided to postpone any further interviews until his gastric secretions returned to normal. That took three months.

After a period of stability we decided that I would simply walk into the lab when he was there, say, "hello," pick up a book, and walk out. Once again his juices went off the chart. His stomach behaved just like one of Pavlov's dogs. On subsequent visits they blocked the secretion with medication, then once again we repeated it without medication and the stomach reacted badly. We concluded the experiment by my treating him and discovered it was his Mother that was the problem. Afterwards his juices no longer increased with my presence. Since those days most ulcer patients do well with drugs, and the surgeons and psychiatrists have lost a little business.

I participated in many other studies, but the last one I wish to share was dramatically different from any study that I've ever been involved in. It all started with a chat I had with a young female friend who told me about her publicity job with the United States Deep Caving Team (USDCT). It was intriguing because a team of men and one woman, with world class climbing and diving experience, were preparing to explore the last great frontier on earth. The cave system they chose is located in Huautla, a remote mountain area in central Mexico. This system of caves, two miles below the earth's surface, had been impossible to explore earlier because scuba gear had been inadequate. So Doctor Bill Stone, a physicist and the leader of the team, set about inventing a re-breathing apparatus that would allow divers to stay under water for periods of at least 24 hours. The machine reminded me of an artificial lung. Because I was able to make contact with doctors doing research for the space agency and elicit their interest and later cooperation for doing some research on this expedition, Dr. Stone invited me to join their board and to head up all medical research.

The agency was interested in studying men and women who had to endure the most hazardous conditions imaginable in order to develop a profile of those who might be selected for living in space or on other planets at some time in the future. This expedition fit the bill; it was the best that they ever encountered. I limited my research to understanding each member as best as I could. They were all built like cowboy wranglers: light framed, slim, strong and remarkably fit. They were basically loners with the intellects of college professors and a life long ambition to challenge the unknown.

With one exception each member volunteered that he had a consistent genuine respect for danger. Each remained cool and objective up to the last second when faced with almost certain death. But one of the team was not honest. He gave the impression of being "real cool," but when I first shook his hand, it was clammy. When the interview was over, his hand was dripping from sweat: a common manifestation of anxiety. On the very last day of a training mission, he panicked and drowned because he was convinced that he was not getting oxygen from the scuba tanks. He died and almost caused the death of his diving buddy. Both tanks were later recovered and it was discovered that they were more than half full of oxygen.

The Explorers Club in New York rated the difficulty of this caving expedition as being similar to climbing a mountain twice the height of Mount Everest for the first time, without any surveillance and in total darkness. The USDCT was successful except for the tragic death of one member, the point man for the last leg of the journey, who died of complications of diabetes. This disease had been diagnosed just six months prior to the expedition. Unfortunately his doctor gave him permission to go.

The expedition was a success. The team worked in total darkness for 45 days, constantly wet and cold, having to climb down wet limestone cliffs often through cascades of water. Then they proceeded to find their way through deep pockets of water, miles of pitch black uncharted caves, expending enormous amounts of energy. In spite of tremendous caloric intake the skinny team members all lost large amounts of weight.

In the years after leaving Canada again in 1958, even though I was a specialist, I worked almost 100% of my hospital time in the medical clinics, seeing hospital patients in consultation in all areas of medicine and surgery. I always viewed myself as a doctor first, my overall training having made me much more alert to the incipient illnesses that are often masked by states of tension or depression and sometimes even by excessive anxiety about health. While I no longer delivered babies or did surgery, it was very difficult not to think as a country doctor, so that even though my patients were referred for problems of the psyche, I was always concerned with the total person. My research during those more than thirty years involved studying coronary artery disease, heart attacks, pace makers, open heart surgery, peptic ulcer disease, complications of ulcerative colitis, intensive care patients and other conditions.

All of this led me to keep up with the physical part of medicine. I set up postgraduate courses in Psychosomatic Medicine for medical practitioners at Temple University Health Science Center. In time, I was also able to have special postgraduate teaching seminars included at the national meetings of the American Academy of Psychosomatic Medicine. It was also at this time that I was honoured to become the second member of this society to receive the Prestigious Achievement Award. Over time I was also given an honourary fellowship in the American College of Chest Surgeons and was an editor for the journals *Geriatrics* and *Psychosomatics*. But I suppose my most important testimonial comes from my wife who tells everyone what a good doctor I am and insists that I see all the people she feels need a medical opinion.

I still regret leaving country practice, but I have been able to rationalize that in the long run I did more through training others. I would certainly urge every new medical graduate to go out into some isolated area and work as I did, and as did most of my classmates, to experience what medicine is really about. It is the best way I know to find out what kind of stuff you are really made of. No matter what specialty one chooses or where one goes after country practice, it serves as an invaluable foundation. It gives the specialist a broader perspective so that he or she is less likely to try to fit the patient into the narrow field of his or her specialty.

As the years have rolled on, I have grown sick inside as I witnessed the changes in medicine in Canada and the United States. Government and business are inflicting a terrible problem on the hearts and souls of medical healers. From the beginning of mankind, gifted, observant men and women, inspired by a need to relieve suffering, have healed others by using a combination of material substances and spiritual rituals. They passed on this knowledge from generation to generation of disciples or apprentices in an evolutionary process dating back tens of thousands of years.

The tradition that has evolved is simple and straightforward, and though over time there have been changes, mostly for the better, the core of the tradition remains the same. As in the past, when doctors graduate from medical school, they swear to uphold the principles of medicine outlined in the 4th century BCE by Hippocrates and reinforced in the 12th century CE by Maimonides. In taking the Hippocratic Oath, each of them solemnly promises: *I will prescribe regimen for the good of my patients according to my ability and my judgment and never do harm to anyone. To please no one will I prescribe a deadly drug nor give advice which may cause his death.....In every house where I come I will enter only for the good of my patients, keeping myself far from all intentional ill-doing.* And like Maimonides, they ask, *Almighty God.....Inspire me with love for my art and for Your creatures. Do not allow thirst for profit, ambition for renown and admiration to interfere with my profession. For these are the enemies of truth and can lead me astray in the great task of attending to the welfare of Your creatures.* With such basic principles as these to guide them, it seems that men and women in the medical profession could not go wrong. And this would be true but for the fact that there are outside influences at work. As with all evolutionary processes, improvement in a craft is a natural byproduct of its practice, but when this practice is disrupted by wars, religious persecution and restrictions, or political or economic expediency, the momentum slows, ceases, or reverses.

In 1949, during my internship in Alberta, physicians had already begun leaving England to settle in Canada, South Africa, Australia and the United States because they were running from government control of medicine. They refused to accept the National Health System's intrusions on their professional autonomy. I empathized with them, but since the British immigrant doctors that I met were bright and well trained and had much to offer, I was happy to welcome them here.

I did not think about their plight for long; after all, what was going on in England had little to do with those of us practicing medicine in Canada. Besides, the Canadian medical profession had a much bigger problem: the "brain drain". A report by the Royal College of Physicians published in the early 1950s noted that Canada was losing the equivalent of one graduating class per year from its medical schools. The American institutions were happy to have Canadian students because they had similar cultural backgrounds, the same work ethic and no language problems. Many of those Canadian doctors remained in the US to take positions in teaching, research and practice. This is borne out by the experience of my own graduating class. Out of the thirty-four who graduated from the University of Alberta's medical school with me in 1949, eleven went to the United States for post-graduate training; four—approximately twelve percent of our class—remained there.

When I returned to Canada in 1956 and set up practice in Vancouver, I had been just in time to witness the beginning of government involvement in medical services, but I left again within two years so it never directly affected me. However, over the years, I frequently visited Canada and was somewhat appalled by the continued government control of medicine. As the economy weakened, taxes went up and services went down. Part of this had to do with the government investing less of that tax money in medical services, but the most critical factor in the decline in services was the accelerating attrition rate on the actual number of doctors in practice.

Canadian medical associations' report that each year since Canada shifted into full government control of the entire medical community, approximately 10% to 15% of established doctors have been migrating to the USA. In addition, 10% of new graduates are still going south, a loss which is compounded by the fact that within this last decade the government in its infinite wisdom has cut enrollment in medical schools by 10% as another means of reducing the cost of health care. Add to this fact that in the normal course of events, another 5% to 10% of older members of the doctor population retire each year. This means that the total annual loss of doctors to the Canadian medical profession is somewhere between 35% and 45%. The annual number of new graduates comes nowhere near offsetting this tremendous drain. This explains why most Canadian doctors are overworked and closing their doors to new patients. The government, however, continues to minimize the numbers.

In 1949 the population of Canada was about 10 million. It is now 30 million. This increase accounts for the drastic shortage of doctors in this country and explains why Canada is actively recruiting doctors from Europe and third world countries to help fill the gap. However, this influx has created two brand new problems. Most of these immigrant doctors do not come close to the level of competence of our own graduates because our medical school system ranks with the best in the world.

It matters little which medical system, Canadian government or American business, that you are talking about, the most vital but also most vulnerable portions of it are within the health profession—doctors, nurses, aides, therapists and others. With cost cutting they are the first to go. Inadequately trained aides replace nurses who, along with physician assistants, replace doctors, resulting in the crumbling of quality care.

In both countries the emphasis in medical care is now on doing more and more in less and less time. Doctors must cut corners to meet the "bottom line". Their practices are being bent and twisted to conform to the reams of paper work designed by the administrators who tell the computers to tell the medical people what to do. They regulate how much time can be spent on each patient, which drugs they can and cannot prescribe, which consultants they can and cannot be referred to, how to deal with waiting lists, how to fill out forms, and what deadlines must be met. The healing profession is now part of a business with the doctor at the bottom of the corporate/government food chain. But how can non-medical people measure the public's best interests in the field of medicine?

Unfortunately, it is the patients who take the brunt in the disruption in the chain leading from healer to hospital. Much like the canaries that are first to show the effects of mine gases, they are the first to suffer from the toxic effect of the health care system. They suffer from neglect, inconveniences and lack of compassion in their frenzied efforts to get some help.

Doctors in Canada and the USA are faced with a dilemma. They can choose to remain aloof and independent outside the system, a difficult position to maintain when government and business are setting the ground rules. They can leave medicine, or they can ignore their oaths and join the systems set up by government or business. Many doctors reflect their unhappiness at finding themselves in this bind with feelings that range from rage to depression to panic. They are becoming increasingly exhausted by the demands placed upon them, and as they become too overworked, they have to close the door to new patients. As a result, the number of frustrated, unhappy patients continues to grow.

But there is another kind of doctor who, feeling lost and apathetic, reacts to the stresses of change by resigning himself to this impersonal system. All the signs of apathy are manifested in his or her personality. The numbers in this last group are swelling. Patients who say, "he just doesn't seem to care" are describing the apathetic doctor. This is the doctor who merely puts in his time shuffling patients in and out, fulfilling the bare minimum of obligations set down in his contract with government or business. The apathetic clinician has lost his passion for his work. He has sold out his freedom and he is contributing to the weakening of the chain of our ancient heritage. As a consequence, the medical profession's old-fashioned, time-tested approach of personal commitment and love is giving way to a more impersonal approach as the focus shifts to writing more prescriptions and ordering more lab tests.

One would think that in a government-controlled system such as in Canada, people needing surgery would not have to wait. However, delays here are caused by staff shortages and operating room closures – both of which are caused by inadequate funding. Now it appears that younger people go to the front of the list and older people have to wait; a recent study done by the Ontario Medical Association has proved just how this neglect of elderly patients results in unnecessary loss of life. This is age discrimination to save money instead of lives.

In the USA this business of age discrimination has been carried to new depths of cynicism by the Health Maintenance Organizations (HMOs) with the introduction of the "kill factor", a business decision not to provide prolonged expensive treatment for those with complex medical or surgical problems. Under this system, the business managers decide that they will take the chance of short-changing the patient to save money, banking on statistics that show that relatively few patients or their grieving next-of-kin will actually sue their doctors for negligence.

I wonder what my old friend Frank Coppock would have done about all this, besides cursing a blue streak and drinking a little whiskey? After all, he had a system in place that provided the best care to all, rich or poor, in his rural community for as long as he lived. He was a dedicated physician, with a well designed and equipped office and hospital, and a readiness to refer patients to the best of specialists. He would have never given in to the system that is currently in place because it is a step backward. He would have fought with all his strength, utilizing his leadership skills and his position in the medical association and his surrounding community.

Frank was typical of the doctors of his day. He and many others like him died early because they worked alone for most of their lives. It was only in the last two and a half years that he had someone to work with him so he could get away for rest and recreation. Unfortunately, he was already worn out and unable to change. I certainly would not advocate a return to his unremitting work regime. Nonetheless, the core of how and what he practiced would work well today in rural as well as urban communities because modern transportation and communication have made doctors less isolated.

If Frank were alive today, he would insist that every person or family have a primary caregiver. He would also insist that the family doctor be given the courtesy and the privilege of inclusion in the team when his or her patient is admitted to the care of a specialist in a large city hospital. That courtesy would help the patient feel better, knowing that the family doctor was there and that he would eventually take over after discharge. Continuity of care would thus be ensured.

When it came to economics in Frank Coppock's day, most caring physicians were generous with their time and did not charge those who could not pay. The family doctor was always willing to see his patient through difficult times by reducing or eliminating his fee for services or bartering services for produce. I would love to have a barter system in return for service, but today that is a little unrealistic. However, during all my years on the faculty of Temple University Health Science Center almost all of the staff worked in the outpatient clinics without pay. This was done as a community service and as a way of teaching young doctors in training.

I do not know where the problems in health care will end. The enforced changes in the old doctor-patient relationship are now resulting in decreased communication, decreased rapport, decreased involvement or caring and, perhaps most ominously, a decrease in trust. If this transformation of medicine continues, the doctor as we knew him will disappear much like the salmon and cod stocks. I note that in Canada many patients are resigned to the system and simply accept what is available, although significant numbers are frustrated and bitter about the care given. Border towns like Detroit, Seattle, New York and others are flooded with Canadians who do not want to be put on long waiting lists for surgery or specialists' services. Yet in the past year the voices of more and more patients and professionals have begun expressing their bitterness and concern.

Certainly changes have to be made in our medical system, but these changes can be accomplished for the betterment of patients and physicians alike. If everyone, rich, poor, young or old, has the right to receive the best of health care, then the parties involved need to sit down and hammer out a better solution. There must be fair representation by doctors, laypersons, business, insurance and government, but the lead must come from the medical profession because it is doctors and nurses who will ultimately be responsible for delivering care.

Kagna, Harvey 35
Karloff, Boris 68
Kennedy, Mr. 18
Kenny, Sister 91
Kidney diseases 23, 110
Kiev 5
King David 35
King, Kingsley 102, 112-115, 149
Klassen, David 54, 63-64, 79, 100, 235
Knudson, Ida 102-103, 107, 136, 213
Knudson, Larry 88, 103, 117, 128, 183, 213
Kroenig, Mr. 13
Kushner, Dave 41, 82
Kushner, Sam 82
Lamont (Alberta) 7, 20
Latin language 30, 48, 52, 94-95, 232
Leduc 69
Lethbridge 237
Leukemia 98, 203-204
Levy, Dr. 32
Library 43
Lindsay, Bill 58
Lithium 165
Lloydminster 100
Lobotomy 76
Loomer, Joe 2
Loomer, Mr. 2, 13
Los Angeles 209
Lutheran 19
Lutzky, Bill 5
Lutzky, Joe 5
Mackenzie, Alexander 218, 222
MacLean, Lloyd 79, 100
Maher, Len 53, 61-62
Maimonides 248

Manning, Premier Ernest 217-222
Martians 115
Masonic 84, 236
Mayerthorpe 100
Mayo Clinic 32, 93, 125, 164, 244
Mcbeth, Dr. Bob 50
McCauly School 29
McDougal Presbyterian Church 30, 70
McGregor, Dr. John (Captain) 43, 50
McKenzie, Dr. Walter 7-8, 93
Measles 21, 23
Medusa 130
Meir, Golda 31
Meisner, Dr. George 94-95
Meniere's disease 64
Mental illness, psychiatry, psychoanalysis 24-25, 31, 61, 68, 72-78, 82-83, 164-165, 223-224, 227-234, 239-247
Mercury diuretics 123
Mexico 246
Microbe Hunters (book) 43
Middle Ages 21, 25
Miller, Abe 7
Minneapolis 100
Minnesota 32, 100 (Minneapolis)
Misericordia Hospital 210
Molander, Freddi 106-107
Montreal 6, 100
Moravian 19
Morphine 88, 139, 176, 186, 207, 236
Moses 35
Mount Everest 246
Mount Sinai Hospital 70
Multiple sclerosis 125, 237

Prince of Wales 34
Prostate surgery 133-134
Psychiatry, see Mental
Psychoanalysis, see Mental
Psychoanalytic Institute,
Philadelphia   239
Psychosomatic Medicine,
American Academy of 247
Psychosomatic Medicine (book)
230
Psychosomatic Society, American
76
Psychosomatics (journal) 247
Quinidine 123
Ragan, John 58
Railways 6, 10, 12, 25, 32, 39-40,
70
Rawlinson, Dr. Herb 41, 60-61, 63
Red Deer (community; hospital)
85,   87, 100, 110, 126, 133,
136,   203, 213-214, 236-237
Reed, Dr. 170
Religion, see Catholic, Greek
Orthodox, Jewish, Lutheran,
Presbyterian
Rheumatic fever 23, 210
Ringers solution 128, 197-198
Rochester (Minnesota) 32
Rocky Mountain House 145, 188,
217-218
Rocky Mountains 102, 217
Rodkey, Julius 145, 147-148
Rodman, Dr. Floyd 79
Roesler, Dr. Hugo 210
Roman Catholic 179
Rosh Hashanah 17, 115
Rosthern (Saskatchewan) 85
ROTC 50
Royal Alexander Hospital 67

Royal Canadian Mounted Police,
see   Police
Royal College of Physicians 249
Royal George Hotel 17
Royal Officer's Training Corps 50
Russia 8-9, 11, 23; see also Kiev,
Odessa, Ukraine
Russian language 7, 9, 15
Salmon 253
Salter, Professor F.M. 54-55
Salvation Army 1, 11, 26
Sandoz Pharmaceutical Co. 231
Santa 18
Saskatchewan xii, 57, 85, 102,
109,   237; see also North
Saskatchewan River
Satanove, Chaim 72
Scarlet fever 22-23, 143
Schizophrenia 68, 73, 77, 241
Schneider, John 23
School 2-7, 15-16, 27-35, 37-44,
58,   103, 232; see also College;
University
Schultz, Carol 233-234
Schultz, Mr. 13, 129
Scott, Dr. John 66-67, 70-71, 137,
240
Scouts 30-31
Seattle 253
Seder 18
Sestrap, Myrtle 106, 144
Sestrap, Ray 105-106, 108, 139-
142,   144-145, 147, 193, 213,
217
Sestrap, Sandy 106-107, 138, 144
Shakespeare 54-55, 211
Shangri-La 220
Shay Institute 245
Shector, Eli 53, 58-64, 70-71

Shector, Morris 70
Sheriff 214
Sherman, Earl 10-11
Sherman, Fred 1-2, 12
Sherman, Maude 12
Shortliffe, Mr. 41-42
Sinatra, Frank 112
Skene, John 79, 100, 110-111
Smallpox 121-122
Socialism 8
South Africa 249
Spaner, Allen 44
Spaner, Dr. Sid 44, 68, 81-83, 130, 227
Spaner, Sylvia 82
Sproule, Bryan 227, 234-235
St. John's Ambulance 42-43
Stampedes 142-143
Stewart, Mr. 13
Stewart, Walter 43
Stone, Dr. Bill 246
Strong, Ashley 12
Strong, Mr. 12
Strong, Mrs. 12, 25
Strong, Velma 12, 36
Sturdy, Dr. John 67
Suicide 25, 162, 242
Sulfa drugs 92, 120, 128
Sun, Dr. David 245
Swedes 106-107
Swine flu 139-142
Sylvan Lake 139, 202
Talmud Torah 29
Temple University Health Science Center, Hospital 77, 179, 227, 229-230, 234, 241, 245, 247, 253
Tetanus 128, 186, 198
Texas 69

Thick Chart study 239
Torah 29, 37
Toronto 9, 240
Towers, Major 50
Trail (BC) 100
Trans Canada Highway 217, 221
Tuberculosis 20, 24, 87, 132
Ukraine 5-6, 8-9, 19, 175; see also Russia
Ukrainian language 6-7
Ulcers 125, 128-129, 244-245, 247
United States, American 3, 54-55, 119, 240-242, 245-253; see also Boston, California, Chicago, Cincinnati, Detroit, Hollywood, Los Angeles, Minneapolis, Minnesota, Nebraska, New York, Ohio, Oklahoma, Pennsylvania, Philadelphia, Rochester, Seattle, Temple University, Texas, University of Pennsylvania
United Way 30
University xi, 44, 48-49, 248; see also   John Hopkins; University of
    University of Alberta
Medical   School; Hospital
8, 32, 41,   43, 49-72, 77, 79-
101, 110,   134, 137, 186, 200,
204, 225,   227, 237, 240, 249
University of British Columbia 240
University of Pennsylvania 227, 230
Vancouver 240-241, 249
Vegreville 45
Veterans Hospital 66, 68

Victoria High School 58
Victorian 39
Vietnam 39
Volkmann's ischemic contracture
96
Walker School 3, 16, 29
War, see World War
Watts, Dr. Ernie (Major) 43, 50
Weinlos, Dr. Morris 7
Weiss, Babs 208
Weiss, Dr. Edward 208, 210, 230-
231, 239-242
Weslowsky, Jim 61
Westend Pool 31, 44
Westmore, Perc 35
White, Miss 4
Whiteside, Dr. Carlton 200-202
Whooping cough 22-23
Willis, Dr. 31-32
Wilson, Dr. Gordon 96
Winnipeg 17, 85, 101
Woodland Dairy 31, 50, 97
World War I, 9, 85, 241
World War II, xi, 43, 49-50, 120
Wright, Al 58
Yerki (Ukraine) 5-6
Yiddish 6-7, 9, 15, 18, 39
YMCA 25, 30, 40, 50, 190
Yom Kippur 17, 115
Young Judeans 30